The Conscience of a Lawyer

Cliff Durr, 1933 (Courtesy of the Alabama State Department of Archives and History)

The Conscience of a LAWYER

Clifford J. Durr and American Civil Liberties, 1899–1975

John A. Salmond

The University of Alabama Press
Tuscaloosa

The University of Alabama Press
Tuscaloosa, Alabama 35487-0380
uapress.ua.edu

Hardcover edition published 1990.
Paperback edition published 2020.
eBook edition published 2020.

Cover image: Cliff Durr, 1933; courtesy of the Alabama State Department of Archives and History

Paperback ISBN: 978-0-8173-6011-5
E-ISBN: 978-0-8173-9354-0

A previous edition of this book has been cataloged by the Library of Congress.
ISBN: 978-0-8173-0453-9 (cloth)

This book is dedicated to
my grandchildren,
Bill, Hilary, Jim, and
Tom Washington,
whose heritage most
satisfactorily combines
Alabama and the Antipodes,
and to the memory of
David Alan Kingsley Jolley.

Contents

PREFACE

At a memorial service for Clifford Judkins Durr in June 1975, his daughter Tilla repeated a story of his childhood, a favorite one, which Durr had often himself told. It was a ghost story, describing an event which occurred when he was about ten years old and spending the summer, as he always did, on his grandfather's farm at Wetumpka, Alabama.

One summer day, so the story went, Durr set out with his trusty horse Belle to visit an old sawmill on a road leading out of Wetumpka. So intrigued was he by the mill's workings that he forgot the time, as small boys will, and by the time he and Belle came to make their return journey through the woods, dusk was falling, and the woods were full of the sights and sounds of impending night. The young Durr was frightened. Then, suddenly, both Belle and he spied a terrible apparition, the figure of a man hovering under a large sycamore tree. Belle bolted home, the terrified young Durr clinging to her back for dear life.

Clifford soon told his black playmates, sons and daughters of the farm workers, what he had seen. They knew it had been a ghost, for a man had been killed in that very spot some years earlier, and rumors abounded that his spirit had come back to haunt the area. Moreover, Durr and Belle were both so clearly terrified by the apparition that this in itself reinforced the veracity of the rumors.

Grandpa Judkins was not impressed—indeed, he was very angry. "You get right back on Belle," he commanded, "and take another look at that ghost, and then you come back and tell me and your friends just exactly what you see." Not only had Cliff been "scaring folks unnecessarily," the old man said, but he had "just about ruined a good horse" as well.

Terrified as Durr had been by his experience, he feared his grandfather's wrath even more, and back he went to the woods, "trembling with fear," to take another look. When he reached the haunted spot, he found that the "ghost" was but a jagged scar in the trunk of a large tree which had been struck by lightning. As the last rays of the summer sun had filtered through its leaves, they had caught the scar in such a way as to create an eerie effect. But there was no ghost.

Humiliated, the boy returned to confess to his friends and his grandfather that his fears had had no foundation, that terror had got the better of him—and of Belle. To his surprise, Grandpa Judkins greeted him as a hero. It took a lot of bravery for him to go back there, he said, to return to the woods and confront that ghost. Yet it had had to be done. When ghosts were not laid, he told his grandson, "fear runs wild," and in that situation, innocent people were often hurt.[1]

Clifford Durr never forgot that experience, nor his grandfather's words. Throughout his life, he was concerned to help people conquer their fears, for he knew well the destruction unchecked fear could wreak. In particular, during those years when Sen. Joseph McCarthy and others like him played on the fear of Communist subversion in America, Durr was one of the few who stood against the demagogues, quietly urging Americans to take another look at that particular "ghost," for in so doing, they would lose their fear. For this courageous stand, he suffered much—and yet he never wavered.

Durr urged his fellow Southerners, too, once he had returned to his native Montgomery, to confront their ghost, that of racism, and the fears the region's traditions had engendered, for again he believed that, having done so, they would be bound to recede, and the positive and decent aspects of Southern tradition would reassert themselves. Once more, in the maelstrom of social change which engulfed the South in the early 1960s, he was attacked and reviled. And yet he lived long enough to see the partial vindication of his commitment. His was a life full of meaning because he always confronted his ghosts and taught others to do so.

Inevitably I have acquired many obligations during the making of this book and have the space to acknowledge only a few of them here. The La Trobe University School of Humanities Research Fund generously supported the initial research on which the study is based, while La Trobe University granted me leave in 1987, which enabled me both to complete the research and to write the first draft. To the School of Humanities, then, and my university, my gratitude.

Like all researchers, I have been the beneficiary of the skill, patience, and dedication of many librarians and archivists in both Australia and the United States. I wish to thank them all, and in particular Mimi Jones at the Alabama Department of Archives and History and Dorothy Jean Smith of the Pelletier Library, Allegheny College, Meadville, Pennsylvania. Their helpfulness and friendliness made working at both these institutions an unalloyed pleasure.

Virginia Durr has been an enthusiastic supporter of the project since its inception. She has been generous with her hospitality, her time, and her friendship, and I owe her a very deep debt of gratitude. Likewise, her daughters Ann Durr Lyon, Lucy Durr Hackney, Tilla Durr, and Lulah Durr Colan have all treated me with real warmth as they shared with me their recollections of their father. I hope they all find something of him in the pages that follow.

In a real sense, this book is the property of Bruce and Carrah Clayton and their family, close friends for nearly thirty years. They have provided me with "a home away from home" during my research trips, they have been frank yet constructive critics of my work, and most important of all, in their support and encouragement over the years they have reinforced constantly the true meaning of friendship. My gratitude to them all is beyond measure.

My colleague and friend at La Trobe University, Bill Breen, carefully read the manuscript, and it has benefited materially from his many suggestions. Johanna Breen also read it, and her comments were both helpful and encouraging. Susan Poynton saved me from scores of errors in spelling and style, as well as providing wise counsel on several crucial points. If the advice of these three people was not always followed, that in no way diminished the spirit in which it was given and received. Shirley Horton typed and corrected the manuscript with her usual efficiency and good humor and was ably assisted by Merelyn Dowling and Brenda Joyce. To them all, my thanks.

I wish also to thank my colleagues at La Trobe University and my friends in Melbourne and its environs, in New Zealand and in the United States, for their continued support. My final debt of gratitude is, as always, to my family.

John A. Salmond — Melbourne

The Conscience of a Lawyer

1

A Southern Boy

Throughout his life, Clifford Judkins Durr took much delight in asserting that, if a member of his family ever had lived north of the Potomac River, the record of such a "shameful event" had long since been destroyed. "Family legend had it," he would say, that "some of my ancestors had passages booked on the Mayflower." However, when they discovered that the ship was bound for Massachusetts Bay, they decided to wait for a vessel with a more congenial, Southern destination.[1]

This was but one of the many ways Clifford Durr made a fundamental point about himself. He was born on March 2, 1899, in Montgomery, Alabama, the first capital of the Confederacy, into an old Southern family. He was always a Southerner, and throughout his long life he loved his region—its geography, its history, its distinctiveness, and the best of its traditions—completely without qualification. It was the very wellspring of his existence.

Clifford Durr's paternal ancestors, it was believed, came originally from Bavaria, settling in South Carolina, where his great-grandfather Michael was born. He moved farther south as a young man, to Warm Springs, Georgia, where he lived for a time. From then on, the record becomes clearer. In June 1835 Michael's son John Wesley Durr was born, and shortly afterward Michael moved his family again, this time westward, to Loachapoka, Alabama.[2]

Like his father, John Wesley Durr soon struck out on his own, moving to Montgomery when scarcely out of his teens. There he became a successful cotton factor, president of Lehman, Durr, and Company, but with active interests also in textile mills, the Southern and North Railroad Company, and the First National Bank of Montgomery. He served as a captain in the Commissary Department during the Civil War and was a Montgomery alderman for two terms and a deacon at the First Presbyterian Church for forty-five years. John Wesley Durr's elegant old white-framed house was situated not far from what was to become for a while the White House of the Confederacy, Jefferson Davis's residence. Indeed, his children and the young Davises were frequent playmates.[3]

John Wesley Durr, then, was a pillar of the Montgomery community, both before and after the Civil War. When he died in 1909, however, he was virtually penniless, his wealth gone in fruitless land speculation engaged in late in his life. By this time, however, his son, also named John Wesley, was himself established as a citizen of some substance. Born in March 1863, he was educated locally and then attended the University of Alabama for one year only before following his father into business. In 1896 he formed with two others the wholesale drug house of Gay, Hardie, and Durr, which became the Durr Drug Company in 1906, one of the most prominent of such enterprises in the South and the financial base for the Durr family's comfortable, upper middle class life.[4]

Clifford Durr's mother was Lucy Judkins. Her father, James Henry Judkins, had had a somewhat colorful career. Coming from a large landowning and slaveholding family, he had served in the Civil War with distinction as a captain in the cavalry. Unwilling to adjust to the changed South at the war's end and, in particular, refusing to accept the reality of emancipation, he formed one of the small band of Southerners who moved with their families to Brazil after the Confederacy's surrender, hoping there to reestablish their lost plantation world. He and his colleagues, he later wrote, had "no faith in their ability to manage freed slaves." Clifford Durr's mother, Lucy, was born just before the family left for Brazil, and thus she spent her babyhood in a world far removed from the conquered South.[5]

The Brazilian experiment was not a success. In fact, as James H. Judkins later described it, "It was but the mad mistakes of a few, and is not to be written as a part of the history of the South." He soon brought his family back to Alabama, settling on the farm near Wetumpka, in Elmore County about twenty miles from Montgomery, which would be so much a part of Clifford Durr's growing up and, indeed, his whole life. He also held a number of local and federal offices, serving as Elmore County solicitor from 1872 to 1874, inspector of the penitentiary from 1874 to 1880, and assistant United States attorney for the Alabama Middle District from 1897 to 1901.[6]

Holding federal office under a Republican president was enough to mark grandfather Judkins as a man to be watched in the post-

Reconstruction South. What really set him beyond the pale, however, was his support in 1904 for Theodore Roosevelt for president against the Democratic candidate, Alton B. Parker, a decision he publicly announced and defended. Though he had returned to the Democratic fold by 1912 and was loud in his praise of Woodrow Wilson, the "shame" of their father's Republican vote haunted his children for the rest of their lives. Nearly forty years later, Cliff Durr's mother told her son how it had nearly broken her, in imploring him not to add to the family's dishonor by attending a dinner for Hugo Black at which blacks, reportedly, would be present. She had, she said, lived with the "shadow of Papa's Republican vote" for most of her life and did not want "another shadow to bear. I just could not stand it," she pleaded.[7]

Clifford Durr loved his grandfather deeply. The relationship between the two of them was extremely close. Some of his childhood's happiest days were spent in his grandfather's company, working in the fields on the Wetumpka farm or fishing and hunting in the nearby rivers and woods. To Grandfather Judkins, Cliff was always someone special. "I am looking more to you than either of the other boys," he once wrote, for "you belong to the days of hope and of visions." Probably this warm, loving man—for this is how he is both remembered and revealed—was a more significant influence on the young Durr than his somewhat austere, preoccupied father. And, if the Republican vote revealed a disinclination to go with the majority, a tendency to stand up for what he believed, regardless of the consequences, then grandfather and grandson were very much alike.[8]

Clifford Durr wrote a little about his parents quite late in his own life, in a fragmentary, unpublished autobiography. Clearly, he adored his mother. She was, he said, "Little, pretty, flirtatious, imaginative—and tough." She was undisputed ruler of her household—there was no question of that—but she was also a gentle lover of nature, especially "the small things that grew in quiet places," who delighted in taking her youngest son on long country walks, hunting for wildflowers. She delighted, too, in introducing him to her favorite poets—Wordsworth, Keats, Shelley, and Tennyson—reading them aloud to the small boy as he sat enchanted at her feet. The bond between mother and son remained strong for the rest of her long life.[9]

Durr was perhaps not as close to his tall, dignified father, though he clearly admired him immensely. He was, he said, "a good provider and a good citizen," scrupulously honest in all his business affairs and a man whose word was genuinely his bond. Yet he was not always at ease with people, he further wrote, not even with members of his own family, while his preoccupation with his business and church affairs left little time for relaxation. In a revealing comment, Durr wrote that he could not recall him expressing the slightest interest in the poetry his wife so dearly loved, though occasionally he relaxed by playing the mouth harp.[10]

Of her parents-in-law and their relationship with her husband, Clifford Durr's wife, Virginia, confirmed that Cliff's relationship with his mother was probably closer than that with his father, but she stressed the stability of the family. "He had grown up in a stable family," she wrote, "with a very firm set of beliefs . . . he was brought up in an extremely loving and protective atmosphere."[11]

It would have been very difficult for Clifford Durr to feel other than protected, brought up as he was in such a large and loving family. He was born the youngest of five children. The others were Kate, born in 1890, John Wesley Durr III in 1892, James in 1894, and Lucy in 1896. Brothers and sisters were all close, and the youngest was certain to be swamped with affection. Clifford, then, was formed in a calm, secure environment, "so greatly beloved," once recalled his elder sister Kate, that she "felt it necessary to inspire a little fight into him now and then." Her brothers, too, tried from time to time to shake the little boy's certitudes. When Cliff refused, she said, against all the evidence and all her assertions, to give up belief in Santa Claus or the Easter Bunny, they decided to help out. "Pinky," they said, "if you don't stop believing these stories we are going to beat you up." Yet not even these threats could shake him.[12]

Contributing greatly to this atmosphere of love and security was Miss Willulah Judkins, Cliff's beloved "Little Auntie," who lived with the Durr family for most of her adult life. She was, he once wrote, as much a part of his childhood as his mother. Little Auntie was Lucy Durr's younger sister, and by all accounts a pretty and vivacious young girl with her full share of suitors. However, in her early twenties she contracted tuberculosis, from which she took years to recover. In accordance with the conventions of the time, therefore, marriage was out of the question for her. Consequently she devoted her life to the welfare of her father and her sister's family. She loved all the children without stint, but Cliff, the baby, was her special favorite and remained so throughout her life. One of her greatest thrills came in 1947, when he named his youngest daughter, Lulah, after her.[13]

Completing the Durr household were the servants. The most important in Cliff's life was his nurse, Henrietta Walker, whom he adored and who looked after him till he was ready for school. Henrietta was devoted to the family and was practically a part of it. Yet Cliff, to whom she was closest, knew something about her that no one else did, something that troubled his young mind deeply. When he was about six, he recalled, Henrietta's nephew was shot by the Montgomery police. Clifford recalled going with his father to view the body, the first corpse he had ever seen, and wondering what offense the frail-looking young man could possibly have committed to have provoked so violent a response. No one told him, but from then on, Henrietta changed. Still ostensibly devoted to the Durrs, when everyone was out of the way except young Cliff, she would often "break into violent diatribes against what she called pure white folks," beating herself in anger and frustration. He was puzzled and a little frightened, as he glimpsed early in his life what lay under the surface calm of a segregated society.[14]

Turn-of-the-century Montgomery was a city jealous of its Old South tradition, and especially of its brief period as "the Cradle of the Confederacy"—its first capital. Occupied only in the last days of the Civil War, it had escaped the destruction that had been visited on other Southern cities and entered the last decades of the nineteenth century a proud New South town, its wealth still resting securely on the buying and selling of cotton and on the presence of the state government, but with high hopes for industrial development as well. By the mid-1880s the city had also become a major railroad junction, with four lines converging upon it, and its leading businessmen, generously fueled by the New South ideas of expansion and progress, were hungry for business growth. Alabama's first cotton mill was built in Montgomery in the late nineteenth century, while the city also boasted that the first completely electrified street-transport system in the world began operating there in 1886. There was much talk, too, about developing the city's cultural as well as its business life. Alabama's first public library opened there in the year of Cliff Durr's birth. A graceful city, combining prewar stately homes with modern brick sidewalks, electric streetlights, and wide avenues, Montgomery's population in 1900 was just over thirty thousand, of which the majority was still black, though the proportion of whites was steadily increasing. Parity was reached, for the first time, in 1910.[15]

Race relations in Montgomery, as in most like cities, had been increasingly strained since the 1880s. As the historian Wayne Flynt has written, "Although Montgomery's black institutions continued to expand, they did so in a community separated by racial barriers." By the time Clifford Durr was born there, Jim Crow laws were thoroughly in place. Montgomery's blacks and whites rode on segregated streetcars to separate neighborhoods, worshiped in separate churches, and were educated in separate schools. The patterns of institutionalized inequality and second-class citizenship which were to become the norm for Southern blacks throughout the first decades of the twentieth century were well established in the city by 1900.[16]

As befitted a lad from a prominent family, Clifford Durr was educated privately, first at Miss Woodruffe's Academy, and then at the Starke University School for Boys. The Starke School was a Montgomery institution. Founded in 1887 and headed until his death in 1940 by Dr. John Metcalfe Starke, it was the city's leading private school. Run on strictly military lines, with all the boys dressed in gray uniforms, its standards were rigorous and the discipline severe. Professor Starke stressed the importance of hard work, self-discipline, and honesty. He reinforced the message with frequent beatings, not only for mischievous behavior, but also for tardiness and slowness at lessons. It was a tough, even Spartan, school environment.[17]

Clifford Durr's report cards show that he performed well under Professor Starke's heavy hand. In 1912, for example, his lowest mark was 97 percent in Latin, and he received 100 percents in history and geography. He consistently made the honor roll, and Starke was delighted with his accomplishments. "Cliff is a dear little fellow," he wrote his father in 1913, and deserved anything "a good, smart, diligent boy ought to have."[18]

Despite his successes, Durr did not enjoy his school days, nor did he take "any great delight in learning." He disliked Professor Starke and his teaching methods, especially resenting being taught with "a stick on the desk" and the threat of up to "fifteen licks on the palm of the hand" for even the most minor of infractions or omissions. "I studied," he later wrote, "not for the joy of learning, but because the consequences of not studying were even more unpleasant than the ordeal of studying." Yet school and study occupied most of his week, for on Sunday there was church and Sunday school. Only on Saturdays were we "free to be ourselves," he recalled. Because of the Starke School, childhood in Montgomery was only "endurable," he remembered, but not much more than that.[19]

Grandfather Judkins's farm at Wetumpka, however, was an en-

Cliff Durr in 1910, in his Starke School military uniform (Courtesy of the Alabama State Department of Archives and History)

tirely different matter. There, life was "close to heaven." As soon as school was finished for the year, he would be off to the farm, and there he would remain "until that sad day when school went in again." The journey was always by horse and buggy or spring wagon, his grandfather always came to fetch him, and as they rode along together, he would entrance the boy with stories of his early life on the plantation and of the Civil War. Then, as familiar landmarks appeared, the excitement would mount, for on the farm were the animals he loved so much—the chickens, the cows, the horses, and, of course, his dog Shiloh. It was here, for a time, that his bantam rooster Dickey resided. Dickey was a magnificent, rich-plumed bird. The young Durr won first prize with him at the Alabama State Fair in 1906, a moment of joy unalloyed.[20]

As well as the animals, there was the natural landscape, "the pastures and woods to explore," small streams to dam up, and a large creek in which to fish. There were plums and blackberries to pick, peach trees and apple trees to enjoy, and Indian arrowheads to be "found in abundance" along the banks of the Coosa River. Sometimes in his wanderings he would stray onto the adjoining state-farm land, and there he would see convicts working in the fields—strangely dressed men, often wild looking. Yet their very familiarity meant that he was not afraid of them.[21]

Clifford Durr's letters to his family in Montgomery revealed just how much he loved being at Wetumpka. Full of accounts of adventures such as breaking steers, killing snakes, hunting and fishing, they are the joyful chronicles of an essentially happy experience. Sometimes he wrote of his companions on these excitements, for he did have playmates on the farm, and very different they were from his classmates at the Starke School, upper-class white boys like Lister Hill, the son of a prominent Montgomery physician who one day would serve as senator from Alabama. Here, the young Durr shared the farm's joys with the sons and daughters of the farmhands and the tenants, who were poor and who were black. Like many Southern white boys who grew up in the country, young Clifford Durr's childhood friends were often not of his race.[22]

His chief companion, however, was his grandfather, whom his wife, Virginia, was later to describe, correctly, as "the greatest influence on his life." Together they hunted and fished, roamed the fields, explored the riverbanks, and talked—about the South and its traditions, about the land and its peoples, and about the war. Sometimes the two of them ranged farther afield than the Wetumpka farm.

In 1904, his grandfather took young Cliff on his first journey, when together they went to the St. Louis World's Fair. Durr recollected little about the visit except the sight of a "cow made out of butter" and the general comforting presence of being with a man whom he loved without stint and who returned his devotion in like measure. It is significant that, when Cliff fell seriously ill with typhoid in 1913, it was Grandfather Judkins, not his mother or Henrietta, who nursed him through the illness.[23]

Describing his childhood many years later, Clifford Durr thought it was "pretty much that of the average Southern boy," in a region "characterized by a rather comfortable poverty." No one was rich, he said; "Only Yankees were rich." Obviously, however, the Durrs were neither poor nor average. As the son of a prosperous businessman of prominent family, given an education reserved for a fortunate few, Durr's childhood experiences were often considerably removed from those of his white contemporaries, not to mention those who were black. His father was indeed no millionaire, but in turn-of-the-century Montgomery, Clifford Durr was a child of relative privilege.[24]

Still, there were experiences held in common with many white Southerners at least. One was the chance to get to know the land. His Wetumpka summers engendered in him a love for the locality and a feel for it which never left him. The fact that, at the end of his life, he was able to live on the farm which had been such an important aspect of his boyhood was a matter of the greatest joy to him. All his life he loved the Elmore County countryside—the rivers, hills, and forests of his growing up—and this he shared with many from his region.

Then, he also shared an early and lifelong adherence to Protestant Christianity. John Wesley Durr, Jr., served forty-six years as clerk of the session of the First Presbyterian Church, Montgomery. All his children followed him into the church early and remained there. Clifford Durr was a Presbyterian all of his life. The church, the Christian message, was central to his own belief system. Nothing made him sadder than his eventual parting with First Presbyterian in the 1960s because of differences over the admission of blacks. He never, however, repudiated his Christian faith. Rather, it became a stronger sustaining force the older he grew and the more he was beleaguered. A strong adherence to the Protestant tradition, then, was something Clifford Durr gained early and which he shared with many of his contemporaries.[25]

Of course, Clifford Durr, along with his white contemporaries, held a particular view of Southern history, a perspective on the recent past colored by a conviction of the essential justice of the Southern cause in the Civil War, the bravery of the Southern men at arms, and the horror of the Reconstruction period at war's end, when the defeated South had a government imposed on it that was dominated by Yankee conquerors, Southern traitors, and ignorant and vengeful Negroes. This was the view of Southern history promulgated at the Starke School, and if it was moderated somewhat by his grandfather, who refused to march with other Confederate veterans, having no use for such windy display, who acknowledged that Yankees could also fight well, and who wondered if the South had always been right, Clifford Durr nevertheless grew up believing implicitly that the South's reasons for seceding had been just and that she had been cruelly betrayed. In this, he also made common cause with his contemporaries.[26]

Nowhere was his upbringing more traditional than on the question of race. Clifford Durr's parents believed implicitly in racial segregation and the inherent inferiority of black people. Along with that, of course, "there was a continuing emphasis upon the obligations and responsibilities that went along with that superiority in status." However, the status was never in doubt, nor the illegalities occasionally necessary in order to maintain it, such as the denial to blacks of the provisions of the Fourteenth and Fifteenth amendments. Moreover, there were times, such as the killing of Henrietta's nephew, when the violence engendered by Southern segregation seemed genuinely to trouble his father at least. Normally, however, there was not much talk about race in the Durr household, at least when the children were in earshot. Conversations about the subject were very likely to die down if one of them appeared, Cliff Durr later recalled.[27]

Grandfather Judkins held similarly paternalist views. He was scrupulously fair to the blacks who worked for him, while at the same time insisting that they "keep their place." He was bitterly opposed to the drafting of blacks to fight in World War I, Durr recalled, because, having fought for their country, they would then be in a position to demand full rights from it, rights in all conscience he believed America could not refuse, deplorable as he felt it to be. At the same time, nothing enraged him more than a black who seemed to take liberties. Clifford Durr recalled once having to hide the shotgun to keep his grandfather from killing "an old Negro of whom I was particularly fond," because he had thought him insolent. Deprived of the weapon, Judkins attacked him with his fists, felling him with a blow to the mouth. "When he saw what he had done," said Durr, "a look of shame and horror immediately came over his face and he apologised." He tried, for the rest of that old black man's life, Durr thought, to "heal the wounds to the [man's] dignity of which he held himself guilty." His sense of paternalism precluded such violence, yet at the same time his grandson always believed he would, in his rage at the man's fancied insolence, have shot him, had the gun been available. Hardly surprisingly, given his background and environment, Clifford Durr grew to manhood holding essentially the same paternalist perspective on race relations as the rest of his family. In this again, his childhood experiences were common to most white Southerners.[28]

Clifford Durr completed the Starke School phase of his education in 1915. He was, as usual, on the honor roll and also won the James T. Holtzclaw Medal for "ready writing." The next step in his formal education was never in much doubt. Like many other Starke graduates, including Lister Hill and his own elder brothers, it was decided that he should attend The University of Alabama in Tuscaloosa.[29]

The University of Alabama in 1915 was on the threshold of a period of expansion synonymous with the name of perhaps its greatest twentieth-century president, Dr. George H. Denny. In the course of more than two decades, as one historian has written, he "converted it from a small old-fashioned institution into a modern State University." Denny, however, took up office only in 1911. When Durr entered the freshman class in 1915, the university retained many of its late nineteenth-century characteristics: a somewhat inflexible curriculum with heavy emphasis on the classics, relatively low scholarly standards, a small, homogenous student body, with the presence of a handful of women scarcely detracting from the overwhelmingly masculine atmosphere. Indeed, the compulsory wearing of military uniforms had been abolished only in 1903. There was also a general lack of resources, the result of a consistently niggardly approach by the state legislature.

Denny's new broom had started to sweep through the campus by the time of Durr's arrival there, however, and the foundations had been laid for the new buildings that were to be one enduring mark of his long tenure of office. Moreover, some aspects of the campus spanned the transition from small college to modern university. The beautiful oaks that dotted the campus were one such landmark, as was Prof. Thomas Chalmers McCorvey. Born in 1851, Professor McCorvey imparted his particular perspective on Southern history to generations of young Alabamians, both before and after Denny's arrival. In his booming tones, as future senator John Sparkman recalled, he told them of the glorious nature of the Southern cause, of the bitterness of Reconstruction, and of his own experiences in the Knights of the White Camelia as he fought the Yankee occupiers and their black lackeys. He spoke, too, of redemption and the need to maintain vigilance lest once again Republicans should try to impose their wicked will on the South. The preeminence of the Democratic party was essential if Southern independence was not to be once more compromised. McCorvey, easily the university's most popular teacher, reinforced in the minds of hundreds of young Alabamians the bitter lessons of the recent past. Clifford Durr became one of his young disciples.[30]

Clifford Durr's initial reaction to the university was one of confusion, compounded by acute homesickness. However, this passed, and as things became less strange, his natural cheerfulness returned. Like most freshmen, he was living in a boardinghouse, with a Mrs. Curry, whom he liked and who seemed "to take a special interest in new boys." Moreover, he had got his course straightened out and had done well in examinations covering work he had done at Starke School. "I can now consider myself a full-fledged freshman," he wrote his mother in October; "I am feeling fine and don't think I will have any more trouble." To his sister Lucy he wrote of meeting girls and watching the football team practice. University life, he thought, was not going to be too bad after all.[31]

By the end of the first semester, he had clearly adjusted to college life. Academically he had done quite well, earning three As and two Bs, which pleased his father immensely. "We have great hopes of you," he wrote his son proudly. He had embraced the university's social and sporting life enthusiastically as well, taking part in the various rites and rituals accompanying the major football fixtures. When Alabama defeated archrival Sewanee for the first time in eighteen years, he was one of the hundreds who took part in a postgame "nightshirt parade." The Sewanee tiger was laid in a coffin and, followed by "400 students all wearing night shirts and pyjamas," paraded noisily through the girls' dormitory and then all around Tuscaloosa, interrupting picture shows and other forms of entertainment. Eventually it was laid to rest under one of the goals on the football field. The lark was not without its unscheduled excitement. "While the parade was in progress," Cliff wrote to his sister Lucy, "one of the esteemed citizens of Tuscaloosa, taking offense because he had been aroused from his slumber advanced toward the line of night shirts with a gun in his hand while his wife had an iron poker by way of reinforcement." It was all very good fun, he said.[32]

The University of Alabama, like most Southern schools, had a strong fraternity tradition. Durr was anxious to join one and was a little nervous during rush week that he would not be asked to do so. He was delighted, therefore, when he was "rushed" by Sigma Alpha Epsilon and wrote formally to his father seeking permission to accept the offer. Paternal approval was duly forthcoming, even though his father warned him that "such organizations encourage the habit of extravagance." Noting Cliff's enthusiasm for sports and social life, he exhorted him to put the same enthusiasm into his studies.[33] Cliff Durr completed his first semester of tertiary education, having survived initial bouts of homesickness and having integrated himself reasonably well into the scholarly and social life of the institution.

One aspect of college life he could not come to terms with, however, was the constant hazing of freshmen by the senior class. Freshmen, rather in the manner of junior boys at an English public school, were required to perform menial tasks for senior students, such as cleaning their boots, carrying their books, or marking off the football field. Failure to perform satisfactorily could result in beatings, usually by the application of bed slats to the exposed rear end. Durr suffered this treatment more than once; consequently, it was with some relief that he reported to his family that the whole senior class had been expelled shortly before the end of his second semester for hazing freshmen, as Denny moved decisively to end the practice. "So from now on I don't have to be afraid of getting beat up," he crowed to Henrietta Walker, "and I can walk about feeling just about as big as anybody in school."[34]

Clifford Durr's own problems with homesickness during his freshman year meant that he viewed the travails of the new students with a sympathetic eye when he returned to the university as a sophomore in September 1916. "I never saw as many homesick boys in my life," he wrote his mother. In their misery they reminded him so much of his own condition the previous year that he was spending a deal of time helping console them and, in a few cases, persuading them not to go home. Otherwise, the routine that had become established during his first year continued. He attended to his studies sufficiently to make quite good grades, he spent time at the fraternity house, he went to the movies occasionally (one which made a deep impression was *Birth of a Nation*), he ran on the track team, and he took part in football parades and rallies. Indeed, it had all become rather boring and routine. University life was monotonous, he complained to his mother in February 1917. Basketball was over, but baseball had not yet started, "so there is no amusement at all of an athletic nature"; classes were unexciting, "studying was monotonous," and since *Birth of a Nation* there had been few good "moving pictures" in Tuscaloosa. It was all a bit of a drag.[35]

The campus was soon, however, to be shaken from its routine, as it became increasingly obvious that the United States was about to enter the European war. Clifford Durr was an avowed Wilsonian. "Today I am 18," he wrote his father on his birthday. "Just old enough to be shot by the Germans, but still too young to vote for the President who will declare war on Germany." However, had he the chance to vote, he would have supported Wilson, "for he has certainly done all he could to keep us out of trouble." As the formal declaration approached, the campus became engulfed in "a patriotic fervor." Military uniforms again appeared, and the students began to drill regularly. It was all very exciting, and he was very pleased to be a part of it, as he drilled daily with the university regiment.[36]

By late April, he reported, the university had "become more of a training camp than a school." All students who were taking military training were allowed to drop three hours of class work, morning class periods had been shortened from an hour to forty-five minutes to make more drilling time available, and afternoon classes and laboratory work had been cut out entirely, as the University of Alabama made its contribution to the patriotic fervor surrounding America's entry into World War I. Soon the university's regulations were amended to permit seniors to graduate without completing their courses, provided they planned to enter officer training school. There was no prospect of studying anyway, Durr said. Every afternoon was devoted to drill, as was the morning hour between 8 and 9 A.M. No one talked of anything except the war and going "over there."[37]

In this heady situation, Clifford Durr, like thousands of others, had to evaluate his own position. Should he join up immediately, thus abandoning his studies, or should he wait awhile? In the end, he decided on the latter course. He fully expected to fight Germany at some stage, he wrote his father, but had decided not to volunteer immediately. He would try to complete his junior year, go then to officers training school, and, he hoped, overseas after that. However, should there be conscription, he would volunteer immediately, thus giving up his studies. "It is the duty of all of us who are able to volunteer," he thought. "To be conscripted would be a mark of dishonor."[38]

He was able to follow his plan. He completed his junior year, performing sufficiently well to be tapped for the Jasons, an elite society comprising the best "all round" men in the junior class. He formed his first real association with a girl, a Miss Spottswood, whom he took to a "society debut," and then, as soon as school was over, he reported for Reserve Officer Training School at Fort Sheridan, Illinois.[39]

Cliff Durr's initial reaction to Fort Sheridan was most unfavorable and reveals graphically the extent of his acceptance of Southern mores and myths. He was on a streetcar, he reported disgustedly, "and the first thing I saw was a black negro with the ROTC insignia on his collar." Profoundly shocked, Durr "felt like coming home immediately," to a world where such disorders could not possibly occur. It transpired that the black trainee was assigned to a Wisconsin company, and thus there would be no chance of their having to mix. Durr's company, fortunately, was safely Southern and white, with only the presence of "a China man" providing any sort of incongruity. He, however, could be coped with; a black could certainly have not been so.[40]

The course at Fort Sheridan lasted a month. Durr returned to the University of Alabama ROTC and in October 1918 went into full-time officer training at Camp Pike, Arkansas. Like many another lad, he was anxious to be up and away and chafed at the relative inactivity of the training camp. As the prospect of peace became increasingly real, he became worried that the war would end before he could get into it and scorned those of his fellow trainees who looked forward to early discharge. "I think I must be in a platoon of conscientious objectors," he wrote to his sister contemptuously of them. "All they can talk about is peace," which was not what he wanted to hear.[41]

Peace came anyway, on November 11, 1918, bringing to Clifford Durr "the biggest disappointment I have ever had." He was genuinely devastated. "My chances of ever seeing service in France are entirely gone," he wailed to his mother. He had come to Camp Pike confident that he would experience some action in the trenches. Peace had "considerably lowered" his spirits, but he still had some hopes of going to France with an army of occupation. Instead, he was scheduled for early discharge. How bitterly he rued his initial de-

Cliff Durr in his military uniform in 1918 (Courtesy of the Alabama State Department of Archives and History)

cision not to join up immediately. "What hurts is the realization that I could have gone over if I had gotten into this thing at the start," as his brother James had done, "instead of waiting until it was over." However, he did not "feel like a slacker," though to the outside world he might appear so, because he knew he "would have been glad to go if I had the opportunity." Still, the end of the war was a bitter pill to swallow. Like many young men, full of idealism about Mr. Wilson's crusade and ignorant of and insensitive to the full horror of the European carnage, Cliff Durr had hoped desperately to have been part of the great adventure.[42]

Instead, it was back to The University of Alabama, and with very bad grace. Still, there were compensations. For one thing, he was elected senior-class president, recognition of his all-round standing with his fellow students, and that was gratifying, even if the office carried with it some difficult social responsibilities. One was to lead the senior dance. Desperately he sought advice from his sister Lucy on "all questions relating to dances and, especially to leading them." His partner, Miss Noxie Lanning, had proved to be of little use in this department—in fact, he said, "she don't dance." Neither did he really, but he wanted "to act like I had been leading dances ever since I shed my Baby teeth."[43]

Lucy obviously worked hard, for the dance went off very well. Clifford Durr—tall, blond, and resplendent in his military uniform—led the grand march with Noxie, whose father had finally given her permission to dance. She loved all the gaiety and color, and even he was quite impressed. "I don't see much pleasure in dancing," he told his sister, "but I would like to know how just for such emergencies."[44]

Cliff's senior year at The University of Alabama thus passed pleasantly enough. However, he was glad it was coming to an end; he wanted "to hurry up and go to work"—but at what? His own thoughts had turned to the law as a profession, and he believed he could make a success of it. His father, however, had other ideas. Brushing aside any talk of law school, he told Clifford to try farming. Moreover, he had arranged work for him over the summer with a local farmer. That would give him the chance to sample the career chosen for him.[45]

Cliff Durr was happy enough to go along with his father's wishes. Besides, it did not do to cross John Wesley Durr. He duly completed his A.B., majoring in English and economics, with a record sufficiently distinguished to be elected to Phi Beta Kappa, and duly went to work on the land, as his father had insisted. He also did something else, however—something quite unusual, something about which he consulted no one, something which would drastically change the direction of his life. On August 9, 1919, he made application for a Rhodes Scholarship.[46]

Clearly this action had been taken on an impulse. He had not thought through its implications, and by early September he had resolved to withdraw his application. He was persuaded, however, by his former dean at The University of Alabama to remain in the race. The references were duly taken up; his father, somewhat reluctantly, agreed to Cliff's applying; and he was formally interviewed on October 31, 1919. By this time he had at least made the decision that, if his application was successful, he would read for a B.A. in jurisprudence at Queens College, Oxford. However, it still seemed very much a shot in the dark.[47]

On December 9, 1919, Prof. Frank Aydelotte, United States secretary to the Rhodes Trust, wrote to the sixty-three young aspirants whose applications for scholarships had been successful. Clifford J. Durr was one of these. As he needed to be in Oxford in January for the start of the Hilary (or winter) term, he had less than three weeks to outfit himself, pack, and bid his family farewell. Clifford Durr had deeply regretted missing the "great adventure" of the battlefields of France and Flanders. Now he was to embark on an adventure of a vastly different kind, in the ancient halls of Oxford University. It was a long way for a boy from Alabama to travel.[48]

2

Johnny Reb at Oxford

Clifford Durr's "great adventure" really began even before he left the United States, with the journey north and then a day or two exploring New York City. He had never been there and, like every other visitor, found the sights, sounds, and smells of the metropolis quite overwhelming. In particular, Brooklyn Bridge filled him with wonder. However, what with arranging his passage on the SS *Adriatic,* getting his visa, and attending to the various tasks of the departing traveler, there was little enough time for sightseeing. His passport, incidentally, revealed that, like his father, he was a tall, well-built young man, six feet one inch in height and seeming even taller because of his erect carriage. His complexion was fair, his eyes blue, and his nose straight.[1]

Clifford Durr sailed for England and Queens College, Oxford, on January 3, 1920. His reports on the sea voyage indicate that it was reasonably uneventful, though he was very sick for a few days. Indeed, he believed "a German torpedo was the only thing I could think of that would end my misery," so unwell did he feel. However, things got better after a day or two, and he was able to observe both his surroundings and his fellow travelers. There were twenty Rhodes men on board, all "fine fellows," even one Tong from Arizona, whom Durr at first feared was Chinese. He turned out not to be, however; indeed, "in spite of a mustache," he seemed to be "all right." The crew were all English and to his surprise were "polite, obliging and very friendly." Also on board was Viscount Grey, who invited the Rhodes men to tea. Durr was very impressed with him. He was "entirely different from the American idea of a lord," he wrote his Aunt Florence, as "he didn't have on spats or a monocle." Indeed, he was nowhere near as pompous as the former mayor of Montgomery, Durr thought, and he particularly enjoyed the polite yet effective way the viscount handled one of the young Americans, a brash young lad from Wisconsin, who had been rather too familiar with him. "I couldn't possibly have enjoyed anything more than the way that Yankee cooled down," reported the young Southern gentleman.[2]

The voyage was soon over, however, and it was straight to Oxford and his lodgings in Iffley Road, with a Mr. and Mrs. Holland, who were very welcoming. He had hoped for rooms in the college itself, but unfortunately there were none available, though he would take his meals there. He had also called on the senior tutor—"a very pleasant and near-sighted old gentleman," was how Durr described him. Yet it was all rather strange, and the pangs of homesickness and loneliness were real. "I am as unsettled as if I was in the Congo Free State or somewhere else in the African jungle," wrote the young Alabamian, and nothing looked natural, not even the admittedly beautiful English countryside. His study plans had fallen into place, however. He had been admitted to senior status on the strength of his Alabama degree and could therefore begin to read law immediately. Moreover, he had begun to puzzle out the intricacies of Oxford's college system and English currency. He had bought a bicycle, he was beginning to like tea, and he had even noticed that English girls had "good complexions and big feet." The English reserve, however, was daunting. No one had spoken to him since his arrival, not even those with whom he ate. They were "as sociable as an iceberg," he complained.[3]

Soon, however, young Clifford Durr had made some friends, despite the coolness of the English. There was an American club at Oxford with over one hundred members which he soon joined, and he also found the Canadians there extremely congenial. Then, he had become friendly with a young South African named Halley. "The negro question naturally brought us together," he told his father. Indeed, Halley had soon convinced him that South Africa was one place that had "a bigger Negro problem than Alabama, and from his account the Negro isn't allowed as many privileges as he is in Alabama." So, he was not lonely "in spite of the Englishmen"; besides, there was plenty of work to be done. He was reading Roman law, constitutional law, and torts, and though he found the permissive educational atmosphere strange after the highly structured one of The University of Alabama, the demands on his time were nevertheless considerable.[4]

By the end of the Hilary term, in March, Cliff Durr was ready for the first of what would be many periods of tourism. With some other Americans, he went to see the sights of London. Most of them he found fascinating—Westminster Abbey, St. Paul's, the houses of Parliament; the beauty and the grandeur of the old city moved him deeply. Moreover, he had his introduction to serious theater during his visit. He saw a number of shows, the highlight being a performance at Drury Lane by "Anna Pavlova and her outfit of Russian ballet dancers," the first ballet he had ever experienced.[5]

There were some things, however, that bothered him. One was the tolerance the English showed for what to the young Alabamian were dangerously alien points of view. He went to Hyde Park and was assailed by radical rhetoric on all sides. While recognizing that "England has a different policy" toward radicals than that of the United States, in that "they believe in letting the radicals speak and get it out of their system," he was nevertheless concerned at what he heard and by the fact that a "good many laboring men" seemed in sympathy with the speakers, even those who praised Lenin and Trotsky. He hoped that the United States would not follow the British example but would "continue to make all of this type go back where they came from," ironic words from one who would later suffer greatly for his principled defense of the right to free speech. Clifford Durr did recognize, however, that because of its class structure and distinctions, "England is more favorable as ground for the red movement than the USA," one of the many reasons he was "thankful . . . that I am an American." Already the experience of being a foreigner abroad was reinforcing his national as opposed to regional identity. When at home he was a Southerner; in England he was, for the first time in his life, an American as well.[6]

It was not long before he was again a tourist, and this time to the Continent. His mother and his sister Lucy arrived in England in May. Once Clifford's Oxford obligations were over, the three of them took off for France. They visited the world war battlefields where American troops had been engaged and spent time in Paris before settling in Grenoble, where Clifford was enrolled in a French course. On the whole, they enjoyed France. Rather to their surprise they found the French "obliging and not very mercenary," while Clifford thought the men "look more like real men than the English." Indeed, "it is surprising how little like foreigners some of them look," he remarked to his aunt, in one of his more ethnocentric utterances. Clifford remained in Grenoble after his mother and sister had gone, and the rather sedate pace of life there gave him time to think about his

"Afternoon Coffee at Oxford." Cliff with some friends in 1920 (Courtesy of the Alabama State Department of Archives and History)

first months abroad and, especially, about Oxford. "Oxford life is the most pleasant life in the world for those who don't worry about the future," he told his father, and though the work was in many ways undemanding and "like a correspondence course," a "while spent there is time well spent." He did not want to be there too long, however. Oxford, he hoped, would provide him with a degree and a means of making a living, nothing more.[7]

As well as trying to learn French, Grenoble provided Clifford with his first real chance to meet European girls. There were two he got to know particularly well, whom he "recommended" to his brother James. One was an Italian lass who was "good looking enough, smokes cigarettes gracefully and is husky enough to sweep out the house" and a Norwegian who was "equally husky," though "not so good looking." She compensated, however, for this relative lack of looks by singing well and was also a good cook. Despite these and other diversions, by September he was looking forward very much to returning to Oxford, never mind the "cabbage, potatoes and roast beef and rain." Besides, he now had a room in Queens, which he was thoroughly looking forward to.[8]

Back in Oxford he quickly settled into college living, aided by his scout, who was "tall, red-headed" and was called Joe James. He found that he had to spend more time on his studies in order to keep up. Before long it was Thanksgiving, which the Americans celebrated with a football game, and then the Christmas break. Once again it was over to the Continent—first to Paris, and then to Spain, which he did not like at all. He attended a bullfight, and the experience fixed his opinion of the Spanish "at about zero," while he found Spanish officialdom and the Spanish military laughable. "If the Negroes could see the Spanish uniform," he wrote his mother, "they would stop going North and come to Spain and join the Army instead."[9]

And so a year had passed—a year full of interest, full of effort, but also with its low points and its unresolved questions. He still had trouble dealing with the English. Their reserve was always a worry, and he was increasingly angered by their ethnocentricity and their superiority. One complaint was that they knew nothing of Alabama—and so he gave them frequent geography lessons. "Last night an Englishman by the name of Richardson showed that he was very ignorant of Alabama," he wrote his mother early in 1921. "He even thought Alabama was below the Equator and didn't even know about the Alabama claims. It is surprising how ignorant Englishmen are." So, after dinner he invited poor Richardson to his room, got out the atlas, "and proceeded to give him a lesson in geography." He also gave him a piece of Alabama cake, a gift from his mother.[10]

Despite their ignorance of his home state, it was the English view of the United States in general that he found most irritating. "The tendency is to belittle the US, and to try to make it out as an inferior sort of country run by men of inferior intelligence," he told his father. "When any remark concerning America is made in a lecture it always brings forth laughter." Like many before him, the young Southerner found that the English sense of superiority brought out in him nationalist sentiments he had not really known he possessed. His American sense of difference was continually being reinforced by his overseas experience, even more than his Southernness.[11]

At the same time, however, he felt he was making some progress toward understanding these strange people. He was getting used to Oxford, his room, and Oxford life generally and was even beginning to come to terms with English sport. The tall, fit young Alabamian had been the star of the Queens College Athletics sports, winning three titles, including the 220-yard handicap, and finishing second in the 100-yard dash. His speed led to an invitation to join the Queens rugby union squad, and he eventually became the regular fullback for the college team. He enjoyed the sport and became quite good at it, but again, playing the game brought out further differences between the English and the American temperament. "The Englishman is just as hard to understand in sport as in everyday life," he opined. "They never get excited but go about the game in a determined sort of way just as if they had a job before them." They did not "get up the same fighting spirit in games as the Americans do," he thought.[12]

Yet there would always be much in Britain that would remain strange, institutions that were puzzling and at times menacing. The young man was particularly bothered by what seemed to be the power of organized labor to dictate to the government on a range of issues. "Labor seems able to do what it pleases in England," he told his father, "in spite of Lloyd George's threats of being firm." He believed in fair treatment for workers, but what he was observing in England was something else again. He hoped fervently that organized labor would "never get as powerful in America" as it had in Britain, for economic ruin would surely follow. The coal miners, currently engaged in a national strike, he found particularly threatening, with their "Bolshevik tactics," their open defiance of government authority, and their frank desire to "start a civil war." Alabama did not have such problems and, "wonderful State" that it was, would, he hoped, continue to avoid them. There was little sign in the young Durr of the convinced defender of the rights of organized labor that he later became.[13]

Much of the formalism, the tradition, and the appeal to imperial values that was so much a part of Oxford life continued to amuse or irritate him. A devout Christian and a regular churchgoer, he found the Church of England form of service altogether too stuffy and circumscribed for his taste, coming as he did from a Southern Presbyterian tradition. Only when he started attending a Congregational church did he begin to feel at home. It was "the first time I have really felt I was in church since I have been in England," he wrote, for there were "no choir boys, no praying by formula or anything else."[14]

As to the monarchy, he found the whole institution rather irrelevant. He was amused by the fuss and the pomp surrounding a visit by the queen to Oxford in the spring of 1921 in order to receive an honorary degree, though he did concede that she at least looked "human." As far as the British Empire was concerned, as a Rhodes

Scholar he had to mingle with its representatives and its celebrants from time to time, notably at the annual Rhodes Dinner. The 1921 one was particularly noteworthy, not only because many of the scholars got drunk, but because among the guests were Field Marshal Smuts, Lord Milner, and the prime minister of New Zealand, William Ferguson Massey. Massey gave the after-dinner speech, and to Clifford Durr it was so bad that it enabled him to think of "Alabama's State legislators with a feeling of pride," something it had never occurred to him to do before. Massey took as his theme "the mighty British Empire" and "how nothing else was of importance." It was, said the less than impressed Durr, "as if William Hohenzollern and not the Prime Minister of New Zealand had been speaking." Naturally, there was no mention of the Americans. Experiences such as these continued to reinforce the young man's sense of nationalism and of national difference.[15]

The Rhodes Dinner was one of the few social diversions Clifford permitted himself in the spring of 1921, as he had decided to present himself for the Schools examination (the final examination for his degree) in June, somewhat earlier than normal. He studied from 9:00 A.M. to 11.30 P.M. each day, with only a two-hour tennis break each afternoon to relieve the monotony. It was during this time that he became a convinced and enthusiastic cigarette smoker, a habit he retained for the rest of his life, despite the increasingly mordant warnings of successions of medical practitioners. The examinations themselves were "not too bad." He sat nine papers in all, including Roman law, legal history, real property, torts, contract, constitutional law, and international law, achieving a second-class pass overall, "the average Rhodes Scholar grade," he called it. He was pleased with his result, and with good reason, because he successfully had covered two years' work in less than eighteen months. Moreover, it brought nearer the day he could return to Alabama.[16]

By the time his results came through, he had embarked on an extensive and diverse summer holiday. First came a cycling tour with four Oxford friends of southern England and the west coast beaches, visiting, among other places, Bath, Glastonbury, Penzance (which he found "over-rated"), St. Ives ("one of the prettiest little towns I ever saw"), and Clovelly. They broke for a week on the Isle of Wight, returned to Oxford for their orals, and then went north to Scotland.[17]

Along the way the lads had many adventures. They went fishing with some locals at Clovelly and took some beer along for the fishermen. They proved to be teetotalers, and so the beer went over the

Four young Oxonians on a beach, summer 1921. Cliff is on the extreme right. (Courtesy of the Alabama State Department of Archives and History)

side. It was, he wrote, "the first time I ever saw an Englishman refuse beer." He attended the Inverness-shire Society picnic, an occasion where "English dignity and stiffness were noticeably absent," and won the single men's footrace. It was in the north of Scotland, too, that he first encountered that burgeoning phenomenon of the 1920s, American tourists, and he was to continue to meet them as he traveled on. They did not impress. "It is no wonder that the American doesn't as a general rule make a very favorable impression in foreign countries," he wrote his mother. "The foreigners don't realise that it is the case of the 'catfish who has left his home in the little creek' taking a swim in the ocean among the sharks." One of the said catfish attacked him vigorously for coming to Oxford, "when there were American universities just as good." She did, however, become friendlier when she learned that he planned to return home once he had completed his studies.[18]

So, there were American braggarts as well as English ones, but somehow they were not quite as offensive. The Americans, after all,

"The Perils of Cycling," summer 1921. Cliff is the heavily bandaged young man. (Courtesy of the Alabama State Department of Archives and History)

only claimed that theirs was "the finest country in the world." The Englishman, on the other hand, thought that not only was England the greatest country in the world, it was the only one that counted. "He even looks on the Scotchman as a sort of inferior being and the Irishman as a brainless sort of animal," while the Welshman was "the lowest type of all." America, claimed Durr, was seen as an "upstart country, full of millionaires but entirely lacking in brains" and owing all its success to its British foundations. This English sense of superiority he could never accept, and it continued to infuriate him throughout his Oxford years, even though he came to recognize that it was directed not only toward Americans but to all non-English, including citizens of the empire like the Australians, who were always accused of "being poor sportsmen." It was, he said, the reason why Cecil Rhodes's money had "been wasted as far as the accomplishment of his main object is concerned," for he had manifestly not learned to love the English. Still, they had their good points, and he did not love Yankees either, yet "the North and South get along." So, presumably, could Americans and the English. Nevertheless, he said, he would never write B.A. (Oxon) after his name, though he had earned the right to do so.[19]

The trip to Scotland did reinforce one perception for him, namely, that not all residents of the British Isles were alike. Indeed, he found the Scots to be "as different from the English as it is possible for members of the same household to be." In general, Clifford liked them better, even though he deplored their addiction to strong drink. In Glasgow, he said, the only interesting thing was to try to count the sober people on any given street—"the number was not high." Edinburgh was scarcely better, and it made the young man glad the United States now had prohibition, "even though it is contended that it doesn't prohibit." Moreover, the Scottish laborers and their plight disturbed him. "They look like degenerates both physically and mentally," he told his father. Of course, the root cause of their problem was the dangerously high levels of unemployment, which appalled him, both because of the suffering it engendered and because of the prospect of revolution it portended. "It is a wonder Bolshevism doesn't get a stronger hold than it already has," he warned.[20]

From Scotland, with both its warmth and its bleakness, it was across the North Sea to Norway, where Durr and an Oxford friend were the guests of Miss Rolsted, the "husky" Norwegian girl he had befriended in Grenoble the previous year. Nothing had prepared him for that country's physical beauty; the scenery overwhelmed him, with all the magnificent mountains and the awe-inspiring waterfalls. He quickly decided that he liked the Norwegian landscape more than the English countryside, because, while England looked like a beautiful garden, Norway had such superb natural beauty that it did not "need the finishing touches of hedge rows and sheep." He liked the people, too, the food (especially the breakfasts), and the beautiful cities. He would not, he wrote, have missed this Norwegian experience "for all the cathedrals in Europe."[21]

From Norway it was on to Germany—and with some trepidation, given recent history. Again, he was pleasantly surprised. His German cabin mates in the voyage across the Baltic were, "despite their nationality," not "such bad fellows," while the country itself seemed to be "on the way back." The people were even more polite than the French, and though they were threadbare, they were eating well, and they all seemed to be working. There were no beggars, "no men on street corners turning the handle of a barrel organ" and bearing the sign "unemployed ex-officer," as in Britain. The cities were beautiful, despite the military monuments. Berlin, in fact, he voted "the prettiest city I have ever seen." Yet the monuments did symbolize something troubling, in that they were so suggestive of war. "The Germans have been in the power of the militarists as the Spanish, Italians and Irish are in the power of the priests," was his conclusion, and this could only be deplored.[22]

Nevertheless, as the young traveler moved through Germany, the prejudices arising from the recent war began to abate. And then, in Coblenz, he observed something which struck an immediate response with his own background and which "aroused great sympathy for the Germans" within him. Among the French troops occupying the city were colonials from Algeria. They were dark skinned, and he was outraged. "I don't see that there is so very much to choose between them and negroes," he wrote his mother in horror. "They are just about as tough looking a bunch of men as I ever saw and I am sure that if they had been put in charge after the Civil War instead of the Negroes, the Ku Klux Klan would have been just as active. They are just as uncivilized as any Negro troops from the Congo would be."[23]

Clifford Durr, a true son of the South, knew his Reconstruction legends well, and the parallel between what he saw in Coblenz and what he perceived to be the history of his own region was obvious. From then on, his sympathy was with the Germans. The British and American press were publishing lies about the hatred the Germans felt for the victors in the war, he claimed. The Germans in fact were a pleasant, friendly people—"even the police"—particularly toward Americans. They wanted no more than to get on with the job of rebuilding their nation, and this they should be allowed to do without the presence of unwelcome occupying forces, especially colored ones.[24]

And so, after being away from Oxford for over three months, it was back to study. With less than a year to go, and that to be interspersed with more travel, it did not seem a long time. "Two thirds of my period of exile is almost up," he wrote his mother as he prepared to resume his academic career, this time to read for the B.C.L. degree.[25]

Clifford Durr's final months at Oxford were extremely relaxed and pleasant. He moved out of the college and into digs "with the best land-lady in Oxford," a Mrs. Bosher, whose dog Gyp became his special pet. The English autumn was beautiful, and even the died-in-the-wool Alabamian was forced to concede that, in such circumstances, "there are few places more pleasant than Oxford." Still, as his period abroad drew to a close, he became increasingly preoccupied with what was to happen when he returned home. Where would he work? Where would he live? He was worried, too, about reports from home concerning the political and social climate there, in particular that President Harding and the Republicans now in power favored greater political rights for blacks. "Political equality isn't a solution," asserted the young Southerner, "and can't very well be separated from social equality." Why could Northerners not see this? He still disliked "Yankees as a whole," he confessed, "although I don't see anything wrong with the individuals." Exposure to other cultures had certainly not diluted his basically Southern perspectives. Indeed, they had been reinforced.[26]

It was perhaps these preoccupations that caused Cliff Durr's Christmas vacation to fall a bit flat. He went to Italy with a fellow American Rhodes Scholar, and though he found the art and ruins wonderful, he was not so impressed with the people. They were, in fact, "the least interesting of any country he had seen." Moreover, the overwhelming presence of the Catholic church repelled the young Presbyterian. He found the veneration of images of saints completely alienating. "I can't see the superiority of this form of Christianity to the religion of the Hindus, Chinese and other heathen," he complained, indicating again that experience of other societies had reinforced his own narrow cultural perspectives rather than broadened them.[27]

Back he came to Oxford for the final preexamination period, though even this was interrupted by another brief visit abroad, ostensibly to study. He and some friends took a house in Dinard, a small Breton village. Clifford claimed that they worked hard all week but reserved the weekends for "dissipation." If so, it was of a milder sort than is normally associated with the word, mainly involving visits to the movies, breakfast in bed, and long country walks. He took his exams in June, again cramming two year's work into one and was far from confident about the outcome. Nevertheless, he was determined to leave. His orals were on July 4, and he had booked a passage on the SS *Melita,* which sailed for Montreal two days later.[28]

Between his written examinations and his orals, Cliff paid a final visit to London, went to Warwick, which he had not seen before, packed, and practiced his Montgomery accent. As it turned out, he secured a third-class B.C.L., the best "I could have hoped for," given the brevity of his preparation for what was a harder examination than the B.A., and he thus left for home well satisfied with his performance. Moreover, he had a job to go to, his father having found him a position with the legal firm of Ray Rushton, a conservative Montgomery lawyer. The worries of the previous months, therefore, had been dissipated. He was coming back home, and coming back with prospects.[29]

There is no evidence to suggest that Cliff was reluctant to leave England. Rather, he wrote his mother, he was glad to be off from "the country where men put brilliantine on their hair and the women smoke cigarettes in public and both get by with it; where the main occupation of the people is running down other people and each other . . . where marmalade takes the place of Nigger in de Cane Patch." The self-assumed superiority of the English irritated him just as intensely at the end of his stay as it had done when he first arrived, and the differences between English and Americans, not their similarities, had continued to strike him. Yet not all Cecil Rhodes's money had been wasted. Despite the irritation, despite their conceit, the English were still "the finest people in Europe." Moreover, Americans, too, could be conceited. The tourists he had met had taught him that. How he wished they would stop their endless chatter about "the superiority of America in plumbing arrangements." The young man had at least learned something from the experience.[30]

Clifford Durr left the United Kingdom on July 6, 1922. When he next returned, it was in the wake of World War II. He was then an important official of the United States government, and the Oxford world he had known—the world of lazy, unstructured days, of rugby and of cycling trips, of cheap rail travel throughout Europe—had gone beyond recall.

It would be hard to argue that Clifford Durr's experience in England was in any sense catalytic. He left Oxford ostensibly little different from how he had entered it—a rather conservative, rather narrow young Southerner. He rarely referred to his English experience in his later life, and certainly never as a time which was decisive in shaping his values, in taking him outside his regional heritage. When he returned to Oxford in the mid 1960s to lecture, it was as a result of the pressure and the influence of young English lawyers and scholars whom he had befriended during their particular "grand tour," that of the embattled South in the 1960s, not through any nostalgic desire to revisit the important places of his youth.

The principles that Clifford Durr came to espouse so vehemently and the social views that he was later to defend were not developed as a result of his exposure to the Old World, to the English class structure, to the rhetoric of class struggle and class violence, and to the sights and sounds of a shattered system. Rather these came, as with so many of his kind, from his American experience—notably from the crucible of the Great Depression. Before that, however, there was more growing up to do, now that he was back in his beloved Alabama, his "period of exile" safely negotiated.

3

Learning the Law—and Other Things

Clifford Durr arrived back in Montgomery in July 1922 to a great welcome from his family and looking forward to his job with Rushton, Crenshaw, and Rushton. Yet, as is so often the case, some things, anticipated with the greatest of pleasure, just do not quite work out. His father, after all, had found him the job at Rushtons; Cliff had had nothing to do with it. John Wesley Durr had also decided that a monthly salary of twenty-five dollars would be perfectly adequate for his son. He was, after all, living at home, his country-club dues were paid for him, and he had the use of the family car. To his father, there was no need for Rushton to pay him more than pocket money. Clifford on the other hand, fresh from one of the world's great law schools, thought he merited a proper job at a proper salary. Rushton, who believed he was doing an old friend a favor, said he simply could not afford more.[1]

Then, the lack of privacy which living at home necessarily entailed was burdensome for a young man used to being on his own and eager for social life, including female companionship. Soon after his return he began to see something of Sara Mayfield, a pretty young Montgomery girl and friend to Zelda Sayre, the city's most famous "flapper." Sara herself eventually became a writer of some note. The two of them would sometimes cycle out to the Alabama River to read poetry together—and to swim. It was on one such excursion that the matter of privacy came to a head. Little Auntie discovered that Cliff's bathing suit was missing. Sara's mother, duly alerted, discovered likewise. The surprised young couple, innocently eating sandwiches and talking about poetry on the river's bank, found themselves assailed by two highly agitated middle-aged ladies.[2]

For Cliff Durr that was the last straw, and he resolved to leave home as soon as he could find a position which paid him sufficiently to do so. Fortunately an opportunity was soon available. His sister Lucy's college roommate, Dorothy Thigpen Shea, had married a young Milwaukee lawyer, a partner in the Milwaukee legal firm of Fawsett, Smart, and Shea. On a visit to Montgomery he met the young Durr, was impressed by him, heard of his restlessness, and, after consulting with others in his firm, offered him a job. Durr was pleased to accept, even though his salary, at seventy-five dollars a month, was scarcely munificent—although it was more than he was earning at Rushton's. Besides, he would be out from under the close scrutiny of his family—especially Little Auntie. Thus, early in September 1923, scarcely a year after his return from Oxford, he moved from Montgomery to a state and city he had never even visited before.[3]

His first letters home were quite enthusiastic. Fawsett, Smart, and Shea did mainly corporation work, and Durr was soon hard at it writing briefs. He enjoyed the new job thoroughly and welcomed the experience. Moreover, he liked being in a new place and exploring it. He was making the rounds of the Presbyterian churches, he told his mother, before deciding which one he would attend regularly. His living conditions were satisfactory; after a brief stint in a single room in a boardinghouse, he moved into a shared room with another young lawyer, Carl Mitchelson, and he had made other congenial friends. He had also made arrangements to take a "home cooked meal" each weeknight with a private family—for seventy-five cents a meal—and the Sheas fed him on Sundays. The move, therefore, had been relatively painless. Indeed, as he told his brother James in November, he was "beginning to feel more or less at home in Milwaukee."[4]

Cliff believed he was doing well at the law, and in 1924 passed both the Alabama and Wisconsin bar examinations. Though he had doubts about some of its workings—the jury system he thought had to be excised "like tonsils or appendixes," for it no longer "served a useful purpose"—he nevertheless was certain that, in deciding to follow the law, he had made the right career choice. Furthermore, the firm seemed to agree, for by August 1924, his name was on its letterhead. Nevertheless, his salary remained at seventy-five dollars monthly, and this eventually was a constantly chafing irritation. While he recognized he could not expect immediate advancement and that he would "have to work my way up," still, after a year had gone by with no increase, he became increasingly angry at the firm. He was, he believed, worth more than the pittance he was being paid, and if Fawsett, Smart, and Shea failed to recognize this, he would take his talents elsewhere. Dissatisfaction, not so much with the work he was doing as with the failure of the firm to reward him adequately, was a major reason for his decision to leave Milwaukee, a decision he took in late 1924.[5]

A second and perhaps the most important reason had nothing to do with his work. Despite the friends he had made, there was something missing from his life, something he was beginning to recognize acutely: female companionship. He and his friend Steve Evans often discussed "philosophies of bachelorhood," and, frankly, though he saw some advantages in the single state, he was becoming tired of it. Bachelors, after all, stayed "in much the same pasture" as married men, even "though no rope was tied to their legs." To his brother John he confessed that on some days he was restless and felt "ready to marry."[6]

"Ready to marry" Cliff may have been, but to whom? To his sister Lucy he admitted that he was having considerable trouble meeting young girls. The reasons were not hard to find: he was shy, he lacked confidence, and he lacked the money to give a girl a good time. He was not "a scorner of women," he told Lucy, "and frequently felt the desire of a little companionship." But, he said, Milwaukee was not Montgomery. "I hate to start out by asking a comparative stranger to go for a streetcar ride when she probably has a Pierce-Arrow in the back yard." On seventy-five dollars a month he could not afford a Pierce-Arrow or anything like it, but the comment meant more than that. He was shy and unsure of himself with the sophisticated, affluent Milwaukee girls, and thus he tended to back away from involvements.[7]

The theme of lack of confidence was an insistent one, especially in his letters to Lucy. He knew a few girls, he wrote in March, but he did not know what to do with them, as he felt nervous about taking them to the movies by streetcar or entertaining them at his lodgings. "So I am still spending my evenings at home," was his lament. When he dated, it was almost always double, with Steve and his partner along as well, and the chance for intimacy, with its attendant stresses, was thus correspondingly reduced. There were some girls who clearly were interested in the tall, good-looking young Southerner, but even these he tended to keep at a distance. He had been to dinner with Miss Elizabeth Wright, he told his mother in October 1924. She was leaving soon for Europe and wanted him to write, but he was dubious about doing so. His shyness, his lack of confidence in approaching the very different young women of a bustling midwestern city, even as he recognized his need for female companionship, was a second major reason for his decision to return to the South.[8]

Besides talking with Steve about "law, Oxford, Russia, matrimony and various other questions" during the long Milwaukee winter evenings, he also went to the cinema (enjoying such minor classics as *The Lost Tribe,* about the headhunters of New Guinea), and he read. Galsworthy he was particularly taken with, especially "The Indian Summer of a Forsyte," which he found "very well written" and quite moving. Throughout his life, Clifford Durr was an avid and wide reader. Virginia, his wife, once described his favorite authors as legion, and he returned to them time and again. Galsworthy, whom he had discovered in Milwaukee, was one such, so was de Tocqueville, while from his youth he was a regular reader of the Bible, as much for the beauty of the King James version's language as for the spiritual uplift he gained from it. On the day he died, he was reading Joseph Heller's *Catch 22*—for the third time. Books then were a solace for the lonely Milwaukee evenings, as they were to be all his life.[9]

He also thought about politics and his own political adherences. Milwaukee, after all, was a polyglot city politically, with a strong socialist presence, as well as a vibrant Republican party. Complicating everything, for young Durr at least, was the city's ethnic diversity and its political effect. His comments on the 1924 mayoral race revealed both this confusion and his rather superior attitude to a very different political world from that of the white Democrat of Alabama. The race, he said, was between "a crook, a fool and a Socialist." The men "naturally . . . thought the crook the least objectionable while the women gave their support to the Socialist." The way the city's various ethnic groups played off one candidate against the other for maximum possible gain he found particularly depressing.[10]

The mayoralty race experience confirmed him in his Democratic faith, though it received a bit of a shaking at the 1924 presidential nominating convention. Like most Southerners he stood resolutely against the candidacy of New York's governor, the Catholic "wet" Al Smith. If he were nominated, Durr thought, "it would be less of a crime to vote for Coolidge." Fortunately right prevailed, and the nomination went to the conservative lawyer John W. Davis, who was predictably thrashed by President Coolidge at the November election. Durr was bitterly disappointed at his defeat and furious that Kentucky and West Virginia had deserted the Democrats. "We had a right to expect better things of those two states at least," he fumed, revealing the essentially regional nature of his political thinking at this time. Milwaukee had not moderated his thoroughgoing Southernness any more than Oxford had done.[11]

Clifford Durr left Milwaukee for Alabama in December 1924 amid a round of farewells and thrilled at the prospect of going home. He was not returning to Montgomery, however, but was joining the Birmingham firm of Martin, Thompson, Foster, and Turner, one of the largest of the city's corporation law offices and general attorneys for the huge Alabama Power Company. Once again he was helped by the family name. His father had business interests in Birmingham and dealings with Martin, Thompson, and he suggested that his son contact them. A job was open, and Cliff was duly appointed at a monthly salary of $150, double what he had earned in Milwaukee. Moreover, he would be able to live with his brother John and John's wife, Annie Paul, as they also had moved recently to the city. Cliff could scarcely believe his good fortune.[12]

Birmingham was in some ways the quintessential city of the New South. Founded after the Civil War, by 1920 it had become a bustling industrial town with a metropolitan area population of more than 300,000, its economy based on iron and steel, on mining, and on its mills. Its middle class, like those in other American cities, enjoyed the general prosperity of the Coolidge era; not so, however, its miners and its mill workers, or the hill farmers in its immediate environs.

Birmingham in the 1920s was a town of bitter social, sectarian, and industrial tensions. There was strong animosity between Catholic and Protestant, between management and workers, and, of course, between black and white. It was, in short, a violent city, one in which the mean and vicious side of Southern urban life was always close to the surface. It was scarcely surprising that Klan activity was strong there throughout the decade; indeed, after 1925 agents of the Invisible Empire were in clear control of the city's government.[13]

The Alabama Power Company, Martin, Thompson's principal client, was formed in 1906, and in 1912 its name was changed to the Alabama Traction Light and Power Company. A holding company, its sole purpose was, as Leah Rawls Atkins has written, "to acquire the common stocks of the isolated electric companies in Alabama."

By the time Durr joined Martin, Thompson, it had become a huge regional power company "supplying much of the industrial and domestic power to Birmingham and its environs."[14]

Durr was quickly hard at work, almost exclusively on power company business, which he enjoyed. He got on well with his brother and his wife, and they made a handsome threesome driving around the city in John's recently acquired Model T Ford. Yet it would have to be said that Cliff's main preoccupation in 1925 was neither his work nor getting to know his new home. Rather, it was getting to know the beautiful assistant librarian at the county bar association's law library, Virginia Heard Foster. They had met first in April, in church, and Virginia had thought the "tall, blond and blue-eyed" Durr was "the handsomest young man I had ever seen." She was particularly taken with his English suits, so different from "the seersucker suits that looked like pajamas that most Southern boys wore," testimony to the fact that, throughout his life, Durr dressed well, not in any ostentatious manner, but always neatly and in good taste. It turned out that Virginia's brother Sterling and Cliff had been fraternity brothers at the university, so there was no problem in inviting him to the Foster home for Sunday dinner. Mrs. Foster got out all the best table settings; the dinner was delicious, the cook having been well instructed, with the pièce de résistance a huge lemon meringue cake. It had actually been bought from a local confectioner, but Mrs. Foster managed to convey the impression to the impressed young guest that Virginia had made it herself. After dinner the rest of the family conveniently disappeared, and courtship began in earnest.[15]

By November, Cliff had proposed. He was promptly accepted and delightedly wrote to his mother to let her know that "Virginia and I like each other well enough to believe that we can spend the next fifty or sixty years together without being bored." Cliff's family was very pleased; both his mother and sister Lucy wrote promptly welcoming her to the family. The couple were married on April 6, 1926, at the Independent Presbyterian Church, Birmingham, the bride lovely in ivory satin, the tall groom, attended by his two brothers, resplendent in a new English suit. It was a large society wedding. Virginia had no less than eight bridesmaids, plus a maid of honor, and there were more than five hundred guests at the reception, all paid for by her father, she later wrote ruefully, with money he "didn't have." Thus began what was to prove an enormously successful, enduring marriage.[16]

Virginia Foster Durr, as she now was, became one of the South's most remarkable women. She was born in 1903, in Birmingham, the youngest of the Rev. Dr. Sterling Foster's three children. Her father was then the minister of South Highland Presbyterian Church. She was, on both sides, descended from landowners. Indeed her father's family, the Fosters, managed to retain most of their land, near Union Springs, Alabama, despite the destruction of the Civil War. At the time of her birth the family plantation was still around thirty-five thousand acres, and Virginia's earliest memories were of visits to Union Springs and its sights, sounds, and smells. Virginia Durr, then, came from old established Southern stock. She grew up, she said, "on the romantic traditions of the benevolent slave system."[17]

In 1913, amid scenes of great trauma, Dr. Foster was dismissed from his position at South Highland Presbyterian for heresy, for he had admitted he no longer believed in the literal truth of the Scriptures. Though financially the family did not suffer at first—in fact with the death of his mother, Dr. Foster became a landowner in his own right—nevertheless, the shame of the event had a permanent effect on him. He started selling insurance but was scarcely a success at it. In the end, his lack of ability to earn an income meant that his inheritance became eaten up, and in his old age he and his wife needed constant financial assistance to survive.[18]

Virginia Durr described her family's economic circumstances during her adolescence as "genteel poverty," in comparing it with the "abject poverty" she saw around her in the mining villages surrounding Birmingham and on the farms. Without doubt her early life, compared to that of most of her contemporaries, was an exceedingly comfortable one, despite Dr. Foster's failing circumstances. The large house on Niazuma Avenue in which the family lived was spacious and gracious. Though not leaders of Birmingham society, the Fosters were well respected, with impeccable "Southern credentials." Virginia was educated in the public schools of Birmingham, but she did take private dancing lessons, and in 1918 was sent to New York, to Miss Finch's finishing school, then to the extremely fashionable Cathedral School in Washington, D.C., to be "polished up" before returning South to find a husband. Like that of Clifford Durr, it was, in Southern terms, a relatively privileged upbringing.[19]

In 1921 Virginia went off to college, not to Sweet Briar, where her sister had gone, nor to any one of the Southern schools deemed suitable for girls of her class and expectations, but to the liberal, academically respected Wellesley College, in Massachusetts. Her father sent her there, though he almost certainly could not afford it, she believed, because he was convinced she had "brains enough to go to college." She loved the place, especially the social life, but she was also challenged to the roots of her Southern being by much of what she found there. For example, she was required to eat at the same table as blacks. When she protested that she simply could not do so, she was told she would have to leave the school. After a sleepless night, she decided to stay, though in fear that her father would find out what she had done. These and other experiences encountered at Wellesley, she reflected later, first raised doubts about the certitudes she, as a Southern girl, had grown up believing. She learned, too, that there were alternatives open to women, that marriage was not the sole means of fulfillment. When her father was no longer able to sustain the cost of her education and she was forced to leave Wellesley at the end of her sophomore year, she returned to Birmingham with a mind open to new ideas, ready to challenge certitudes and shibboleths. This was the girl to whom Clifford Durr became so quickly attracted and whom he wed, beginning a mutually sustaining partnership that lasted nearly fifty years. Very different in temperament and outlook, they became, as Jessica Mitford, the English-born author and friend to them both, once wrote, "intertwined like two trees of utterly different species."[20]

There was one other facet of the merging of the Durr and Foster families which had a most important and continuing influence on Clifford Durr's life. Virginia had an elder sister, Josephine, whom she adored. In 1921 she had married a successful young lawyer named Hugo Black, who was already making a name for himself in Alabama political circles. Not every one approved of the young man, and his close identification with labor unions was bothersome at first to Dr. Foster and his friends. However, he won the family over. Black and Josephine wed and quickly had two children, and by the time Clifford and Virginia married, Hugo was deeply involved in his successful campaign to enter the United States Senate. Black had a deep influence on the political thinking of both Virginia and Clifford. The connection was a crucial one for them both.[21]

After an idyllic honeymoon in Pass Christian, Mississippi, which was "just full of spring blossoms and the air smelled fresh and sweet" and from which Virginia returned pregnant, the young couple set about creating a life together. Initially they moved in with the Fosters in the house on Niazuma Avenue. This was not something they particularly wanted to do; they would have much preferred to get an

Cliff and Virginia on their wedding day (Courtesy of the Alabama State Department of Archives and History)

apartment of their own, and on Cliff's salary they could easily have afforded to do so. But Virginia's mother did not want her to leave. Moreover, the Foster's economic circumstances were now so bad that even the rent money was important to them. This was one of the first of many fictions through which both Cliff Durr and Hugo Black helped support their parents-in-law, while at the same time protesting that they themselves were being done a favor.[22]

The arrangement naturally enough had its tensions, and these were increased when Ann Patterson Durr, their first daughter, made her appearance early in 1927. Both Virginia and Clifford longed for the privacy of a home of their own, but the more they talked of leaving, the more distressed Mrs. Foster became. Virginia found the situation increasingly upsetting, and her health broke in 1930 after a severe miscarriage, forcing Clifford to take the matter into his own hands. He was able to convince Virginia that her recovery really depended on their moving out, particularly since he had recently been promoted and was well able to afford to buy a place of their own. He superintended the house hunting, and when they had found a little house in the same neighborhood, he both arranged the move and reconciled Mrs. Foster to it, displaying, as he did so, qualities of quiet but firm resolution and determination which would become increasingly obvious in his public life. Fortunately, the Blacks returned to Birmingham in 1931 and were able to protect the Fosters' pride by themselves moving into Niazuma Avenue.[23]

Of Clifford Durr's years with Martin, Thompson, Foster, and Turner (shortly to become Martin, Thompson, Turner, and McWhorter), there is little that is recoverable, for the firm's records have long since been destroyed. Moreover, in the various oral history interviews Cliff recorded, he passed over his eight years with the firm in but a sentence or two. The firm's main responsibility was to represent the Alabama Power Company, and Cliff worked almost exclusively on power company business, mainly drafting the legal documents to do with the expansion of its operations. In so doing, he gained a sound grasp of corporation law. He was clearly good at his job, becoming a full partner in 1927 and receiving frequent pay rises thereafter. Moreover, he supplemented his income by moonlighting. He reported to his mother in 1928, for example, that he had accepted the position of secretary and treasurer of the Greater Birmingham Investment Company, at an emolument of twenty-five dollars monthly. Yet it was work which could be done on an occasional Saturday afternoon. His income was such that he was little affected financially by the onset of the depression in 1929.[24]

Nevertheless, the changed economic circumstances affected the young family in other ways. First the economic problems of Virginia's parents were compounded. Her father had borrowed far too much money and was simply unable to make the repayments. Hugo Black and Cliff helped out as best they could, but there was nothing that could be done in the end. The plantation had to be sold, and this duly occurred, though the amount he received did little more than pay the accumulated back taxes on the property. Moreover, the effect of financial ruin was devastating to Mrs. Foster in particular. She became extremely depressed and was eventually hospitalized. There was no alternative. Mr. Foster moved in with the Durrs, a ruined man financially.[25]

The plight of her own parents was one reason why, as the depression deepened, Virginia Durr began to question assumptions about the American economic system which she had formerly accepted uncritically. She was, as she later described herself, "leading the life of a young married woman in Birmingham," in comfortable economic circumstances, while around her the signs of social and economic disintegration became increasingly obvious. She began, she said, "to wake up to the world," to see for the first time the human misery which surrounded her. She did volunteer work for the Junior League and the Red Cross, as a driver for officers charged with certifying people as eligible for relief. The accumulated misery she saw appalled her, as did the fact that the destitute blamed no one but themselves for this situation. These experiences affected her deeply, she began to read contemporary political and economic theory, and she discussed these new and sometimes radical ideas with her still rather conventional husband. In so doing, she later recalled, she broadened his horizons, until he too began to question the moral validity of a system which could allow people to suffer in this way. The depression years in Birmingham, she said, were a time of real political growth for them both.[26]

It was this developing awareness of the inequality and injustice which characterized many responses to the economic collapse that caused Clifford unexpectedly to part company with Martin, Thompson, Turner, and McWhorter early in 1933. He was by now a full partner, his senior colleagues liked his work, and despite the severe economic troubles, his future there seemed safe enough. However a crisis suddenly erupted in the firm over the treatment of certain members of the junior staff. The senior partner, Mr. Logan Martin, began to fire people without either explanation or consultation. When a young stenographer, on her own and with a child to support, was summarily let go, Clifford protested at the injustice of her treatment and suggested that the more senior members of the firm take a pay cut in order to prevent future firings. The suggestion certainly did not meet with Logan Martin's approval, nor was it supported by other senior staff. Clifford thus found his continued association with the firm to be untenable. Whether he was fired by Martin or resigned before that could happen is beside the point. What is clear is that he suddenly found himself in the depths of the depression, with a young family to support and no job, having taken a stand, as he was so often to do, on principle. "The prospect is somewhat frightening," he wrote to his mother.[27]

Clifford was not certain as to what to do next, though it seemed the only viable alternative was to open an office of his own, not the most inviting of prospects, given the economic climate. He thought, nevertheless, he might be able to make it, though Virginia would have to give up her voluntary work to become his typist, and the house would need to be sold to help meet the debts they would necessarily incur. However, he wanted more time to think the matter through. He and Virginia decided, therefore, to spend two or three weeks at a little fishing cabin they owned near Clanton, before taking up the new challenge. Accordingly, they sold their automobile in order to finance the trip and prevailed upon Cliff's brother John to drive them to the river, there to plan in more detail the next phase of their lives.[28]

Events, however, took a quite unexpected turn. Cliff's own personal crisis had occurred against a backdrop of the deepest national significance as Franklin Roosevelt assumed presidential power and the New Deal began permanently to alter American life. Though, good Democrat that he was, Clifford Durr had voted for FDR, as well as supporting Hugo Black's successful bid for reelection to the Senate, yet the importance of what was happening in Washington seems to have eluded him. Certainly, there is not the slightest evidence that he thought of himself as having a role to play there, of himself becoming part of the New Deal. His father-in-law, Dr. Foster, an early and enthusiastic Roosevelt supporter in Alabama, had hopes of a job with the new administration; Cliff, however, entertained no such notions.[29]

Someone else did, however. Cliff and Virginia had been at the river only about a week when a messenger came by truck to tell Cliff that there had been an urgent phone call from Washington for him. Would he please return it immediately? In some bewilderment they drove to Clanton, to find that it was Hugo Black who had called. His message was clear and direct. A federal government agency, the Reconstruction Finance Corporation, was to have greatly expanded functions under the new administration and was looking for bright young corporation lawyers. Black had been asked for recommendations and had supplied a half-dozen names, including Cliff's. Was he interested in such a position? If so, "he had better go right on up there," because the RFC wanted people immediately. Clifford Durr, though bemused, certainly was interested and left immediately for New Deal Washington.[30]

He went straight to the Blacks to find out more about what had been happening and to get Hugo's assurance that, should he be appointed to a position, it would cause his brother-in-law no embarrassment. Hugo readily gave him this and said that in fact he had been quite impartial in his recommendations, suggesting Durr solely because his experience in corporation law seemed exactly what the RFC was looking for. Next, he was interviewed by the RFC's chief counsel, Mr. Stanley Reed, who seemed impressed. He told Durr that, though certain appointment formalities had to be taken care of, the job was his if he wanted it.[31]

Excitedly Clifford reported all this to his wife. Reed had promised him that "I would have full charge of the work assigned to me and all the responsibility I will be willing to shoulder," he said. Though his duties at first would be general, once he had learned the ropes, he would be given an area of specialization, which at this stage looked like working with insurance companies seeking RFC aid. Whatever it was, the experience would be marvelous, something he could not "get anywhere else." Moreover the pay was good (his annual salary would be $6375), and Josephine assured him they would be able to live on it comfortably, and even keep a servant or two. Accommodation would be no problem. They could stay with the Blacks until they had found a place of their own.[32]

There was, however, one note of caution. Hugo was insistent that the news of Durr's appointment be kept quiet in the meantime, and in particular, that nothing appear in the Birmingham papers about it. If she was asked where her husband was, Virginia was simply to say he was on vacation, otherwise Hugo would be flooded with job applications which he could not possibly do anything about. Cliff wanted his wife and daughter with him as soon as possible, but their departure, too, must not be the subject of any publicity. In the meantime, he needed a few things sent to him. There was no time for him to return home and fetch them himself, for he was to begin work right away.[33]

Thus, in a most unexpected manner and in an atmosphere almost of secrecy, began Clifford J. Durr's career as a public servant. For the next fifteen years home would no longer be Birmingham but New Deal and wartime Washington. It was a decisive change in direction.

4

NEW DEALER

The Reconstruction Finance Corporation was a key weapon in President Herbert Hoover's fight to bring about economic recovery, a product of his belief that the depression was largely a crisis of confidence and that "employment and industrial production would not begin increasing until private bankers were more willing to make business loans." Loosely based on the War Finance Corporation, RFC was created in January 1932 and was capitalized at $500 million with the ability to raise a further $1.5 billion. Its purpose was to make "low-interest loans to commercial banks, savings banks, savings and loan associations, mortgage companies, credit unions and railroads." In short, it would provide loans to the nation's collapsing institutions, who would presumably themselves increase their lending, thus promoting a revival of confidence. For the public perspective, the need to shore up the banking system was particularly crucial. For, as Susan Estabrook Kennedy has written, "One of the most devastating blows to national confidence was the increased tempo of bank failures." These had increased from 491 in 1928, in itself a disquietingly high total, to 2,294 in 1931. Banks in trouble protected themselves as best they could, and invariably the customer and the community suffered. Hoover, then, was responding partly to public pressure in creating the RFC, but he was also convinced that through its activities the depression could be beaten.[1]

In an attempt to avoid politicizing the new agency, Hoover appointed a bipartisan board of directors, of which the most important members were Eugene Meyer, chairman of the Federal Reserve Board; Charles G. Dawes, former Republican vice-president; and Jesse Jones, a Texas Democrat and Houston's biggest banker. Quickly the RFC began to lend and by July 1932 had already disbursed over $1 billion. More than four thousand banks had received loans, and though at one level the RFC seemed to work, in that there was some reduction in the rate of bank failures, yet it was also becoming apparent that increasing a bank's liquidity temporarily would have no lasting effect on the banking crisis and was only postponing collapse. What banks required was an improvement in their capital structures; they needed to be able to raise more capital in order to counteract the depression-induced deflation of their assets. Moreover, in the crisis winter of 1932, the period of interregnum between Roosevelt's election and his assumption of office, the RFC was powerless to prevent the bank crisis from worsening dramatically, as panic set in, and institution after institution closed its doors, including some of the nation's largest banks. By the time Hoover left office, the banking system had virtually collapsed, despite all the efforts of the RFC to save it. The new president would have to direct himself immediately to this emergency.[2]

Roosevelt, as is well known, speedily met the challenge. The Emergency Banking Act of 1933, passed within days of his inauguration and building on Hoover's own efforts, was a multifaceted attack on the crisis. One of its provisions was to expand the role of the RFC. Under its new head, the Texas banker Jesse Jones, it was permitted to invest in the preferred stock and capital notes of commercial bank and trust companies in order to provide liquidity for new loans and to build up the capital account.[3] This, as Albert Romasco notes, was a historic departure. "The government, in short," he wrote, "was now going beyond its established practice of making loans to endangered banks to a new practice of investing money in them by buying capital stock." It became, as a result, part of the ownership and management structure, and under Jones the RFC turned itself into the world's largest and most powerful bank and America's biggest single investor. Eventually, as William Leuchtenburg points out, "Jones ruled an empire of RFC subsidiaries: federal mortgage agencies; the Commodity Credit Corporation; the Electric Home and Farm Authority; . . . and the Export-Import Bank."[4]

The RFC began buying bank stock at once; the scale of its investment in bank capital was immense. By 1937 it had invested well over $1 billion dollars in more than six thousand commercial banks, and though it had not achieved the ultimate goal of increasing bank credit, yet it had saved the banking system. President Hoover's creation had survived the watershed of 1932 to become one of the most important of Roosevelt's recovery agencies—and the most successful.[5]

The RFC's purchase of private bank stock and its consequent involvement in the management structure required complex contracts and agreements. These needed precise legal drafting and close scrutiny. One of the immediate requirements of the expanded RFC, therefore, and especially its legal division, was for well-trained corporation lawyers with a capacity for hard work. This was the context which lay behind Black's opportunity to nominate such men and his immediate call to Cliff Durr.[6]

Durr officially started with the RFC on May 4, 1933. Initially, his work had to do with the reorganization of insurance companies, but in July he was transferred full-time to "the reorganization of banks and am very happy about the change," though he had to work extremely hard to learn about these matters. He was to remain with the banks until 1936, becoming head of the Preferred Stock Section of the legal division in 1935. His letters home to Alabama give a sense of the pace and intensity of the work, especially during those first few months, and of his growing commitment to Roosevelt and the New Deal. His office hours were still 9 A.M. to midnight, he told his mother in October, and yet he and his colleagues could not keep up with the work. The RFC had become the spearhead of the recovery drive, he said, and the "bank reorganization division is the point of the spearhead." Often they worked blind, in the sense that they had no precedents to guide them. "We can only hope we have guessed right as to the view the Supreme Court will take a year or so from now," he commented. The pace of the work and the long hours left him extremely tired, yet—and here he echoed the views of hundreds of similar recent arrivals—he had "never done work so interesting and I get a 'kick' out of feeling that I have a very definite part in the big 'experiment.' " Cliff J. Durr, the rather conventional young Southern corporation lawyer, was on his way to becoming a New Dealer.[7]

By the end of May 1933 it was already clear that Cliff was going to be in Washington for a lot longer than the few months he had originally thought his job might last. Accordingly, Virginia joined him. They stayed with the Blacks for a time, and then she went back to Alabama to fetch Ann, while Cliff began the process of house hunting. Affordable houses in Washington were hard to find in those heady days of the early New Deal, for as hundreds of newly hired, young federal employees poured into the capital, demand far outstripped supply. Initially the Durrs settled for an apartment on Wisconsin Avenue, but the twelfth floor was no place for an energetic youngster like Ann. Besides, both Virginia and Clifford wanted to get out into the country if they could. Soon they were able to do so. Virginia discovered Seminary Hill, in Alexandria, Virginia, an area of beautiful old houses so named because the Virginia Episcopal Theological Seminary was located there. She fell in love with it and was lucky enough to find a place there to rent. Seminary Hill became the Durrs' home for the rest of their time in Washington.[8]

To write extensively about Clifford Durr's work with preferred stock and bank recapitalization generally is difficult. His was not an activist role, and he was not in a visible position. He did not make newspaper headlines (that the RFC left to Jesse Jones), nor did he, unlike lawyers in the Labor or Agriculture departments, for example, shape through his draftsmanship and advocacy broad public policy, often with an ideological slant, which became the subject of debate and contention. In this respect, his role was very different from young lawyers like John Abt or Lee Pressman, both of whom, incidentally, Durr knew well. There was little that was ideological or politically divisive about the purchase of preferred stock in private banks.[9]

Nevertheless, Durr, equally with Abt or Pressman, should be considered an example of one of the most important aspects of New Deal Washington, the unparalleled opportunities it gave, as Jerold Auerbach has perceived, "for men of legal talent—who were sick of corporate practice or who could not get into it." The New Deal agencies attracted to Washington hundreds of young lawyers, not always from the most prestigious law schools in the land, often from minority or ethnic groups, "who satisfied personal, professional and ideological needs in public service for a liberal reform administration." Clifford Durr was one of these young professionals, and though his coming to Washington resulted more from the need to earn a living than from a loftier commitment to government employment, he soon came to hold a perspective on service in the public interest that was to provide a coherence to his whole government career.[10]

The RFC records reveal Clifford Durr's work as being multifaceted. He superintended the legal framework of individual bank recapitalizations, drew up contracts, checked the legal draftsmanship of others in the division, provided opinions and rulings on complex matters of equity or transfer, and answered thousands of queries from individual bankers and state and city RFC counsel, the men in the field. For example, when the Birmingham, Alabama, counsel for the RFC prepared a draft policy statement on preferred stock dividend rates, to be circulated to all participating banks, it was Durr who corrected it and gave it final approval. It was Durr who drafted changes in the standard form articles of incorporation for California's banks in order that RFC policy would continue to conform with the state's banking laws. He it was who provided the agency's local counsels with detailed instructions on how preferred stock was to be purchased, who unraveled for them the mysteries of federal taxation laws as regards such stock, and who finally approved all contracts drawn up by local agents for stock purchase.[11]

One problem that quickly became his exclusive area of expertise was fraud and forgery. He handled all cases concerning the government's liability when banks in which the RFC owned preferred stock had been defrauded. Thus, when the Carter Council Commercial Bank of Olive Hill, Kentucky, was in dispute with the attorney general's office over certain government pension checks cashed with forged endorsements, it was Durr who provided an opinion as to the limits of the bank's liability, an opinion which was accepted. He also advised the RFC Board on general matters of policy or of problems arising in changes in policy, often highly technical in nature, because of the knowledge of individual cases he had acquired through the drafting or the scrutiny of thousands of contracts, opinions, and appeals. His duties, though neither headline grabbing nor easily explicable to the layperson, were nonetheless fulfilling and important.[12]

By 1936, Clifford Durr had established himself as an important member of the RFC's legal team, hardworking and competent. He had earned the respect and friendship of his colleagues, like Bill Livingston, and had even gained the favorable attention of Jesse Jones himself on occasions. Jones had been particularly impressed by an early opinion he had written which held that the RFC could not buy preferred stock in Iowa's state banks because of the restrictive nature of that state's banking laws. Indeed, by 1934 his legal skills were sufficiently respected for him to be offered the assistant directorship of the Land Acquisition Division of the Tennessee Valley Authority, but he preferred to stay with the RFC. He had "never done more interesting work," he said, and felt a real part of a team.[13]

Being part of a team came to mean something wider than just the RFC, however. It meant becoming caught up in the excitement of the Washington atmosphere, of thinking about directions and possibilities, of recognizing the potentialities for change possible through enlightened use of the public purse, and of rethinking one's own political perspectives as a consequence. Clifford Durr had never thought deeply about politics—he had never had to. He was a Democrat, his grandfather's brief apostasy notwithstanding; he, like most Southerners, regarded voting any other way as something akin to betrayal of the region. Moreover, again like most Southerners, he had an instinctive distrust of the powerful state, or of central government in general, and this he took a long time to lose. Two years a New Dealer, and he could still confess to his mother that he was bothered by big government. "The whole show can't be run from one place whether New York or Washington," he argued.[14]

Yet, working for the New Deal forced him, along with thousands like him, to rethink fundamentally their responses both to the strong state and to public as opposed to private employment. He had not expected to stay in Washington for long. Black's phone call and the subsequent offer had certainly come at a good time, but his aims had nevertheless been to get back to private practice as soon as possible. A year later, however, his views had changed. "Now nothing seems as interesting as staying where I am and watching developments," he confessed. By the end of 1936 his transformation was complete. "Uncle Sam," he told his mother, was "by far the best and most satisfactory boss" he had ever worked for, and he had no intention of leaving government service for "any corporation with head quarters in New York." Clifford Durr, private corporation lawyer, had become a dedicated public servant.[15]

The main reason for this shift in values was his growing identification, despite all his residual fears of bigness, whether in the public or the private sectors, with the aims of federal policy and his developing commitment to what seemed to be its reformist directions, confusing as the actual path seemed to be at times. As early as 1934, he told his mother that the next year or so would be crucial and would "tell definitely whether or not we are going to have more than a temporary 'new deal.' " He himself was optimistic. "I believe that something permanent will come out of the business that will make life pleasanter for Ann's children," he thought. He would rather have Washington as the umpire, he mused a year later, "rather than the preceptor or fairy god mother"; nevertheless he had become a convinced New Dealer. "No better deal has been offered so far" to the American people was his conviction. Moreover, though he had "heard all my life" about the rut government employees got into and had believed this, his own experience had convinced him otherwise. When there was a sense of common purpose in government work, when one felt part of a great project, then public service was creative rather than stultifying. By the end of Franklin Roosevelt's first term, Clifford Durr had become a committed member of his team.[16]

Given his competence and his capacity for hard work, it came as no great surprise when Durr was appointed the RFC's assistant general counsel in 1936, which meant a move from the agency's banking section to the litigation section. He was pleased with the promotion at the time, though he later confessed that he had enjoyed the work with the bank recapitalization more than his new, more general duties. Though he still dealt with preferred stock matters, providing his usual crisp memoranda of advice on questions of retirement, of dividend rates, and so forth, he was also required to keep a general superintendence over a host of other matters.[17] He advised local loan agency chiefs, for example, on changes in legislation affecting their operations and on the implications to them of court decisions. When the Texas Supreme Court ruled in 1938, for example, on a matter concerning double liability of bank shareholders, Durr, who saw the decision could have general implications, sought information from, and gave advice and direction to, all local agency counsel.[18] One area that became his entirely concerned the consolidation, merger, or takeover of banks, mortgage associations, insurance companies, and building societies in which the RFC had an interest. When the Tennessee Valley Bank proposed to take over the Sheffield National Bank in Sheffield, Alabama, for example, it was Durr who scrutinized the proposed agreement of purchase and sale, who stated certain objections to proposed procedures, and who saw to it that those procedures were met. He was also responsible for ruling on allowing certain claims for reimbursement and expenses.[19] Though he may not have enjoyed his widened duties as much as working exclusively with preferred stock, yet it is clear from the RFC's records that he performed them with his usual diligence, attention to detail, and legal skill.

There was, of course, still plenty of work to do. After Roosevelt's triumphant reelection in 1936 and its vindication of the New Deal, Congress quickly acceded to his request that the RFC be continued. This prompted a further flood of work and a protest from Durr that it was "hard to act out the part of a good family man when there is so much at the office that needs doing." Underneath, however, he reveled in it and was learning more about himself all the time. The RFC experience had convinced him that he "worked best under the whip." He needed that sort of constant pressure to bring out the best in him, and this was an added reason, he thought, for not returning to private practice. Without the whip of continuous work he would, he believed, "soon become a victim of my natural mental inertia." Durr was even more determined than ever to stay in government, despite "the parade back to private life" he saw beginning as the business climate gradually improved. He, however, would not be joining it. He had cast his lot in with FDR for the duration of his presidency, at least. A measure of how far he had traveled down the New Deal road was that he even defended FDR's "court-packing" bill of 1937, an action which outraged his family. The Supreme Court, he wrote his furious mother, "has been sufficiently isolated from human affairs to constitute a symbol, like the British king, and an object of reverence. The President has scratched through the gold leaves and exposed the lead underneath and a lot of people don't like it." Still, he did admit that had Hoover, rather than FDR, attacked the Supreme Court, he would have felt "rather indignant," but his growing New Deal faith was such that, despite a little misgiving, he stood firm with FDR, even on this most contentious of issues.[20]

Clifford Durr's growing reputation as a skilled legal draftsman resulted in his being asked to assume certain duties outside the RFC ambit. When, in 1939, Franklin Roosevelt set up a committee, chaired by Supreme Court justice Stanley Reed, to recommend ways of improving conditions in government service, Durr was appointed to an advisory panel investigating the conditions of appointment and service for government lawyers. Other members included the general counsel of the Pennsylvania Railroad, presidential adviser Jim Rowe; Dean Acheson, the dean of the University of North Carolina Law School; and Alex Harris, a lawyer with the National Labor Relations Board. Their task was to recommend conditions of appointment and service which would satisfy both those who wished all government lawyers to be brought under civil service provisions and those who believed that lawyers worked best without the inflexibilities which this was seen to entail. Most of the lawyers who came to Washington with the expansion of federal power had come, like Durr, as the result of patronage. Few positions had been filled by examination. Yet, clearly they were now here to stay. The need to bring some order to the federal legal service, to establish a career structure, was obvious.[21]

Clifford Durr thought the group was a great one, and he thoroughly enjoyed being a member of it. His papers indicate that he was a hard-working contributor indeed, preparing discussion papers on a range of issues and having a major role in the preparation of the committee's final report. Given his own growing commitment to public service as a worthwhile vocation, it is not surprising that the final report recommended a career structure for government lawyers which provided for reasonable standards of emolument and job security but discarded some of the more restrictive civil service practices, such as the seniority system. The report, in large part Durr's handiwork, was submitted to the president's Committee on Civil Service Improvement in June 1939, and some of its provisions were eventually adopted.[22]

Durr was able at times to devote his attention to the particular problems of his region—the South. He became a member of the Southern Policy Committee, a group of young Southerners, either members of Congress like Lister Hill and John Sparkman or working in New Deal agencies like Durr, Clark Foreman, or Abe Fortas, who would meet for dinner from time to time to discuss Southern issues. In 1938, stimulated by Roosevelt's characterization of the region as the nation's most serious economic problem, they, or rather Foreman, persuaded the president that a detailed report on the South's situation, together with recommendations as to future directions, should be prepared. The president asked Lowell Mellett of the National Emergency Council to direct the project. Several distinguished Southerners, such as Arthur Raper, a sociologist from North Carolina, were drafted to serve as advisers, and the result was the *Report on Economic Conditions of the South,* a stark description of the region's severe problems and some recommendations for change. Cliff Durr had an important role to play in the drafting of the report—apart from providing, in his living room, the venue where much of the work was done. He wrote section 13 of the final report, on credit, arguing for the provision of more government capital and credit for Southern agriculture and industry, to stop the tradition of dependence on outside financiers, and also drafted, for Roosevelt's signature, the report's introduction. Again, despite the further inroads it made on his limited amount of spare time, Durr was delighted to have been involved on the report. It contributed to his conviction that he was engaged in a great and important endeavor.[23]

Life in Washington, then, was exciting for Clifford—and it became so for Virginia as well. Seminary Hill was isolated, she later recalled, "but it was a real neighborhood," and she soon made friends. They were, in fact, the first New Dealers to live on the Hill. Most of the other residents were of old Virginia stock and had been there for generations. However, they were welcoming to the new arrivals, and even though Cliff worked such long hours in the office, Virginia was rarely lonely. In the long evenings of spring and summer, she and Ann would stroll among the spacious gravel roads, greeting old "Mr. Jim," who liked to talk to his trees in the evening; or Mr. and Mrs. Herbert, who ate only raw food themselves, though serving their guests delicious, beautifully cooked meals; or Mrs. Randolph, a Virginia lady so refined that she even wore gloves when emptying the garbage. Virginia loved the life there, and though her sister took her to official government receptions from time to time and there were also RFC functions to go to, she lived the first year or so of her life in Washington remote from official circles—and liked it that way.[24]

In 1935 the Durrs were able to buy, for only $6,500, an old farmhouse on Seminary Hill on two acres of land. It needed some work done on it—after the purchase Clifford said his greatest desire was "for a good negro, a mule and plow for about two weeks"—but it had all the makings of a wonderful family home. They were delighted with their good fortune. Moreover, they needed the extra space. After two difficult miscarriages, with attendant doubts as to whether she would be able to conceive successfully again, Virginia gave birth on September 18, 1935, to Clifford Judkins Durr, Jr., who quickly became the apple of his father's eye. The boy was his constant companion as he brought his two acres under control and found how much he loved gardening, something he had not done much of since his boyhood days on his grandfather's farm. "I didn't realise at the time how much enjoyment my Wetumpka experiences were providing for the future," he once wrote his mother. After the birth of Lucy Judkins Durr in January 1937, the two Cliffs, as "the men in the family," formed "a strong defensive alliance." They would, Cliff, Sr., reported, have long political discussions, "lack of vocabulary" not in any way affecting young Cliff's fluency. It was a very happy time for the young family.[25]

Tragically the defensive alliance was soon to be shattered. In April 1938 the little boy got appendicitis. It was not diagnosed as such, the appendix burst, and peritonitis set it. Eventually a correct diagnosis was made, and he was rushed to the hospital, but it was too late. After three days of helpless watching, young Cliff died. The effect on the family was devastating. Clifford could only cope at the time by "trying not to remember" and "realizing how much I have in Virginia and Ann and Lucy." Fortunately, he said, Lucy demanded "cheerfulness," and these demands had to be met. But the loss left him inwardly scarred and at times visited by overwhelming guilt. Virginia, writing in 1959, said that Cliff still found it impossible to look at young Cliff's picture or even to mention his name. It was a lastingly sad experience.[26]

The support and love of family and friends were of great comfort to them in coping with young Cliff's death. The Durrs had been fortunate in that they had acquired a wide circle of friends in Washington, the majority of whom shared a New Deal commitment. Some were neighbors on Seminary Hill, such as James Landis, a brilliant young lawyer from the Securities and Exchange Commission, with whom Cliff rode to work each day, and his Mississippi-born wife, Stella. Next door to them, too, on the Hill, was a house which a number of New Deal "girls" had rented. They had frequent parties, the Durrs usually went, and there they would meet interesting people, some of whom became friends. Sometimes, too, they went to the parties at presidential counsel Tom Corcoran's bachelor establishment on R Street. They were always good fun, especially if Pete Seeger was there and they could all sing along with him. The Durrs, too, held frequent parties of their own. Then, of course, there were numbers of young Southerners in Washington whom they got to know. Three couples who became particularly close were Clark and Maire Foreman, Aubrey and Anita Williams, and, a little later, the young Texan Lyndon B. Johnson and his pretty young wife, Lady Bird. Virginia had actually known Clark Foreman, who was from Atlanta, when she was at Wellesley. Now, here he was in Washington, working in the Department of the Interior as Secretary Ickes's adviser on Negro affairs. Aubrey Williams was Harry Hopkins's deputy at the WPA and also head of the National Youth Administration. From Alabama like the Durrs, he and his charming wife, Anita, often held Sunday lunch parties where all sorts of people would gather. Then there were the Johnsons, the young Texas congressman, "thin as a stringbean," and his quiet, shy wife. They called Lyndon the "drugstore cowboy" because of his boots, but they liked him, and he too became part of their circle. These and many other friends supported the Durrs through the sad times following Cliff's death, as well as more generally being part of a glittering, intelligent social network. Hard as Durr and the other New Dealers worked, there was still time for fun. The New Deal community was full of vitality, shared ideals, and the sense of being part of something bigger than oneself. Even at the parties, the talk would most often turn to politics, their jobs, what they all thought they were accomplishing, and their hopes for the future. For Cliff Durr, working as he was in an agency that could scarcely be said to have an obvious social or even liberal dimension, contact with people like Aubrey Williams and Clark Foreman was of great importance in giving shape and structure to his own deepening liberal commitment. They helped the New Deal become whole for him; they took him far from the world of banks and stocks into the world of people, of social programs, and of social possibility.[27]

Probably the couple they saw most of, however, was Hugo and Josephine Black. They stayed with them when they first moved to Washington, and they tended to dine with them frequently thereafter. Family occasions such as birthdays and Thanksgiving were almost always shared. Josephine introduced Virginia to the wives of various justices, senators, and New Deal officials, while Cliff increasingly enjoyed Hugo's company and learned from him about the ways of Washington. His own thinking about the legitimate concerns of government was very much shaped by his discussions with Black. When Black was nominated to the Supreme Court in 1937 and a scandal erupted concerning his brief membership in the Ku Klux Klan, they happened to be staying with the Durrs at the time, and it was in their living room that Black held the crucial press conference at which he announced that he would not resign the nomination. Later, he gave a radio speech, admitting KKK membership as a young man but assuring Americans that he had had no dealings with it since his election to the Senate. The speech was composed in a vacant RFC office, to which Durr ferried him at five o'clock each morning so as to avoid the press. For his part, Cliff was delighted to have helped. When the Blacks finally left the Durr household on November 13, he wrote his doubting mother that the Constitution was not "going to suffer at his [Black's] hands." However, there was no danger, either, of the "Court making a conservative out of him." If, in fact, Clifford Durr had become a liberal, as that statement might indicate, then Hugo Black had had a lot to do with the change.[28]

So, undoubtedly, had Virginia. Initially she was rather isolated in Washington and somewhat cut off from its political world—not that she minded that. Gradually, however, as they got to know people, this changed as her own political awareness grew. Her friend Stella Landis was very much involved in what was happening. She loved to go to Supreme Court and congressional hearings, and Virginia would go along with her. Then, of course, all the different people she met at parties, with their bold ideas, interested and challenged her.

She decided that she, too, wanted to be part of the New Deal in a rather more substantial way than simply being the wife of a public official. Fortunately, servants and child care came cheaply; she was able to leave the house and her children to do volunteer work for the Women's Division of the National Democratic Committee. She enjoyed the work thoroughly, she met interesting people, and she developed her own political perspectives. It was through the Women's Division that she was first drawn into the movement to abolish the poll tax, something that would soon assume great importance in her life. Then, indirectly resulting from the death of her son, she gained an insight into the problems facing labor organizers in the United States. Robert La Follette's subcommittee of the Senate Committee on Labor had begun holding hearings into the violation of civil liberties in America, and in particular it concerned itself with the violence between employers and employees. These hearings were in full swing by 1938. In an effort to divert her mind from brooding on Cliff's death, Virginia would attend the sessions daily. "This is where I got my education," she later claimed.[29]

As Virginia Durr became more involved in politics, an involvement she retained throughout her life, and as she became drawn more and more to the causes of the dispossessed and downtrodden in the United States—the poor farmers of the South, the blacks, unskilled and unorganized industrial workers, women—the more radical her political thinking became. The radical temper suited her. She had, in time, no difficulty professing her faith in a socialist future, for example, though for her socialism always had to be accompanied by "democratic controls." She came to move rather more easily in the world of the American left than Cliff, who was, as Jessica Mitford correctly discerned, "not one of nature's radicals" but rather was "flung by history into a radical role." Yet, it is clear that by 1939 his political position was very different from what it was in 1933; the New Deal had seen to that, as had FDR, Hugo Black, and his own wife. Some of her own growing involvement with the liberal left doubtless rubbed off on him.[30]

By 1939, Clifford Durr was as much concerned with events in Europe as he was with more domestic matters. The outbreak of war profoundly disturbed him, and unlike many Americans, he did not see how the United States could eventually avoid involvement. Moreover, he was not sure that avoidance at all costs was the morally correct policy, given the repugnant values of the Third Reich. He believed that England and France had been right to go to war; he was certainly not, he said, "a neutral in thought," nor did he see any chance for peace while Hitler was in control. A few months later, the attack on Norway, the country he had enjoyed visiting so much, depressed him utterly. "They have—or had—all our ideas about democracy," he lamented, and did a "better job" than the United States in effecting them. Now the countries "where the individuals don't count" were "on top," and he was not sure that the United States should stay out of the war in such a situation. At the very least America should be prepared for involvement. In a personal way his words were prophetic. Shortly, he was to be very much involved in the politics of preparedness, as he became one of the men behind the formation of the Defense Plant Corporation.[31]

The story of the DPC deserves to be better known than it is, for of all the agencies involved in the financing of the expansion of America's industrial plant to meet the needs of wartime production, it was probably the most important. Its function was to build and hold title to new plants, which would then be leased to manufacturers who had received government defense contracts, or, alternatively, the plant could be operated on the government's behalf through management contracts. As its historian, Gerald T. White, has pointed out, it was by far the most important of four RFC defense subsidiaries set up during the summer of 1940. As such, it was not only a crucial component in enabling American industry to meet the demands of preparedness and war as successfully as it did, it also provided a precedent which could again be drawn upon "whenever ventures of great public consequence seem too risky to be undertaken by private firms." Moreover, as White further points out, one of the architects of the DPC was Clifford J. Durr.[32]

With the outbreak of war in Europe in 1939, Americans for the second time this century were forced to think about national defense, and this need, as White has written, was dramatically underscored the following year, when the Nazi blitzkrieg subdued Europe and Britain stood alone. When Roosevelt addressed the Congress on May 16, 1940, on the need to strengthen defenses, he dwelt at length on deficiencies in air power, calling for the production of at least fifty thousand planes a year and for the putting of factories with defense supply contracts on a round-the-clock basis.[33]

The need to increase defense capability was obvious. The massive military establishment which had been decisive in the winning of World War I had been rapidly dismantled, until by 1939, the United States Army was smaller than that of Spain and only slightly bigger than Bulgaria's. As White points out, the crucially important aviation industry employed fewer people than the confectionery industry. Defense planning had been desultory, with the presumption that private industry could and would finance the production of additional supplies and equipment out of its own capital resources.[34]

The president, however, recognized that the scale of the emergency was such that private capital could not be expected to meet the demands about to be put on industry for expanded production. He therefore made it clear that government aid would be forthcoming. "The Government of the United States," he told the nation on May 26, 1940, "stands ready to advance the necessary money to help provide for the enlargement of factories, the establishment of new plants, the development of new sources of supply for the hundreds of raw materials required, the development of quick mass transportation of supplies. The details of this are now being worked out in Washington, day and night."[35]

Roosevelt spoke to a divided business community, a community, many of whose leaders, however myopically, had for years considered the New Deal as the thin end of a socialist wedge, and who, in White's words, "could be expected to examine the defense program with great care for any taint of socialism and to seek a large degree of control in its development." They could also be expected to take care to prevent any expansion of productive capacity that might be a threat to profits once the emergency had ended. Above all, they would not be willing to finance the expansion of plants and the purchase of new equipment even with government money, unless both profit was guaranteed and risk absorbed. Many New Dealers, on the other hand, deeply distrusted business, and were resistant to the idea that a program of expanded defense productions, essentially paid for out of the public purse, should be turned over to private industry to run. It is little wonder then, that, despite the president's insistence on speed and cooperation, the relationship between business and government continued to be one of suspicion, as confusion grew.[36]

One area of concern was the method of financing expanded industrial facilities. For many of the "dollar a year men" whom Roosevelt had called to Washington to help plan and develop the defense expansion program, the answer was simple. Men like William S. Knudsen, the president of General Motors, whom Roosevelt had appointed commissioner of industrial production, successful products of private enterprise themselves, were deeply suspicious of any sustained government involvement in the private sector. Government should simply furnish the money in the form of generous loans and with few strings attached and let industry get on with the job. The ownership of the expanded facilities should be negotiated on an individual basis, but the implication was that private industry's views should be decisive here as well. The whole expansion program should be carried out, men like Knudsen believed, as far as possible along normal business lines, with the profit motive dominant.[37]

This was a view congenial to the thinking of the former RFC chairman, Jesse Jones. Now federal loan administrator, he retained close connections with the agency he had headed for so long and which he now saw as likely to play a crucial role in defense financing. He prepared to use his considerable influence to persuade its recently appointed head, Emil Schram, to bring it into line with Knudsen's views. However, there were in the agency men whose thinking differed from that of Knudsen, Jones, and their supporters, men who believed that, if the government was to be the source of finance for defense production expansion, then the public interest dictated that the government should retain control over what this finance bought. Of these, none were more important than Clifford Durr and his colleague Hans J. Klagsbrunn, a graduate of both Harvard and Yale law schools and since 1933 a member of the RFC legal staff. Earlier in 1940, both men, along with others such as Oscar Cox from the Treasury Department and Tex Goldschmidt from Interior had been part of an interagency team charged with devising means of financing American industrial facilities to support the British war effort. Bitterly opposed to Nazism, they were also advocates of the public interest and believed, as they turned their thoughts to the best ways of financing American defense-plant expansion as efficiently as possible, that it had to be protected. The DPC, in essence, grew out of this conviction.[38]

The story of the creation of the DPC is worth telling in some detail, for it illustrates both the depth of the conflict between the public and the private interest endemic to the agency's history and the important role Clifford Durr played, not only in its creation, but in setting its parameters. As Durr was to recall, Roosevelt's speech of May 26 gave real urgency to the problems of bringing together the financial resources of the government and "the organization and productive techniques" of private business. To Durr, the solution was simple. "Klagsbrunn asked how I thought the matter should be handled," he later wrote, "and I stated that in my opinion the bulk of the money would have to be put up by the Government, and that if the Government put up the money, it should own the plants." Because of the need for speed, it would probably be impractical for the government to operate such facilities, but it would turn them over to the private sector, either on a lease or a fee-for-management basis. Nevertheless, the public interest dictated that title should remain with the federal government.[39]

Klagsbrunn had been thinking very much along the same lines, and a few days later laid on Durr's desk a proposed bill extending the lending authority of the RFC for defense purposes. The general thrust of the bill was in conformity with suggestions made by the president, but Klagsbrunn had added a provision authorizing the purchase of critical and strategic materials and authorizing as well the construction and lease of plant facilities, along the lines of their shared thinking. Durr suggested a few minor changes and a major one. He proposed that the RFC should have the authority to "create directly the corporations required for handling the plant leases and the purchase of the critical and strategic materials," thus avoiding the "expense, delay and confusion" of having to resort to state law for their creation.[40]

Drafting a bill which incorporated their ideas was all very well, but the collaborators knew that it would not get very far without the approval of the powerful Jones and that he was unlikely to be receptive to the idea, given his preference for defense expansion to be funded through private borrowing. However, Jones often used the phrase "a shotgun in the corner" to describe a threat, something to be used if a preferred option failed. With Durr in the background, Klagsbrunn presented the RFC expansion bill as such a "shotgun," something to threaten manufacturers with if they should show "too great a reluctance to expand through private borrowing." Surprisingly, and perhaps a little absentmindedly, Jones agreed. The bill very quickly passed through Congress and was signed by the president on June 25, 1940, containing, as Durr said, "in its substance the provisions . . . in the first draft prepared by Klagsbrunn," together with his own suggestions.[41]

Passage of the law, however, proved to be the easy part. Even before the bill clarifying the RFC's defense powers had become law, a crucial battle unfolded as to whether the public interest would in fact be maintained in the arrangement of such contracts, or whether the preferences of private industry would be followed, despite the spirit, and even the letter, of the enabling legislation. The battle concerned the expansion of aircraft construction, and in it Durr was to play a central role. In June, Jones gave to him a proposal he had received from Knudsen that the RFC finance a large aircraft engine plant to be operated by the Wright Aeronautical Corporation, a subsidiary of Curtiss-Wright. Knudsen proposed a form of agreement with the RFC which he hoped would prove a model for the future. Highly complex in its drafting, it essentially gave the manufacturer the plant at no risk. The RFC was to lend the full cost of the plant at 3 percent, the cost of the loan to be repaid, not out of resultant profits, but from "an agreed portion of the sales price to the government of the articles manufactured." Thus, the Navy Department, the War Department, or whatever government agency purchased the factory's output ended up, in effect, repaying the loan.[42]

To Clifford Durr, such an arrangement made a mockery of any notion of protecting the public interest, and he told Jones so, suggesting at the same time that they propose to Wright Aeronautical that the lease arrangement provisions of the RFC bill now about to become law be used instead. Jones was unconvinced, especially after Knudsen made it quite clear to him that he had the strongest objections to the government's retaining title to any plant whatsoever. Instead, he came up with his own draft agreement, which essentially followed Knudsen's. Durr, for his part, produced a long memorandum for Jones in which he argued strongly for the government's retention of title on the plants and either leasing them to manufacturers or operating them under a management contract. The advantages, he said, were obvious. In the first place, it gave the government title to property it had paid for; it eliminated the possibility of large war profits financed out of public money; it meant that plants could be located where they were needed for military and strategic purposes, and not from considerations "such as proximity to other plants of the manufacturer"; and it gave the government a capacity to retain the plants in peacetime should this be deemed necessary. It was a clear, direct statement of Durr's conviction that to turn wartime expansion over to the private sector to run unchecked was an abrogation of the public interest; in time, his view was to prevail.[43]

In the short term, however, it failed to persuade Jones, Knudsen, or the management structure of Wright Aeronautical. At a meeting in mid-July, M. B. Gordon, its general manager, stated that the company was far from satisfied even with the favorable terms of the Knudsen proposal and that the RFC lease arrangement could not remotely be countenanced. Knudsen had taken a stand, he said, against the government's retaining title to any of the aircraft plants, and he agreed with this position. After much fruitless discussion, Durr was instructed to prepare a resolution for the RFC's board of directors in terms most favorable to the company. Essentially, it gave Wright the chance, after an initial period of lease, to buy a $40 million facility, constructed by the federal government, for a mere $200,000.[44]

Clifford Durr could not see how this could possibly be construed as being in the public interest. Loyal public servant as he was, he drafted the resolution but refused to approve it or even initial it. Instead, it was presented to the board of directors on August 7, 1940, together with a memorandum outlining his reasons for disapproval. The form of the arrangement, he said, was far too cumbersome, at a time when speed was essential. Much more to the point, the War Department and the RFC, between them, under the resolution he had drafted, would be donating to Wright Aeronautical something the public had paid for. Furthermore, the resolution had within it devices to enable the firm to avoid taxes on its profits, scarcely a patriotic action at a time when the need to sacrifice was much in the air.[45]

Jones was furious, but other members of the RFC board were impressed both by Durr's stand on principle and by the coherence of his argument. The Wright deal was postponed, and a few days later the RFC's chairman, Emil Schram, the only member of the board not under Jones's domination, told Durr that he agreed with Durr's argument and asked for further information in support of the leasing arrangement. Durr gave him a copy of his June 29 memorandum to Jones, and, as he put it, "Mr. Schram was convinced, and with his blessing we proceeded with the organization of the Defense Plant Corporation." The DPC was the fourth RFC subsidiary to be organized in the summer of 1940, the others being the Rubber Reserve Company, the Metals Reserve Corporation, and the Defense Supplies Corporation. These were little more than paper organizations, operating virtually out of Jesse Jones's office and holding no regularly scheduled meetings. Schram determined that DPC would not be like that but would be kept as independent as possible from Jones and his cronies, though Jones would have to be given a place on its board of directors. Nevertheless, he was also able to include people like John W. Snyder, formerly the RFC's St. Louis director and no friend to Jones, whom he made executive vice-president. Durr was designated the new subsidiary's general counsel, eventually becoming a director himself in May 1941.[46]

Schram's determination to maintain some independence from

Jones gave Durr some hope. "The defense program has kept me going at a terrific pace, with discouraging results to date," he wrote in August 1940, but he finally saw some light at the end of the tunnel and no longer felt he was fighting a lone battle, "with everyone else concerned determined to let the manufacturers loot the country under the guise of national defense and even help them at it." At one stage he had thought he would have to leave the RFC, but now he had some supporters in the agency, including Schram, and there were also some allies on Capitol Hill. So, instead of being "put in the dog house," he told his mother, he had just been made the DPC's general counsel. Nevertheless, the battle was far from over, with Knudsen, Jones, and other powerful men still "championing the manufacturers," but with the creation of the DPC and Schram's support of leasing arrangements, the fight was no longer hopeless. To Clifford Durr belonged much of the credit. His concept of the public interest, developed over years of service in the RFC, was thrown in conflict against powerful and ambitious men. That his views prevailed to the extent that they did is a tribute not only to his commitment to principle but also to his persistence and to his skills as an advocate.[47]

Nevertheless, there were still hurdles ahead for the DPC. Conservative members of the National Defense Advisory Committee, exemplified by Knudsen and his closest ally, John D. Biggars, remained deeply suspicious of government ownership of industrial plants. Moreover, as White points out, "Every plant built and paid for by government diminished the opportunity for money making by investment bankers." Consequently, a committee of the NDAC devised its own plan for the financing of defense expansion, one based essentially on private funds supported by government guarantees, which, its architects hoped, would effectively check the development of the DPC. The Emergency Plant Facilities Contract, as it was called, provided for the construction of defense facilities by private contractors who would then be repaid by the government in equal monthly payments over the next five years. The contractor's claim against the government would be assigned to a private bank or lending agent, who would initially provide the necessary funds. Contractors would also be given the right to purchase the facilities once the emergency was over. While this mechanism was being developed, and in the attendant publicity surrounding its announcement, Knudsen stopped referring manufacturers with defense contracts to the RFC.[48]

The EPF contract, however, proved to be a failure, despite the publicity and despite Knudsen's enthusiastic support. Contractors found it altogether too cumbersome; even Gordon of Wright Aeronautical decided in the end on a DPC lease because of its simplicity; moreover, he was not willing "to risk banker control of his company" through the large bank loans the debt assignment provision would necessarily entail. By the end of 1940, despite the hostility to it and the lack of significant publicizing of its activities, the DPC was beginning to play an important role in the financing of America's defense effort. Durr, however, knew that its potential was far greater than its performance. In a successful effort to secure publicity for it, he contacted his friend and former Oxford colleague, the syndicated columnist Ernest K. Lindley, who agreed to write an article on DPC activities. Lindley's piece, entitled "The Lost Defense Agency," was published in the *Washington Post* and then widely syndicated. As well as dealing with the origins of the DPC and highlighting Durr's role, it discussed in detail the lease arrangements, noting their simplicity, especially when compared with the EPF contract. The DPC's "contracts are more simply negotiated than EPFC contract," Lindley claimed; moreover, there was no need for the banks to become involved. Lindley's article certainly did not hurt the subsidiary. The numbers of contractors seeking its assistance steadily increased, until by April 30 its investment in plant and equipment had grown to more than $500 million. Clifford Durr could well feel satisfied at the progress of what he had come to regard as his creation.[49]

White states that, at its Washington headquarters, the DPC "was chiefly an organization of lawyers, for the principal activity was drawing up the terms of contract." Certainly the records show that Durr's days as general counsel were spent mainly doing just that—drawing up contracts himself, scrutinizing those drawn up by others, resolving points of legal detail, answering queries from manufacturers on DPC policy, and generally assuming responsibility for the subsidiary's legal requirements. Even before he became a director, he attended the frequent meetings of the board of directors, at which all lease agreements were formally approved and other matters of policy were discussed. The work was time consuming but, once precedents had been set, became fairly routine and generally concerned with detail.[50]

The question of safeguarding the public interest, however, was never far from his mind, and in the end, a renewal of his dispute with Jesse Jones over what it constituted caused him to leave the DPC. Even after the publication of the Lindley article, he recognized that "the battle is still going on" and that he still got desperate when he saw "power turned over to men who use it for their own purposes." Ironically, the favorable publicity engendered by the Lindley article caused Jones to take a greater interest in the DPC, and he began to claim exclusive credit for its accomplishments. This, Durr found a little hard to take, given the loan administrator's original opposition. Still, he recognized that "the only thing for me to do is keep my mouth shut and try to do my job, which I am doing."[51]

In the end, Durr was unable to stomach Jones's increasing interference in the negotiation of contracts and agreements, particularly after Schram's departure in July 1941 to become president of the New York Stock Exchange. He was replaced by Sam Husbands, a longtime Jones crony. In February 1941, DPC's powers were increased to include the production and acquisition of "strategic and critical materials as defined by the President of the United States." This enabled DPC, in the following months, to enter into contracts for facilities to manufacture synthetic rubber, magnesium, aluminum, iron, and steel, and it was in the negotiation of these usually very large undertakings that Jones began to take an increasing role.[52]

Durr was opposed to his involvement for two reasons. In the first place, Jones would not use the standard contract the DPC had developed. Rather, he insisted on bargaining with each firm, drawing up individual contracts, and this inevitably slowed up the pace of DPC activity. Much more important, Durr believed Jones was ignoring the spirit of the DPC lease systems and, in so doing, ignoring the public interest. Contract negotiations with two large producers of strategic materials, the Aluminum Company of America (Alcoa) and Bethlehem Steel, brought matters to a head. Alcoa, which had a virtual monopoly on the production of aluminum in the United States, had been under investigation by the Antitrust Division of the Department of Justice since 1937. With the need to expand aluminum production obviously an urgent one, Jones naturally turned to the huge company for assistance. The proposed deal he made perpetuated and even strengthened its monopoly. Durr, who like other New Dealers, had hoped to use the emergency to bring new firms into the aluminum industry, and others like it under monopoly control, was outraged. "It does not seem sound to me, from the defense angle," he wrote the new DPC chairman Husbands, "to rely almost entirely on one operator for aluminum." If there was "no other way of getting aluminum except from Alcoa," then there was nothing to do but go along. However, he was convinced that there were alternatives. He had earlier stated similar objections in a long memorandum to Jones on August 2, adding that Alcoa had been given altogether too much freedom over plant operation and prices. "The present monopoly situation which eliminates the spur of competition is contrary to the Government's interest," he protested, "and we should avoid creating a situation which would be a further aid to monopoly." Neither Jones nor Husbands was in the slightest bit moved by his arguments, however, and the contract was duly ratified, leaving Durr bitterly unhappy at the result.[53]

The Bethlehem Steel decision similarly deeply distressed him. The company, a tough bargainer, secured from Jones conditions covering the construction and operation of pig iron and plate mill facilities far more favorable to it than those secured by other steel firms. Even Jones recognized there were problems with the contract; however, once Knudsen had pronounced it "fair and considering the circumstances equitable," he recommended its acceptance. At the board of directors meeting at which the contract was to be approved, an angry Durr requested that his dissent be recorded, the only time during his period with the DPC that such a request was made. Even prior to this he had decided to leave the DPC and to accept an appointment to the Federal Communications Commission. On his very last day with the DPC, October 27, 1941, he submitted to Jones a blistering attack on the Bethlehem lease provisions. The two men parted, therefore, on less than the best of terms.[54]

Almost thirty years later, in a letter to his son-in-law, Durr described his work with the DPC in these terms. "I conceived it," he wrote, "borned it, midwifed it and stood guard over its cradle to keep it from being kidnapped and quietly drowned." Jesse Jones, on the other hand, failed to mention Durr by name in his autobiography. Writing on the origins of the DPC, for whose success he largely claimed credit, he stated that, in the winter of 1940, he asked Klagsbrunn "and another lawyer" to join a group considering ways of aiding the British war effort, and from their deliberations came the germ of the DPC idea, which he, Jones, developed. Durr was doubtless the other lawyer but was not mentioned by name in the book, thus, as White says, erasing "from the record DPC's principal architect." For Durr's judgment was more accurate than that of his superior. If Durr remained proud of his DPC achievements for the rest of his life and a little chagrined that neither they nor the agency itself were not better known, he had a right to be so. There were others besides Clifford Durr who had a hand in the DPC's creation, but none had battled for it more resolutely than he. Moreover, he had fought as hard as he could to ensure that, in its operation, the public interest, as he had come to see it, remained paramount. Perhaps events did not always turn out as he wished, yet, to the extent that the DPC did not ever become totally a creature of private business, much of the credit belonged to Clifford Durr.[55]

Durr left for his new job with some regrets. As he told David Lilienthal of the TVA, the DPC had been his "absorbing interest," and he was finding it hard transferring to "the role of spectator." Nevertheless, he left with the satisfaction of knowing that, as far as he had been able, he had not given in to those who wished to make money from the world crisis. He had kept the public interest in the forefront of the debate, as he was to do for the rest of his career.[56]

Moreover, there was still a private life to be lived, though not enough time to do it. The sadness of little Cliff's death was still hard to bear, but it was at least tempered by the birth of a third daughter, Virginia, soon to be known forever as Tilla, in September 1939, while Ann and Lucy continued to be great sources of joy to them both. Sometimes Cliff felt that Lucy realized "what a big hole" she had to fill, so delightful an infant was she. Moreover, the household was soon to be augmented in a most unusual way. When the Battle for Britain started in earnest and the evacuation of British women and children had begun, former Rhodes Scholars were asked to do their bit. Durr had the room at Seminary Hill to accommodate visitors and the inclination to do so. Thus the family prepared to make welcome Mrs. A. C. Woozley, wife of the librarian of Queens College, Oxford, and her baby. Mrs. Woozley, however, did not come, preferring to take her chances in England rather than risk the dangerous Atlantic crossing. Virginia was relieved. Increasingly busy with her own political activities and with a full household already, as her parents were often with her, she had little inclination to bring a stranger into the home, particularly one who had asked for a room with a private bath and a nanny. So, Mrs. Woozley's change of mind was not regretted.[57]

Nevertheless the Durrs were to get their English "refugees," in the unlikely personage of Jessica Romilly, now much better known as Jessica Mitford, daughter of the second Baron Redesdale and a member of one of Britain's most eccentric aristocratic families. In 1940, however, when she and the Durrs first met, she was the young leftist, idealistic wife of Esmond Romilly, nephew of Winston Churchill, newly arrived in the United States after many adventures, including a period in civil-war Spain. The Durrs had first met the Romillys at a cocktail party and had liked them both very much, and they became frequent visitors to Seminary Hill. When Esmond joined the Royal Canadian Air Force in 1940, the pregnant Jessica, or Decca, as she was called, was glad to accept their offer of accommodation. And there she remained, together with baby Constancia, for two and a half years. When Esmond was reported missing, presumed dead, in 1941, it was the Durrs who helped the young woman through the worst of her grief. They maintained their connection for the rest of Cliff's life, and Virginia and Decca continue to do so.[58]

Later, Jessica Mitford described the household on Seminary Hill as "large, disorganized and animated" and said that it "radiated warmth and affection," always full of interesting people, including "judicial dignitaries, Southern legislators, . . . New Deal functionaries, earnest young radicals." It was also full of children—their own, Constancia, known as "Dinky-donk," and Hiroshi, son of a Japanese couple whom Virginia also had taken in. All of them addressed the "tall, rather stoop-shouldered" Durr (whose appearance, Jessica Mitford recalled, "was casual yet scholarly, reminiscent of a softened edition of Abe Lincoln") as "Daddy." Disorganized the household may well have been, but it was also full of love, and this was a sustaining force for Clifford Durr as he prepared to leave the RFC, where he had worked for nine rewarding years. He knew he had done "a good job" there, he told his mother. Moreover, he had developed, as a result, a clear concept of the public interest, which he had constantly articulated during his time with the DPC and which he was now to carry with him to the strange new corridors of the Federal Communications Commission.[59]

5

Wave-Length Warrior

The Federal Communications Commission grew out of the Federal Radio Commission, created by President Hoover in 1927 to provide some regulatory overview to the infant but booming radio industry. As the industry mushroomed, listening to the radio, as the historian Kent Anderson has pointed out, "often became a frustrating experience," as stations tended to ignore the restrictions placed on them by the secretary of commerce. For example, says Anderson, the evangelist Aimee Semple McPherson operated her Los Angeles station on whatever frequency the Lord chose for her. In an attempt to bring order to this chaos, something the industry itself was clamoring for, Hoover established the FRC.[1]

Franklin Roosevelt both expanded its powers and changed its name in 1934, merging the FRC with the telephone and telegraph regulatory functions of the Interstate Commerce Commission and the postmaster general. As far as radio was concerned, the newly created Federal Communications Commission was charged with the twin tasks of allocating wave lengths in order to provide satisfactory program service to as large an audience as possible and of protecting the public from control of the airwaves by persons operating against the public interest. The FCC was, however, given no control over the selection or content of programs.[2]

Though the seven-member commission performed the technical aspects of its task well enough, in that stations were duly licensed and transmitters approved, its activity in other areas was less obvious. It showed little concern about the general question of public interest in broadcasting and, in particular, how this was affected by the growing control of large networks over the nation's airwaves, with the consequent subordination of independent educational or community programs to the needs of the networks' sponsors.

Throughout the reform decade of the 1930s, the FCC remained moribund, and the radio industry developed with a minimum of regulation or even scrutiny. As the most important historian of the industry, Erik Barnouw, has written, "The New Deal came late to the FCC." However, when it finally arrived, he further notes, "it came strongly," in the person of James Lawrence Fly, formerly general counsel of the TVA, who was appointed FCC chairman in late 1939. He might also have noted that it came in the person of Clifford J. Durr, who became Fly's loyal and committed lieutenant.[3]

With Fly's appointment, the FCC entered the only activist phase in its history. A combative, assertive man, a convinced democrat, and a strong New Dealer, he had a proven reputation as a battler, having won victories in the Supreme Court over private power interests during his years with TVA. The president brought him to the FCC because of these very qualities. Roosevelt had become concerned about the growing trend toward monopolization in the communications industry. In particular, newspaper ownership of radio stations bothered him. Given that most of the nation's newspaper owners opposed the New Deal vehemently, he could see that "unified control of press and broadcasting" could produce a powerful, anti–New Deal communications monopoly, and this he was determined to prevent. In this connection he was also concerned about the growing power of the national networks and their control over programming. Fly's appointment to the FCC was both a recognition of this concern and an attempt to do something about it.[4]

Fly, then, brought a desire to act in the public interest to the FCC, together with a determination to assert some public control of the airwaves. He immediately joined battle with the networks and achieved success. In a landmark decision, just before Durr joined it, the FCC in May 1941 ordered that the NBC network, the nation's largest, be divided in two in the interests of competition. Bitterly opposed at the time, the decision was ratified by the Supreme Court and eventually resulted in the creation of the ABC network from the discarded components of the NBC empire. It marked the beginning of a new and activist phase for the FCC, one whose beginning was coincident with Durr's joining the agency.[5]

Durr's appointment to the FCC had nothing to do with his technical expertise or even prior interest in radio, because he had none. Rather, it arose from the complex exigencies of Alabama politics. His predecessor, Frederick I. Thompson, a Mobile newspaper publisher, had been a political rival of Rep. Lister Hill. Hill, who planned to challenge incumbent senator Thomas Heflin in 1938, wanted Thompson out of the way, lest he muddy the waters, and had persuaded Roosevelt to appoint him to the FCC to fill an unexpired term. This the president had done, but the term was up in 1941, and Thompson had proved to be such a poor performer that FDR had no intention of reappointing him to a full seven-year term. However, to replace him with other than an Alabamian would cause Hill to lose some political face in his home state. The administration therefore decided that Clifford Durr was their man, and White House aide Jim Rowe approached him early in 1941 to sound him out. At first, deeply involved in DPC affairs as he was, Durr was unenthusiastic about making the shift, but after Schram's resignation and Jones's consequent intrusion in DPC contract negotiations, he recognized that his effectiveness with the subsidiary was at an end. Consequently, he let Rowe know that, if the FCC post was still available, so was he.[6]

Durr's nomination occasioned no controversy. His confirmation hearing on October 30, 1941, took about ten minutes, and he was eventually sworn in for a seven-year term by Hugo Black in a brief ceremony in Fly's office. His appointment, however, did prompt a fulsome letter of commendation to the president from the young congressman Lyndon B. Johnson. "Dozens of hardworking patriotic little fellows all over town were very happy this morning when they waked up and read that you had appointed Clifford Durr to the Communications Commission," he exulted. "This was a rebirth of faith. It proved again that there is a reward for conscientious service, intelligent effort and hard work." These qualities Durr had shown during his years with the RFC, and they would be obvious again in his new position.[7]

In November 1945 the magazine *Tide* published an article surveying Clifford Durr's four years with the FCC. Entitled "Dissent by Durr," it asserted that that phrase had become a byword in recent FCC decisions. Representatives of the broadcasting industry, it further stated, had come to consider him to be a "threat to the established system," given his frequent public criticism of the "commercial aspects of radio." In analyzing Durr's recent dissents in some key FCC decisions, *Tide* believed it could discern a pattern to his positions. Two perspectives seemed to inform his judgments. One was "a distrust of big business"; the other was a concern for the public interest. These, the magazine stated, were the principles on

Cliff during an FCC hearing (Courtesy of the Alabama State Department of Archives and History)

which his FCC work had been based and which had made him, within four years, easily the commission's best-known member.[8]

Opposition to bigness, whether in the private or the public sector, was always a cardinal aspect of Durr's democratic faith. Undoubtedly his experience with the DPC had sharpened his distrust of unregulated corporate powers, while his view of what constituted the public interest and of the need to assert its legitimate claims had grown steadily over his years of government service. *Tide* was probably right in identifying these as the twin impulses behind his FCC work. They can be found in the positions he took on key cases before the commission, most frequently in the dissenting views he held, for he was rarely in the majority. They can be found in the reforms he fought for within the commission, and they can be found in the scores of speeches he made during his seven-year term. These twin impulses can be seen in Durr's vigorous advocacy of policies aimed at breaking the power of the networks and their sponsors in determining what was broadcast, in his insistence that applicants for broadcasting licenses and for their renewal should have to convince the FCC of their concern for quality and breadth in their programming policy, and in his tireless advocacy of the causes of educational and public radio, his insistence that some frequencies be kept safe from the networks and commercial channels for educational and community use. By the time his term was up, Durr had become clearly identified as the leading spokesman for the public interest in radio and, as such, a figure of some concern to the network executives, to the commercial station owners, and to their sponsors. It was the time of his greatest public visibility.

Analysis of three of Durr's more important dissenting statements reinforces this point. The first of these to gain public attention occurred in 1943 and involved, not radio stations or licenses, but the nation's only commercial telegraph companies, Western Union and Postal Telegraph. The commercial telegraph industry had been in decline for years, steadily losing business to the long-distance telephone companies and to airmail. In an effort to prevent the collapse of Postal Telegraph, by far the smaller of the two companies, they jointly applied to the FCC for permission to merge. Public hearings were held from July 7 to September 23, 1943, at which the companies' representatives argued that the merger "would permit a unified management of the domestic telegraph industry," would lead to plant modernization and improved services, and was therefore clearly in the public interest. The FCC agreed, authorizing the merger in the expectation that it would place the whole industry on a sounder financial basis. Commissioner Durr, however, dissented sharply. He had long been a critic of the telegraph industry's performance and had opposed applications for rate increases for that reason. Given the economic state of the industry and the reluctance of management to take steps to improve performance, he could not see how the constriction of that competition still existed could possibly result in better service. Rather, he considered it would make it less imperative for the industry to smarten itself up, and therefore he could not agree that the merger was in the public interest in any way. The public would be far better served, in his view, by the maintenance of the existing, competitive situation. Though the merger was duly approved, Durr's strongly worded dissent was noted. Carroll Kilpatrick, in a syndicated column, said Durr was becoming one of the capital's "best known figures" and spoke approvingly of his refusal to compromise on matters of principle and his "fundamental honesty."[9]

In 1945 he dissented in an application which did receive wide national attention. This involved the application of the Aviation Corporation to purchase the radio licenses of Powel Crosley, Jr., as part of the package in which AVCO bought a controlling interest in the Crosley Corporation as a whole. The application, as Barnouw has noted, was a real challenge to the FCC, for it presented to them "in one spectacular package . . . all the issues of multiple-station ownership and license trafficking. If the FCC wished to face these issues, its chance had come."[10]

The background to the application was complex. The Crosley Corporation was predominantly a manufacturer of household appliances, though since the outbreak of war it had also been extensively involved in war production. However, since 1922 it had also held a number of radio licenses, the most important of which was WLV in Cincinnati, the largest station in the area. It operated a number of smaller stations in the Midwest as well and was also involved in experimental television work. AVCO was a holding company, with extensive interests in the manufacture of aircraft and airplane parts, as well as in other industries. It controlled the Consolidated Vultee Corporation, a large airplane manufacturer; it had interests in Pan American Airways and American Airlines; it owned the New York Shipbuilding Company; and it was developing strength in the manufacture of kitchen goods. Notably absent from its concerns was an interest in, or prior experience of, the operation of radio stations. Indeed, when AVCO and Crosley first started their negotiations, the holding company did not even know of the existence of the radio stations. Certainly, there was no initial interest in them. The company wanted Crosley's holdings for the manufacturing facilities and distribution outlets, but when Crosley, for tax purposes, refused to separate the stations from the package, AVCO agreed to take them, and an application for the transfer of the licenses was duly filed with the FCC.[11]

Some members of the FCC favored quick approval of the transfer, but not so Clifford Durr. At the transfer hearing his probing questions of the AVCO management revealed that they were quite ignorant of the operation of radio stations. In particular, they had no knowledge of WLV's past programming arrangements and no thoughts as to how these might be improved. They had not wanted the broadcasting facilities in the first place and were acquiring them only as part of a business deal. Nevertheless they were clearly paying for them and for the right to operate them. They were part of the package. Yet the FCC Act clearly stated that the airwaves were free—the right to use them could not be bought and sold, but granted by the FCC. What had occurred here, then, was a clear case of trafficking in licenses.[12]

The FCC was unhappy, extremely so, with aspects of the transfer, but a majority thought they had no choice but to go along with it, at the same time formulating new rules, which they hoped would prevent any such occurrence again. In future, they decided, in any such transfer proposal, there would be a chance for others to compete for the channel or channels being vacated. As there was no inherent property right in a radio license, they could not possibly be bought and sold automatically. Having tidied things up in this way, the commission approved the transfer by a 4-3 vote.[13]

Clifford Durr was one of those in the minority, and because he had been so critical of the whole proposal, he was chosen to draft the minority statement of dissent. Again, he kept the question of the public interest in the forefront. The transfer, he argued, was clearly against such an interest and should not have been approved. The granting of a radio license did not involve the granting of property. It could not be assigned or transferred but had to be applied for. "Broadcasting channels are public property," he argued, and "the Commission has the responsibility for seeing to it that such public property does not become the subject of private sale," a responsibility which in this case he believed the FCC had abrogated.[14]

Even worse, it had become clear that AVCO had not "demonstrated even minimum qualifications" to operate the stations. "Not a single witness for the transferee," he thundered, "demonstrated more than the vaguest idea about the kind of program service which would be rendered, the availability of program talent and sources, the needs of the people in WLV's service area, or even about the type of program service being rendered under the previous management." The idea, therefore, that the public would not be affected by the transfer was quite untenable, and for this reason he could not possibly support the majority view, though he did favor the new rules governing transfers which the case had made necessary.[15]

Durr's strong statement again occasioned considerable public comment, not all of it favorable. Even before the decision, Durr had replaced Fly, who left the FCC for private practice in 1944, as the favorite target of the broadcasting industry. Indeed, the industry's magazine *Broadcasting* had coined a new word, "Durrmocracy," to define his views. Mr. Durr, ran one attack, is "dead set against the present system." He was a "misguided bureaucrat" who believed the public should be told what it could listen to and who "feels stations should be limited as to how much they can earn, and what type of programs they can present." The AVCO decision was deplored, despite the fact that the transfer was approved, because of the new rules that had eventuated, with the implication that licenses could not be bought and sold like any other piece of property, and Durr was blamed for these. Not all the comment, however, was critical. Lowell Mellett in the *Washington Evening Star* drew attention to his succession of stands on behalf of the public interest, and he was even given a great reception in his hometown when he went there to address the local Rotary club. Earlier, the *Birmingham News* had asserted that all Alabama was proud of him. "There is comfort in the fact," ran an editorial, "that a man like Durr, so candid, simple and free, so open-minded and so daring in the pursuit of democratic right is in a position to keep the FCC 'on the people's side.' " And that is how he was coming to be perceived, both by the representatives of the industry and by their critics. He was the commissioner who most consistently articulated the public interest.[16]

A second dissent by Durr in 1945 again illustrates the point. This involved the voluntary assignment of the license to operate station WSRR, in Stamford, Connecticut, from one Stephen Rich Rintoul to the Western Connecticut Broadcasting Company, the controlling interest in which was held by the publisher of the *Stamford Advocate.* The *Advocate* was Stamford's only daily newspaper, so the town's media outlets would effectively be concentrated in the same hands. The commission showed some concern at this but noted that, given Stamford's proximity to New York's multiplicity of stations and papers, a divergence of views would still be readily available. Moreover, the company had given assurances that the paper and the station would be operated entirely separately. The transfer, therefore, was approved.[17]

Again, Durr's dissent was vigorous, and again it was couched in terms of defending the public interest. "I cannot agree," he wrote, "that the public interest will be served" by the termination of the competition between radio and newspaper and the consequent concentration of ownership. The FCC, he reminded his colleagues, had previously taken the view that "concentration in the media of mass communications is undesirable and not in the public interest," and he did not see how granting Western Connecticut's application could be reconciled with that statement. "The argument that because Stamford was close to New York diversification was still available to its residents was specious," he said, for "the local community remains of basic importance to our way of life, and diversification in the control of outlets of news" there was of equal importance to diversification at regional and national levels. Again, of course, his views were deeply resented by the industry, and its attacks on him continued. But then, so did his dissents.[18]

A final example of the way Durr's concept of the public interest influenced his position on cases before the FCC, and one of a very different flavor, concerned the application of Robert J. Harold Scott for the revocation of the licenses of two stations in San Francisco and one in San Jose. The stations had refused to make time available to him to present the atheist point of view, yet they all used their facilities to present arguments against atheism, as well as regularly to broadcast church services. The stations' response was simply that it would not have been in the public interest to allot time to Scott, given the general unpopularity of his views. The commission, agreeing that the complaint was no basis for removing the stations' licenses, was inclined to accept their view of the matter and to dismiss the complaint without a hearing.[19]

Durr, however, thought differently and insisted that the complaint be heard. There were serious issues of free speech at stake, he believed, and certainly to accept the view that radio stations could decide what views should be presented purely on the grounds of their popularity profoundly disturbed him. In the end, his colleagues came to agree with him. Though Scott's petition was rejected, this was done not because his views were considered unpopular but rather because not every point of view could be presented; there simply were not enough hours in the day for that. Some selection had to be made.[20]

The commission, however, in rejecting the complaint, made a strong statement about freedom of speech and the public interest, and for this Durr was responsible. The licensees, he argued, "seem to have treated atheism as a special sort of controversy and to have interpreted their obligation to operating in the public interest as requiring or permitting them to bar access to their facilities for the presentation of the atheistic point of view, not because of the manner in which the point of view is to be presented, but because they believe its substance to be distasteful or objectionable to a large majority of the listening audience." This was not good enough; the First Amendment guaranteed both religious freedom and freedom of speech. Freedom of religion surely carried with it "freedom to disbelieve," while freedom of speech included freedom to express disbelief. Moreover "freedom of speech can be as effectively denied by denying public access to the public means of making expression effective," such as the airwaves. While licensees might not be able to grant air time to all who wanted it, they could not simply discriminate against those whose views they did not share. Again, the public interest argument was paramount. "The criterion of the public interest," Durr concluded, "clearly precludes a policy of making radio wholly unavailable as a medium for the expression of any view which falls under the scope of the constitutional guarantee of freedom of speech." This was a strong statement and, again, was not universally popular. *Broadcasting Magazine* advised its readers, in fact, to "jot down July 1946 A.D. as the day the FCC took jurisdiction over God." Yet, though very different from his dissents, it reinforces the view that, in all his FCC judgments, Clifford Durr's prime concern was to identify clearly where the public interest lay and to stick staunchly by it.[21]

If Durr's dissents and judgments showed the development of his role as the FCC's leading defender of the public interest, so, equally clearly, did his work within the commission to promote educational and community radio, to limit radio advertising, and to establish minimum standards of public responsibility to which all applicants for radio licenses would have to conform.

In September 1944 a long article on Durr appeared in the *Progressive,* a Madison, Wisconsin, newspaper. Entitled "Cliff Durr: Wave-Length Warrior," it discussed Durr's growing reputation as a fighter for decent public radio. "Cliff Durr has been the champion of diversified non-commercial radio since 1941," argued the authors, and stressed his determination to keep as many of the channels opened up by the new frequency-modulation process as possible free for public use, especially by educational institutions. It was a fight he welcomed, as he saw in FM radio a second chance for colleges and universities to develop an alternative system to network radio.

When the industry was in its infancy, educators had made enlightened use of it, but gradually the commercial broadcasters had persuaded them to give up their frequencies and had effectively frozen them out of AM channels. Now with FM radio about to develop, here was the prospect of trying again.[22]

Durr worked extremely hard to try to convince college professors that this was something worth doing. "I am doing all I can to get Colleges and Universities on the air, and I hope my missionary work was not wasted," he wrote his mother in 1944, after a visit to Harvard. It was a long process, however, and the educators were not always as quick as they could be to recognize the potential of what he was advocating. They had, he thought, "fallen down on the job very badly in not recognizing that education is a continuous process." Still, he battled on, trying to persuade educators to bid for FM frequencies, and his fellow commissioners to listen to his argument. Eventually, his persistence was rewarded. Impressed by his advocacy and by the support he eventually received from some college presidents, especially the heads of land-grant institutions, the commission set aside 15 percent of the new FM frequencies for educational purposes. It was one of his most significant victories while on the commission, and one of which, as he looked back on his life, he was always justifiably proud.[23]

Durr was less successful in persuading the FCC to introduce new rules governing the licensing and operation of FM stations, rules which would insist on separate programming for the new channels and which would allow newcomers to enter the industry. At first his colleagues were inclined to go along with him when he proposed that any AM licensee who was given an FM license as well had to provide at least two hours per day of independent programming on the new channel, one in the morning and one in the afternoon. He also thought they had agreed that twenty of the new channels would be reserved for later assignment, ideally to permit newcomers to enter the industry. These proposals were bitterly opposed by the industry, however, and after receiving intense lobbying pressure, the FCC removed them from its list of rules to govern FM broadcasting.[24]

Durr, predictably, dissented vigorously, again referring to the public interest for justification. The introduction of FM broadcasting, he said, could, if properly handled, provide the public with a far wider range of program choices than currently available—but only if the FCC required some independent programming, especially if current

AM licensees were granted the new licenses as well. If not, there would be no need for them to innovate. "The listening public," he warned, "would receive little more than the same program traffic carried over improved highways." The use of two radio channels for the same program service was, he thought, a tragic waste of frequencies, the abrogation of a real chance to develop alternatives to the current network system.[25]

He was equally discouraged at the commission's decision not to reserve channels for later assignment—except for those already set aside for educational institutions. He was particularly bitter that no consideration had been given to servicemen and women who may well have wanted to bid for the channels but would now be prevented from doing so. "There are undoubtedly men and women still in the armed services who would like to apply for broadcasting licenses and who could bring to broadcasting the imagination, energy and freshness of approach which it so urgently needs," he lamented.[26] Without channel reservation, they would be effectively prevented from doing so, as by the time they were discharged they would almost certainly find that the best channels in their communities had already been snapped up—by AM operators. In giving in to industry pressure, the FCC, he believed, had taken no account of the needs of the listening public.[27] Durr was bitterly disappointed by the outcome. "I have been losing decisions steadily for the past few weeks," he complained to Charles Siepmann. His failures to win either independent programming or reservation of channels were but the latest in a long line. "If the trend continued," he thought, "broadcasting may soon be democracy's greatest menace instead of its greatest hope." As he learned more about the broadcasting industry, its potential as an educative medium, a cultural medium for the uplifting and the enriching of American life, became increasingly obvious to him. His consequent despair when performance ran so far behind promise, when opportunities were so recklessly squandered, intensified.

Nevertheless, he continued to fight, and in the matter of the reservation of channels, he was eventually successful. In June 1946, again reversing itself, the FCC decided to hold open ninety FM channels for a year, to give returning service personnel a chance to bid for them. That it had finally decided to do so was entirely due to the dogged persistence of Clifford J. Durr.[28]

Durr's concern about the growing dominance of the network advertisers over program content arose from the same frustrating sense of possibility denied. The heart of the problem, he told a friend early in 1945, was his fear "that broadcasting is becoming primarily an advertising medium rather than a medium of public service supported by advertising." Yet he did not want radio simply to be a government monopoly; that carried its own dangers. What was needed was "diversification of control, with a maximum of competition" for listeners, from both commercial and noncommercial stations. He did not believe "that advertising agencies should hand us our culture, all ready made to their pattern," or that radio should become their allies. For this reason, he had decided to warn Americans whenever he could against the dangers of allowing advertisers too much power and to attempt to persuade other FCC members to his point of view.[29]

Durr had, predictably, little success in the later endeavor, but he was able to voice his fears about the need to curb the power of the advertising agencies in the public arena, as he began not only to receive more speaking invitations but to have his views reported. Speaking in 1945, for example, to the Conference of the Independent Citizens Committee of the Arts, Sciences, and Professions in New York, he warned against the dominance of advertisers in commercial radio and called on his audience to press for "diversity and for democratic radio. Let us have a radio," he concluded "that is truly free—as free from economic domination and overweening greed as from government censorship; that is free for the fullest expression of ideas and music and art. Let us have a radio that is competitive for listeners as well as for advertising accounts. Let us have a radio that is regulated by the people and that gives the people full access to all information needed for intelligent regulation." It was as clear a statement as he could make about his thinking of radio's potential as a "people's medium," his hopes for future developments, and, by implication, his fears of what would happen if his warnings went unheeded.[30]

Nothing angered the industry and the advertising agencies more, as Durr himself recognized, than that sort of attack and evocation. Editorializing after a similar speech in 1944, under the headline "Durr's Slurs," *Broadcasting Magazine* sneered at him as "the latest crusader" attacking the industry and its sponsors and implied that FCC commissioners should stick to regulating the airwaves and let those who knew how to do so run the radio industry, free of interference from the likes of him. "These gratuitous slurs and attacks on commercial radio and programs do not appear to fall within his official province," asserted the magazine.[31]

There was, however, also strong support for his views. In a December 1944 column reviewing Durr's work, the *New Republic* pictured him as a convinced liberal, "fighting quietly and steadily for the people's interests." Durr was "widely known as a high principled, courageous fighter against advertising control of radio, against the lack of radio service for millions in the U.S. . . . for balanced presentation of controversial issues on the air, allowing labor and consumer groups to buy their share of time as easily as the commercial group, for developing more public service program." Durr, the column concluded, was "fighting on the people's side." Without doubt, that was the way he was being generally perceived. Washington senator Homer T. Bone, as he prepared to leave political life, felt disposed to drop Durr a note of appreciation. "All through the years," he wrote, "I have had to fight a spirit of depression that almost overwhelms me at times as I contemplate the fact that there were so few men in public life, even in our own New Deal, who were willing to carry on a real fight for worthwhile things. This wretched place has a tendency to cool the ardor of men," he thought. But Durr was such a man, said Bone, and he had always sincerely admired his "courage and vision." Durr himself had come to accept the role of the people's advocate, albeit uneasily. He was not, he admitted, naturally "the 'happy warrior' type." But "every now and then" the time came when there was nothing to do but fight, "whatever the consequences may be."[32]

In later life, when asked what his most significant accomplishment was while on the FCC, Clifford Durr had no hesitation in nominating his involvement in the investigation which resulted in the production and eventual endorsement by the commission of the report "Public Service Responsibility of Broadcast Licensees," then popularly known as the "Blue Book" because of the color of its cover. Produced in March 1946, the Blue Book was in one sense a cooperative endeavor, but there was no doubt with whom it had originated. It was Clifford Durr's creation.[33]

The Blue Book was the end result of Durr's growing dissatisfaction with the way the FCC routinely renewed broadcasting licenses solely on the basis of engineering reports, despite the clear statement in the act that such renewals ought to have been governed by the same considerations as had the original granting of the license. This should have included a review of the station's programs, but under Fly, preoccupied as the FCC had been with the matter of diversity of ownership, this requirement had been all but ignored.[34]

Clifford Durr thought it should be brought back. He began to refrain from voting on license renewals when he believed there was no broad base on which to make a judgment, insisting that past programs, especially a comparison between what had been promised at the original hearing with what had actually eventuated, should be central to any license renewal. Stations which had promised one thing but then had delivered another without reference to the FCC should, he thought, be very carefully scrutinized. Some of his colleagues eventually came to agree with him. In 1945, FCC chairman Paul A. Porter started a policy of systematically comparing promise and performance in programming when considering renewals. The result was disturbing. Clearly many stations had made little attempt to implement the program standards they themselves had set and had made no attempt at all to keep the FCC informed of changes made, despite their clear obligation to do so. A number of stations, therefore, were put on temporary licenses, pending the production of a report which would describe the state of the industry and make clear the FCC's reasons for concern. It would also "outline future standards of public interest" to which stations should conform. Clifford Durr, as the commissioner most responsible for its inception, was chosen to superintend the investigation.[35]

Durr in turn delegated the spadework to three friends, his Seminary Hill neighbor Charles Siepmann, formerly director of talks and program planning for the BBC but now an American citizen; Edward Brecher; and Dallas Smythe, the FCC's best statistician. Working virtually round-the-clock, and with Durr vetting the successive drafts, they produced the Blue Book in a month. The FCC endorsed it on March 7, 1946, and released it to the public. Given the speed at which it was compiled, it was a most impressive achievement. Giving copious examples, it outlined deficiencies in past programming, and it set programming standards for the future—emphasizing the need to provide for balance and diversity—to which all applicants for licenses or renewals would be expected to conform. Predictably, it was condemned by the industry as an example of unwarranted government interference with freedom of the air, and Durr was referred to as "radio's Cassius." Some members of the public, too, were outraged, like Leah E. McClelland, who wrote to the new FCC chairman, Charles R. Denny, complaining bitterly about the influence of "that wretched Commissioner Durr whose wife is an active member of the CIO-PAC," a reference to Virginia's ongoing political activities.[36]

Nevertheless, the public generally responded well to the Blue Book. Durr's files were soon filled with letters of support and requests for copies. The press, too, was generally favorable and correctly identified him as the motive force behind it. "He has established himself as a national figure worthy of the people's confidence and esteem by insisting that the public weal is a matter of prime concern to the Commission," ran an editorial in his hometown newspaper. Montgomerians would like to have him home, it continued, but that was a selfish wish. Rather, he should stay in Washington and continue to "serve the whole nation with such high distinction."[37]

So emboldened was FCC chairman Denny by the positive reception accorded the Blue Book that he vowed, "We do not intend to bleach it." Yet bleached it was; the FCC failed to uphold the standards it itself had set. As the nation moved on to other concerns, the power of the radio industry proved to be too strong. The FCC hectored recalcitrant stations, it threatened them, but in the end it renewed their licenses, usually with Durr in dissent. He had won his fight to have the commission set programming standards. However, it lacked the will to do so: the Blue Book, sadly, was soon ignored.[38]

As it became clearer to Durr that his position on a range of issues was not necessarily shared by his FCC colleagues, it became more important to him to get his message across to the public. From 1943 on, he accepted as many invitations to speak as he could, even if it meant longer hours of traveling when he would have much preferred to be home with the family. "I have had my fill of travelling," he wrote his mother in 1946, "and want nothing more than to settle down with my family, chickens and gardens"—but he could not do so. The need to alert people to the problems ahead was too important. Virginia told her daughter the next year that there was a real urgency now about his speechmaking. "He seems to feel he must speak as often as he can while he has a place to speak from so he will be heard," she said.[39]

Sometimes he spoke on general themes. One of his earliest such speeches was to the American Economic Association, in January 1943, on "The Post War Relationship between Government and Business," in which he predicted a general extension of the DPC experience to all sectors of the economy, something "which is not capitalism and a new kind of private enterprise which is not based on private initiative." It would be a system in which the federal government provided the capital and took the financial risk, while business was paid a "management fee" for its technical skill and organizational ability. The government, however, would determine what was to be produced and in what quantity. "The methods used to harness our great productive strength for war purposes have been democratic," he concluded, and they must continue to be so, thus showing how deeply the DPC experience had affected his thinking on the economy and how much a New Dealer, with an optimistic faith in a cooperative future, he had become.[40]

Mainly, however, he spoke about radio and the need to keep it free. A few examples will suffice to give the flavor of his message. In March 1944 he urged an audience of Nieman Fellows at Harvard to fight for diversification of the airwaves. Leaving control of radio to the broadcasters and the advertising people "leads to an end to diversification," he warned, for they "shun controversy." Throughout 1944 he stressed the need to reserve FM channels for educational programs and for public radio. "You can insist that the more timorous or more commercial-minded broadcasters make time available for the frank discussion of issues that are vital to us all," he told the New York Federation of Women's Clubs. They could insist, too, that the decisions as to what they could hear be publicly arrived at and not simply "pass into the hands of a few advertising agencies whose sole function is to sell the goods of their customers." The Conference on FM Education, in 1945, heard him describe his vision of educational broadcasting. FM stations, he said, could make education "a living part of our community life." They could be civic centers, serving "the cultural, intellectual and recreational needs of every man, woman and child" in the community. The following year, to a group of religious educators, he spoke directly of broadcasting as a public trust. "The broadcasting licensee," he argued, "must be regarded and held accountable as a trustee to the public." The people, after all, owned the channels; they had simply entrusted them to the licensee's care, and it is their interests that the licensee must serve, not his or her own. In dozens of similar speeches and articles, Durr spelled out his visionary messages—of a broadcasting system open to all, accessible to all, and ultimately operated under government regulation in the public interest, not by a few large networks in the interests of their own profit margins and those of their sponsors. It was a noble dream.[41]

If Durr's public utterances were anathema to the broadcasting industry, they certainly added to his reputation as the "people's" FCC commissioner. Groups began to honor him with awards and citations. In 1947, *Variety* gave him a special award in its "annual survey of Show management." Dubbing him the "Great Dissenter of the FCC," the citation praised him both for his work on the commission in protecting "the property of the public" and for "stumping the country from end to end to preach the gospel of democracy in radio." He was, concluded the citation, "the guardsman of the American people's stake in the air they nominally own." Later that year he was voted "man of the year in educational radio" by the Schools Broadcast Conference, for being a "staunch supporter" of educational radio and in particular for his successful fight to secure for it those FM frequencies. In 1948 the Ohio State Institute for Education by Radio honored him for similar reasons. Recognition that his message was being heard and appreciated was important to him. It kept him going week after week, despite the fact that his concrete achievements were modest in scope and extremely hard-won.[42]

Stumping the country had to cease completely for a time in 1946. In September Durr went overseas for the first time since he had returned from Oxford. His purpose was to be a member of the American delegation to the Seventh International Conference on Tele-Communications and to the five-power preliminary meeting which preceded it. The conference had the urgent task of repairing and restoring the international communications network, which had been severely damaged and disrupted by World War II; the venue was Moscow. For Durr, the trip was a fascinating and important experience, the more so because it took place at a time when American perceptions of the Soviet Union were changing and the wartime ally was seen as metamorphosing into an implacable foe, bent on global conquest. There is no doubt that the views he came to hold on Soviet ambitions and, by implication, the validity of the approaching Cold War itself were colored by this visit. The conference itself, mainly on technical matters, was a great success. The meetings were conducted in a friendly atmosphere and accomplished more than he or anyone in the American delegation, for that matter, expected. There was plenty of Russian hospitality, though none of it was private; there was the opera and the ballet—"Hollywood looks pretty small stuff compared to the way Russians do things," he said—and there were the historic buildings of Moscow, including the Kremlin, which he visited. He liked the Russian people he met and had not noticed any obvious anti-American feeling among them. Moreover, he had developed some understanding of, and sympathy for, their revolution. He found it hard to believe that the old, repressive institutions had been swept away in his lifetime. "If I had been here 30 or so years ago, I would have been strongly inclined to shoot me a Czar or a few dozen priests," he mused to Virginia. Perhaps that was why Americans found it so hard to understand the Russians, for they were nowhere near as close to their own revolution. "We got rid of George III 170 years ago," he wrote, "and he was a comparatively innocuous fellow at that."[43]

Above all, though, it was the evidence of destruction that stuck with him. The "pitiful condition" of Russian houses, many of them still half-destroyed, the obvious signs of privation everywhere, the scarcity, the drabness, the immensity of the task of rebuilding the shattered economy, together with the physical reconstruction required, made an indelible impression on Durr. He found it impossible to believe that a nation so obviously crippled, that had come so close to destruction, that had suffered so terribly, could possibly entertain ideas of global conquest. It defied all logic to believe that; it belied the evidence of one's eyes and ears. There can be no doubt that the experience of his four weeks' sojourn in the Soviet Union had a profound effect in shaping the attitudes he was soon to adopt on the course of American foreign policy, as Cold War tensions replaced the brief euphoria of peace.[44]

Durr stopped over in Berlin, Paris, and the United Kingdom on the way home. In Berlin, too, he was staggered by the devastation, more than a year after the war's end, and the extremely high standard of living enjoyed by the American forces there. The main occupation of the Germans, he thought, "seems to be looking after the comfort of the Americans." He could not understand, he said, why the Germans acted "as if their greatest pleasure in life was to serve their conquerors" and instinctively distrusted their "smiles and excessive friendliness." Paris he found superficially gay but rather seamy underneath. He reacted to the prostitutes much as he had done when he was twenty-one. "I am glad I passed them up then," he said, because he now knew his instincts had been sound. Sex without love was an empty, imperfect thing. As for Britain, it was pleasant to be back briefly at Queens, though all his teachers were long dead. On the whole he thought the British had survived the war surprisingly well. "They look better than they did after World War I," he noted, much "healthier and bigger." He was, however, very keen to be home. He missed Virginia terribly; being away from her made him realize, he said, just how much he loved and needed her, and he missed his home and family. He "would eagerly trade off Paris" for Seminary Hill, he confessed ruefully.[45]

The love and support that Clifford Durr gained from his family was a prime reason he was able to survive sometimes bitter disappointments in the public arena with such equanimity. Despite the passion and the effort that went into his advocacy of causes in which he deeply believed, they could never be the sole sum of his life. There was always Virginia and the children to come home to. Indeed, from 1947 there was one more—Lulah, born in February, when Virginia was 43, and named after Little Auntie. The war years had not been the easiest of their marriage, for Virginia had been quite ill for part of the time with what was eventually diagnosed as "fatigue neurosis." At times she was hospitalized, and Cliff's sister Lucy came to look after the lively family. Then, of course, his frequent absences from home put strains on the relationship. It survived, Virginia recovered her health, and she continued, too, with her own political concerns, especially under the aegis of the Southern Conference for Human Welfare.[46]

She was particularly active in the bitter battle over the abolition of the poll tax, eventually becoming vice-chairman of the National Committee for the Abolition of the Poll Tax (NCAPT), as well as chairman of the Washington committee of the Southern Conference for Human Welfare. As such, she worked closely with blacks; Paul Robeson became a friend, as did Mary McLeod Bethune. Once she was with Louis Burnham, head of the Negro Youth Conference, when he was refused a room at the Hermitage Hotel, in Nashville, Tennessee. Quickly she helped him wind a towel around his head, and together they convinced the desk clerk that he was, in fact, from India. Virginia's friendship with an enlarging circle of black people, her commitment to her poll-tax work, and her resultant increasingly frequent confrontations with Southern politicians all served to heighten her radicalism in these years. In particular, she became utterly convinced that all vestiges of Jim Crowism must be rooted out if the South was ever to progress economically and socially, and her poll-tax activity was increasingly directed to that end. Much more clearly than did her husband, she believed she was able to see the South for what it was, a region where the rights supposedly guaranteed all Americans were ruthlessly trampled on in the interests of a selfish and self-perpetuating ruling caste; unlike him, she became increasingly pessimistic about its capacity for change.[47]

Her deepening commitment to racial equality, however, had its effect on Cliff's own views on race, though these had been changing anyway—his growing liberalism had seen to that. Nevertheless, though he never himself joined either the NCAPT or the SCHW, he strongly supported Virginia's work with them, in the face of distinct family disapproval, and as he talked with her about it and met those who felt equally committed, his own perspectives began to shift as well. One incident involving Hugo Black resulted in Clifford Durr's having to devastate his mother, whom he loved deeply, over the fundamental question of race, and in so doing, he revealed how far he too had departed from his traditional Southern views on that matter.[48]

In 1945 the Southern Conference for Human Welfare, with which Virginia was heavily involved, decided to honor Hugo Black at a dinner to be held in the Statler Hotel in Washington. Reports of the forthcoming event in the Montgomery newspapers stressed the fact that it would be an interracial affair, that Negroes of both sexes would be present. In desperation, Mrs. Durr implored her son not to attend. She had, she said, lived with the shadow of her father's Republican vote for most of her life, and she could not bear it if her son also became a traitor to his region's traditions, if he, too, besmirched the family's honor. In particular, the idea of black women being present as guests was just too much for her.[49]

Gently, but firmly, Clifford told her he would be attending, and he told her why. "Our differences," he said, "are no greater than are to be expected in the transition of one generation faced with one set of conditions to another faced with a set of conditions somewhat if not basically different." He had always tried to be true to Southern traditions, he said, and "they still are and always will be essential parts of my make-up." He had also been taught that, "in our particular scheme of things," race lines had to be drawn and rigidly maintained, and this he had gone along with. But "the line may not always be a fixed one." Changing conditions may mean that it had to be shifted from time to time, he had come to see, "if we are to maintain the racial division with the minimum of hurt and unfairness." He had several times taken an oath to support and defend the Constitution, and the Constitution gave blacks the same rights of citizenship as all Americans. More fundamentally, they too were human beings; "if we forget that, we are likely to do more terrible things to ourselves than they would ever do to us." The purity of the white race, he now knew, could never be secured by "bloodshed, regardless of how much blood we are willing to shed," but by treating all people with equal dignity and compassion and by recognizing that "the line has got to shift a little."[50]

This was an important statement, the more so as he knew that his mother would still find his position incomprehensible. He hated to hurt her, but he had no choice. Clifford Durr was never the passionate advocate of integration his wife had become. Yet he too had cut his Southern painter on the race issue. The New Deal had helped, Hugo Black had helped, but most of all his own sense of fairness and justice, his fundamental human decency, and his passionate commitment to democratic values had prompted him to part company with his family and his region on this, the most central of all Southern issues.[51]

It is possible that his departure from traditional Southern views on race may have cost him an important federal job in 1945. From time to time he was mentioned as being in the running for various government positions. In 1944, for example, he was considered seriously both for the chairmanship both of the Surplus Property Board and of the Federal Communications Commission. Though he always disavowed any desire to move, there can be no doubt that the prospect of becoming federal loans administrator, for which he was a top candidate in early 1945, greatly appealed to him, quite apart from the irony of his succeeding Jesse Jones. He was strongly supported by Lister Hill; the secretary of the treasury, Henry Morgenthau, Jr.; and by the former vice-president, Henry Wallace, now secretary of commerce. A note in the president's own hand, written on April 9, indicated that FDR was clearly considering him very seriously indeed.[52]

When the president died on April 12, the appointment had not yet been made. If Roosevelt, as some believe, had decided to offer Durr the job, he left no record of it. On the same day, however, Alabama's senior senator, John H. Bankhead, had written to Durr on the matter. In particular, he wished to know his attitude on three things: the elimination of the poll tax, federal antilynching legislation, and the Fair Employment Practices Commission, all issues very dear to Southern hearts. Durr, in his response, said that he did not believe the matters raised fell within the loan administrator's authority, but he would tell Bankhead anyway. He supported the FEPC; he abhored lynching but did not feel that federal antilynching legislation was "a sound or helpful approach to the problem of mob violence," much preferring state action; and he had not yet made up his mind on federal legislation to eliminate the poll tax. His support for such action, again, "would depend on my appraisal of the possibilities of accomplishing the objectives" through state legislation. The objective, however—the scrapping of the poll tax—he supported. More generally, he took the opportunity to urge Bankhead not to "contribute to the laying down of irrelevant standards which may serve only to deprive our Section of the country" of its fair share of federal appointments. "You may well block a Southerner whose views on the issues you have mentioned do not coincide with your own," he argued, but he could not block the appointment of anyone else on those grounds. Bankhead was not impressed and decided not to sponsor him for the position.[53]

Clifford Durr did not become federal loans administrator. On April 17 the new president, Harry S. Truman, sent the name of Durr's old RFC colleague John W. Snyder to the Senate. Even if FDR had lived, Durr may well not have been appointed. The president's administrative assistant, James M. Barnes, had warned him against the appointment the day before he died. "I am rather certain that tremendous opposition would develop on the Hill" if Durr got the job, Barnes had written. There had already been two bruising confirmation fights that year. Wallace's nomination for secretary of commerce had been bitterly opposed, while the fight to confirm Durr's friend and fellow Alabamian Aubrey W. Williams to head the Rural Electrification Administration had but recently been lost. Roosevelt may have had no stomach for another and may have heeded Barnes's warning. Nevertheless, for Durr to have responded to Senator Bankhead in the way that he did, knowing full well what the consequences would be, is again testimony to his integrity and fearless honesty.[54]

These were qualities much mentioned when Clifford Durr decided not to accept reappointment to the FCC at the expiration of his term. At a luncheon in his honor on June 19, 1948, Wayne F. Coy, the new FCC chairman, spoke at length about his "shining integrity, his keen intellect and his disarming charm." The name of Clifford Durr, he said, "stands high on the roll of those who have contributed to American broadcasting in the public interest. He has always had before him the vision of broadcasting as a palladium of the people's

A family portrait, taken on Cliff's last day at the FCC. From left, Virginia, Tilla, Cliff, Lucy, and Ann (Courtesy of the Alabama State Department of Archives and History)

liberties. He has had high aspirations for the fulfillment of broadcasting's destiny as a dynamic leader in moving this nation towards the realization of the American dream," as he set goals of achievement for the industry which it had not yet attained. Durr had not won all his battles, he said—far from it—but he had influenced for the better even his sternest adversaries. It would "be a sad day for America,"concluded Coy, if Durr's "long range objective of a more socially useful and a more democratic broadcasting system ever became a lost cause." Durr had exemplified by his example "the highest type of public service in the American tradition."[55]

This type of plaudit was echoed in the nation's press. The *New York Times* praised Durr's contribution and his devotion to principle, while at the same time criticizing the trade press "which delighted in subjecting him to petty and carping criticism." The *Washington Post*, talking of his consistent fight for "freedom of the air," thought it a "public misfortune" that he could "no longer afford

At lunch, on leaving the FCC. From left, unidentified man, Lowell Mellett, Cliff Durr, Thurman Arnold, Hugo Black, Josh Lee (Courtesy of the Alabama State Department of Archives and History)

the luxury of public service." *Newsweek,* reporting his retirement lunch, spoke of him as the "lone dissenter" on the FCC. "Few there were who appreciated his clarity of vision in safeguarding the use of radio for the public interest," ran the article. "Few assisted him in his courageous fight to retain the balance of power between the vast listening audience and the station operator." Now, of course, they all came to raise "the cup of eulogy," when it was safe to do so. The praise must have been very gratifying to Durr, as he prepared, after fifteen years, to leave government service. At the end of his life he wrote that,though he had failed in much of what he had attempted at the FCC, yet he was even prouder of his work there than his much more successful period at the DPC. It was the high point of his public career.[56]

In his June 19 address, however, Wayne Coy had talked about far more than Durr's contribution to American broadcasting. He made extensive reference to his patriotism and his commitment to basic democratic values. "He is an exultant believer in democracy," he declared. "If he is capable of wrath, all his wrath would fall on those reckless sons of America who would sell our soul of liberty for restraints to be imposed by a few." Durr was not afraid, as so many in 1948 were afraid. "He sees no danger in the other fellow enjoying the same freedom as he enjoys. He has no easy tolerance for things that should not be tolerated."[57]

Coy's audience knew very well to what he was referring. Paralleling Durr's fight for a democratic radio system operating in the public interest had been another struggle, arising from incidents within the FCC ambit but having far wider implications. This was his concern to preserve civil liberties in America, to preserve for all Americans those rights guaranteed by the First Amendment to the Constitution—basic rights like freedom of speech and of association and, above all, the rule of law. In the course of this struggle, he was to confront the House Committee on Un-American Activities, the Speaker of the House of Representatives, the director of the Federal Bureau of Investigation, and, ultimately, the president of the United States himself.

6

THE LOYALTY ISSUE

In January 1942, Clifford Durr wrote to his mother that his "quiet time" at the FCC was over. The reason was that he, as a new member with no previous connections to the commission's staff, had been assigned to investigate allegations that one of its employees, a Dr. Goodwin Watson, was either a Communist or sympathetic to Communist causes. These allegations stemmed from the House Committee on Un-American Activities. Set up in 1938, largely resulting from the pressure of antifascist congressmen for an inquiry into the extent of fascist penetration in America, HUAC had become instead a vehicle for the discrediting of FDR and the New Deal. Shrewdly exploiting the popular anti-Communist strain in American life and showing little regard for established rules of procedure, it became under its flamboyant chairman, Texas Democrat Martin Dies, a focal point for anti–New Deal hysteria and propaganda. The Dies Committee, in William Leuchtenburg's words, "served the purposes of those who claimed the New Deal was a Red stratagem." Clifford Durr was now to do battle with it, and the experience would become his personal "Road to Damascus." The result of the Goodwin Watson investigation was to leave him an implacable opponent, not only of HUAC, but of all institutions and individuals who tried to circumscribe the minds of men and women in the name of "loyalty," who considered unsubstantiated allegations tantamount to proof of treachery, whose concern for constitutional guarantees ran a poor second to a desire for conformity.[1]

Goodwin Watson, a Columbia Teachers College social psychologist, had joined the FCC staff in November 1941. Because it possessed the most sophisticated technical facilities, the FCC had recently been given the task of monitoring and analyzing the propaganda broadcasts of the Axis powers, and Watson had been appointed chief analyst of the Foreign Broadcast Monitoring Service. A man of decidedly liberal views, he had not applied for the position but had been sought out by the FCC because of his acknowledged expertise in propaganda analysis.[2]

On November 18, HUAC chairman Dies gave to the press copies of a letter he had sent to Fly alleging Watson's close connection with Communist groups and listing thirteen organizations to which he had allegedly belonged which would fall within that category. Why he did so remains a mystery, although there was some suggestion that the chief target was Fly, who was currently in deep trouble with conservative congressmen over his outspoken criticisms of broadcasting monopolies. In any event, Fly replied to Dies promptly and unequivocally. The charges were utterly without foundation, he said. Watson was not a Communist party member, nor had he "indorsed the Communist system." Of the thirteen organizations Dies had listed, Watson had in fact been a member of only one, the Consumers Union, though he had supported several others. Fly stated his complete confidence in Watson's loyalty to the United States and hoped that that would be the end of the matter.[3]

It was, of course, a pious hope. Dies had no intention of letting the matter rest. He attacked Watson and Fly in the House of Representatives, claiming he had clear evidence of Watson's association with Communist fronts and of his sympathy for the Soviet Union. Fly was forced, therefore, to launch a more detailed investigation of the charges, and Durr, since he had just joined the commission himself and had thus had no hand in Watson's appointment, was asked to do the job.[4]

Durr began by examining Watson's personal file and found there strong recommendations as to his character and competence but no evidence of subversive activities. He then interviewed him, cross-examining him "in my best courtroom manner," but could find nothing which "would lead me to regard him as a dangerous character." Rather he seemed to be "an intelligent and responsible citizen." Next he asked his staff to investigate closely the alleged Communist fronts to which Watson had either belonged or supported. There were some real surprises. One was the League for Non-Participation in Japanese Aggression. Its president was Henry L. Stimson, secretary of state under Herbert Hoover and presently Roosevelt's secretary of war. Watson had supported the activities of the Council Against Intolerance in America. Its cochairmen were William Allen White, the Republican publisher of the *Emporia Gazette,* and Sen. Warren Barber, a New Jersey conservative. Among the members of its national board were Thomas E. Dewey and Sen. Carter Glass—scarcely men of a radical stamp. Then, Watson had joined the Marian Anderson Concert Committee, a hastily formed group of citizens outraged by the refusal of the Washington Chapter of the Daughters of the American Revolution to allow the famous Negro contralto the use of Constitution Hall. The committee arranged for her to sing at the Lincoln Memorial instead. Its chairman had been the chief justice and former presidential candidate, Charles Evans Hughes. As Durr worked through the list of supposedly subversive organizations, the utter absurdity of the charges against Watson became clear. If membership on these bodies was an indicator of disloyalty, then he was in distinguished company. The nation should "purge itself" of, apart from Watson, the vice-president, every single member of the cabinet, five Supreme Court judges, twelve senators, and thirty-six members of the House including Rep. Jerry Voorhis, himself a member of HUAC.[5]

Finally, Durr read Watson's published work. It was true that some of his writings did indicate a sympathetic interest toward the Soviet Union and that he had commented favorably upon the progress the Russians had made in certain areas, notably education. It was true, too, that he had some good words to say for socialism in general, as a possible means of solving America's economic problems. But, in none of the articles, Durr said, did "he attack or question the American form of government or advocate changes in the political structure of the country as opposed to the economic." To call them subversive, therefore, was ridiculous.[6]

Durr duly reported to his fellow commissioners that the charges against Watson were absurd and was scarcely surprised that they unanimously agreed with him. The evidence, after all, was irrefutable. What did surprise him, and shocked him to the very core of his being, was that three of the commissioners thought Watson should be fired anyway, for fear of offending Congress, on whom the FCC appropriation depended. Durr was utterly appalled. "This sort of behavior was to become typical less than a decade later," he subsequently wrote, "but at the time I found it almost unbelievable in its callousness."[7]

By a vote of 4 to 3, the FCC decided not to dismiss Dr. Goodwin Watson, the charges against whom, all were agreed, had no foundation. The majority then made a public statement, in which the Dies allegations were answered in detail. There was also a declaration of principle. "We said," Durr recollected, "that we could not, consistent with our oaths of office to support and defend the Constitution, deprive a man of his job and his reputation as well on the basis of any such ridiculous charges." The House of Representatives was not of a similar mind. On January 22 it added a rider to the FCC's appropriation bill, barring the payment of any portion of it to Dr. Goodwin Watson.[8]

Fly was infuriated, as, of course, was Durr. At a press conference he bitterly attacked the House's action and said he would press for its reversal in the Senate. More than anyone else, Durr would be doing the pressing. "Commissioner Durr has been designated to handle the matter actively on behalf of the Commission," he announced, "and he will undoubtedly be in touch with some of the Senators." For his part, Durr was glad to do the job, as he was outraged by the whole procedure. Watson was a loyal American, he told his mother, yet now "by an Act of Congress and without any opportunity being offered him to answer the charges, he is to be declared to be disloyal to his country." He was increasingly frightened by the spirit in the land that made such action possible. "I have seen it growing for some time," he said, and it had to be resisted. Resist it he would, for the rest of his life.[9]

Durr went at his task with a will, sending the material he had gathered on Watson to key senators, attempting at first simply to secure a hearing for him before the Senate subcommittee dealing with the Independent Offices Appropriation Bill so that "full evidence may be presented as to Dr. Watson's ability and loyalty." This took place on February 4. Throughout February, Durr kept up the pressure, concentrating particularly on three key members of the Appropriations subcommittee—Burnett Maybank of South Carolina, James M. Mead of New York, and Harry S. Truman of Missouri—and on his friend and fellow Alabamian, Lister Hill. He sent them materials and visited them in their offices. To Mead, for example, he provided a copy of his investigation of the alleged subversive organizations with which Watson had been connected, not failing to point out that he, Mead, was also a member of some of them. He hoped, he said, that the senator was not also "a dangerous red in disguise."[10]

Durr's efforts were successful. The Senate subcommittee struck the rider from the House bill, but it was restored by the full Appropriations Committee, largely through the efforts of Sen. Kenneth D. McKellar, by this time an implacable foe of the New Deal. Debate in the Senate took place on May 1, and Durr was gratified at the success of his lobbying effort. The senators on whom he had concentrated his efforts were solid in their opposition to the rider, but what he had not expected were the numbers from both sides of the chamber with whom he had not communicated who rose "on the floor to express their sense of outrage over the affront to decency and basic American principles presented by the rider and the charges behind it." It was easily defeated.[11]

There would therefore need to be a House-Senate conference, so Durr kept up the pressure. He wrote long, carefully argued letters to the House conferees, in which he pointed out that no charges had been made against Watson, nor was it alleged that he was disloyal. Rather, the only objection to him seemed to be that he had "expressed some views which did not accord with the general pattern of thought in the country." However, there was no suggestion that these views somehow affected his capacity to do his job. There was a basic question of freedom of speech involved, he said, which should be paramount. "I did not know Watson prior to his employment by the Commission," he concluded, "but I have followed his work closely since that time and am thoroughly convinced of his complete loyalty to the Government." Then came a statement which typified Durr's position on this and many similar cases in the decade ahead. It explains why from this time on he was such an uncompromising, resolute defender of those civil liberties guaranteed by the Constitution, during a period when they were increasingly under attack. Indeed, it explains much of the course of his future life, including his decision to leave public service. "I could not maintain my own self-respect," he wrote, "if I should fail to stand up for any lawfully employed subordinate who I felt was performing his duties loyally and competently." Durr's defense of Goodwin Watson was but the first in a long line of principled stands against those whom he perceived as trampling on basic civil liberties. It was to become his most important commitment, and he was to suffer for it in the years ahead.[12]

The House conferees agreed to the Senate amendment rejecting the rider on June 22, 1942. There can be little doubt as to Durr's importance in affecting the outcome. Certainly Watson had no doubts. "I realize how completely the Senate victory depended on you," he wrote in gratitude after the May vote, expressing the hope that the defeat had made that sort of rider unlikely in the future. On that he was wrong. The House passed the same rider the following year, adding for good measure the names of William Dodd, another

FCC employee, and Robert Morss Lovett, then secretary-general of the Virgin Islands. Once again the rider was resoundingly defeated in the Senate, but this time the House conferees refused to yield. The Senate, in fact, was forced to reject it five times in all, with substantial though diminishing majorities each time. On the sixth vote, with agencies fast running out of funds and a war to be won, the Senate was reluctantly forced to compromise. The three men were permitted to hold their jobs until a date a few months hence, after which time they could no longer be paid unless personally reappointed by the president. Roosevelt, reluctantly, signed the appropriation bill, while at the same time denouncing the rider and making it clear that only the urgency of the wartime situation was forcing him to accept it. The FCC let Watson and Dodd work for a few days longer than their specified deadline and then sent them a paycheck that did not include payment for these extra days—in accordance with the rider.[13]

By so doing, the FCC had laid the basis for a challenge to the rider in the courts. The three men, accordingly, sued the federal government in the court of claims for uncompensated service. Normally, the attorney general, Francis Biddle, would have defended the suit on behalf of the government. He felt so strongly, however, that the rider was unconstitutional that he excused himself, Congress appointing a special counsel in his place. The plaintiffs won their case. The special counsel appealed the decision, and eventually the Supreme Court, in the landmark case of *United States* v. *Lovett, Watson, and Dodd,* supported the plaintiffs. It was the final vindication for Clifford Durr's fight, but any satisfaction he may have felt was tempered by the recognition that the United States Congress had agreed to what was virtually a bill of attainder affecting three federal employees against whom no charges had even been brought. It was a grim preview of what lay ahead during the time of the "Great Fear" and the excesses of Sen. Joseph McCarthy and his cohorts.[14]

The Watson case brought to Durr a second preview of the future. A few days after the Senate vote in 1942, a Seminary Hill neighbor told him that FBI men had recently been in the neighborhood asking questions about him and his political opinions. Soon afterward he was interviewed by FBI operatives and questioned about his loyalty. He was incensed, both that this should have occurred at all and because he could get no information as to the nature of the allegations against him or who it was who made them. He complained bitterly to the attorney general about what was happening. Complaints such as the one against him often resulted from personal political vendettas, he was sure, and the FBI failed to appreciate this. Moreover, "the nature of the examination to which I was subjected is neither fair to the person under examination nor calculated to obtain helpful information," he claimed, given that neither the nature of the accusations nor the name of the accuser could be known. He had been profoundly disturbed by the whole experience.[15]

A few days later, J. Edgar Hoover released a copy of the report on Durr to Fly, with the routine explanation that, as a complaint had been made, the Bureau had had no choice but to investigate. Durr was given a clean bill of political health, however; in fact, the report said much more about Virginia's activities with the SCHW than it did about his own. This scarcely mollified him, however, the more so because he was convinced that the original complaint had come from HUAC and would not have occurred had he not been so prominent in Goodwin Watson's defense. To Alabama congressman Joe Starnes, a HUAC member, he wrote detailing his anger and his concern, in so doing setting out a position on investigatory committees, loyalty procedures, and the abuse of power by the FBI which he was to repeat many times in different contexts throughout the decade. "If this is the Committee's idea of Americanism," he thundered, "we would hardly be worse off letting Himmler set the standards. By building up meaningless dossiers on reputable private citizens," he went on to argue, "by bringing public charges reflecting upon the loyalty of Government employees without giving them any hearing or opportunity to answer, by making Americans suspicious of their fellow citizens and undermining their confidence in their future . . . and by employing procedures which violate the fundamental principles of real Americanism, your committee is doing incalculable harm to this country and playing directly into the hands of its enemies." Durr was angry, and he remained so the rest of his life. If his ongoing struggle to preserve the fabric of American civil liberties was one of the themes which gave his life consistency, then the Goodwin Watson investigation and its aftermath were crucial in explaining the strength of his convictions.[16]

Durr did not let the issue of his own investigation rest and complained to Edwin Dickinson, the Department of Justice officer directly responsible. He was, he said, "impressed by the simplicity of the procedure under which a smear of suspicion may be applied," in contrast to the time and trouble required for its removal—if it ever could be removed. He knew that his persistence would scarcely make him popular, but he did not care. "I can't stand to see people kicked around by those who hold power over them," he told his mother. Moreover, he thought the right of free speech to be "basic Americanism," and the subject ran "pretty deep" with him. Indeed it did.[17]

As his FBI file, eventually obtained by Virginia under Freedom of Information provisions, shows, Durr was to be placed under FBI surveillance again. Indeed, by the end of his life he had come to expect it. This first time, however, he was shaken and outraged to the core of his being. Yet as Virginia later recalled, even outrage had its funny side. In late 1941 the Durrs had acquired a Japanese butler, Yamasaki, who lived with his wife and small child in their rambling Seminary Hill home. His presence, it transpired, thoroughly confused the FBI's investigators. They were, after all, investigating allegations of Communist sympathy, allegations which, incidentally, Jessica Mitford's continued presence at Seminary Hill seemed to substantiate. Yet here was a possible enemy alien living there as well, and one whose clothes trunk, they discovered, had a false bottom. Not until an investigation disclosed that concealed in the trunk was, not the secret radio transmitter they had expected to find, but simply a collection of salacious postcards, was their perplexity assuaged. Yamasaki, accordingly, was given a clean bill of health.[18]

Durr's next battle with the abuse of Congress's investigatory powers occurred in 1943. In this instance, his adversary was the influential Georgia congressman Eugene E. Cox, a member of the House Rules Committee and a friend to the powerful, including the Speaker of the House of Representatives, Sam Rayburn, and to Martin Dies. In 1942 a routine FCC relicensing investigation turned up clear evidence, including a canceled check, that in 1940 Cox had been paid $2,500 for services rendered to the Herald Publishing Company, Albany, Georgia, in its successful application to get a license for radio station WALB. Cox had, in fact, used his influence to permit the company to operate the station on an incorrect frequency, despite opposition from FCC engineers, and in return the grateful owners paid him $2,500 in cash, which he immediately returned for stock in WALB. This was so clearly illegal that FCC investigators believed that they had no choice but to turn the matter over to the Justice Department for possible criminal prosecution. This was duly done, the case was prepared, and eventually it was sent to the attorney general with a recommendation for "immediate presentation" to a Washington, D.C., grand jury.[19]

The case, however, was never submitted—Cox was too powerful for that. Rather, the congressman began a campaign of systematic abuse and calumny against Fly and the FCC, culminating in his introduction of a resolution on January 6, 1943, calling for a congressional investigation of the commission and alleging that the "FCC had set up a Gestapo the equal of which had never been seen under a free government," and, then, in an eclectic switch of metaphor, claiming it to be "a nest of Reds" and "the nastiest nest of rats to be found in this entire country." The Rules Committee, not surprisingly, supported the resolution; a Select Committee to Investigate the Federal Communications Commission was set up; and despite his obvious bias and personal interest in the matter, Cox was appointed its chairman. It was, commented Durr wryly as he prepared for the fight, a situation where "the defendant is trying the judges." Still, he did not think the FCC had much to fear. "I don't think Congressman Cox can prove anything on me than that I am a New Dealer," he told his mother—and that he certainly continued to be "without apology." It was not yet a crime to be so inclined.[20]

Durr and his fellow commissioners, however, were simply not prepared for the vehemence and viciousness with which Cox and his handpicked counsel, Eugene L. Garey, a right-wing New York lawyer, went about the investigation. There was systematic harassment of witnesses, some of whom had been subpoenaed in clear violation of the law; some were questioned without a single member of Congress being present, again in clear violation of the law; the transcript had been altered; the sessions were often held in quite unlikely places, in an effort to keep them secret; and there had been improper use of the congressional power to seize records and files. Indeed, most of the FCC's files were subpoenaed on what was clearly a fishing enterprise. The committee seemed less interested in finding out anything about the FCC than in punishing it, in reducing its independence, and in destroying the morale of its staff. As Eugene Meyer, the conservative editor of the *Washington Post* later stated, the investigation was "a mockery of basic American traditions of fair play. It has been a star chamber; it has been black with bias."[21]

Something had to be done, and again it was Clifford Durr who made the move. His opportunity came when Garey wrote to all the commissioners requesting full details of their personal finances for the period from January 1, 1937. Durr flatly and publicly refused to comply, saying that such information was of an entirely personal nature and thus no business of the committee's—unless, of course, "it was for the purpose of ascertaining whether or not I have been guilty of accepting bribes or similar misconduct in the performance of my official duties." If so, he suggested that the matter be referred to the Department of Justice. Cox and Garey were both furious. The congressman said he would get the information anyway from other sources, while Garey described Durr's action in making public the original request as "highly discourteous."[22]

There was more such "discourtesy" to come, and Durr decided to put his public life on the line over the matter, for, as he wrote to his brother John, "decent government" could not possibly survive if "individual members of Congress are permitted, without protest to use its investigating power for their own private purpose." Even worse, in this particular case, the purpose was to evade the consequences of the "violation of a criminal statute which Congress itself passed." Accordingly, on May 13, 1943, he petitioned Speaker Rayburn, seeking Cox's removal from the committee investigating the FCC because of his "bias" and "prejudice" toward the agency. He also raised the matter of Cox's personal interest, drawing the Speaker's attention in particular to the matter of the $2,500 payment to him for services to WALB. All this he released to the press, including photostats of the canceled check. The battle was well and truly joined, a battle he certainly did not want for a number of reasons, not the least of which was Virginia's health, but which he could not avoid, even if he was to fight it on his own. His six FCC colleagues, he said, preferred to "keep their necks tucked in." Durr, however, could not be like that.[23]

Rayburn was not pleased and immediately referred Durr's petition to the House Judiciary Committee, where it lay for the summer while the Cox investigation proceeded apace. Nothing was heard of it, in fact, until September 18, when Rep. Hatton Summers, chairman of the Judiciary Committee, advised him that his committee had concluded "it had no jurisdiction and no responsibility" in respect to the petition. The responsibility for deciding on it was now firmly back with the Speaker, as Durr forcefully reminded him by letter, in insisting that the House now consider it without delay. This letter he released to the press, together with copies of his original May 13 petition and, once again, the telltale photostats of the Cox check.[24]

He did one more thing. He enlisted the aid of a powerful ally, Eugene Meyer, the editor and publisher of the *Washington Post.* Meyer had supported Durr's May 13 stand and had decided to pursue the issue further once Congress reconvened. He asked Durr to see him, they talked at length, and Durr gave him copies of all his documents. Meyer then took over. In a public letter to the Speaker, published in the *Post* on September 27 and widely reprinted, he drew his attention to "a matter . . . which goes to the very roots of public confidence in the House of Representatives." After rehearing the facts of the matter and dwelling in particular on Cox's alleged offense and the reluctance of the attorney general to prosecute, a reluctance he deplored and which he attributed to the House's continuing to show a "sense of confidence in Mr. Cox," Meyer turned to the investigation itself and to Durr's petition. Attacking the conduct of the investigation as biased and an affront to American traditions, he laid the responsibility for this departure firmly at Cox's door. "Mr. Cox has corrupted the high function of the investigatory power of Congress," Meyer asserted. "If there was ever ground for the House retaining confidence in Mr. Cox . . . what ground is left now?"[25]

The House, Meyer concluded, must act on Cox without delay. "The Durr petition which now again lies on your desk, Mr. Speaker, must be taken up." The *Post*, he said, called on Rayburn and his colleagues "to submerge whatever there may be of personal loyalty to Mr. Cox to the far higher compulsions which derive from your proven loyalty to the integrity of the American legislative process." Given the intensity of the support throughout the country for Meyer's position, there was little Rayburn could do but comply. Newspaper after newspaper echoed his views in the next two or three days, and Meyer received hundreds of letters of support from private citizens, together with copies of telegrams sent to congressmen urging Cox's removal. By September 30, the Speaker had persuaded Cox to resign from the committee. He did so in an atmosphere characterized by the *Louisville Courier Journal* as a "Farce with Tears," loudly protesting his innocence of any wrongdoing and claiming to be a victim of "the poison shafts of slander." So vicious had the attacks on him become, however, that the real issue, the incompetence of the FCC, had become "beclouded," and he was stepping down, therefore, in order to redirect the focus of the investigation back to the commission.[26]

His congressional colleagues, doubtless relieved to see him go, nevertheless contributed to the sense of farce. Cox was applauded from both sides of the aisle, and his honesty and integrity were generally held up as shining examples of selfless public service. House majority leader John W. McCormack set the tone when he called

Cox's decision "the greatest act of personal sacrifice any man ever made while a member of this distinguished body," on the face of it a quite extraordinary claim. Speaker Rayburn spoke of the great love he bore Cox and assured him that his integrity remained intact. The newspapers were generally less fulsome, however. Most followed the line of the *Louisville Courier Journal,* who after expressing the profoundest relief that an inquiry "so flagrantly star-chamber, so fiercely one-sided" would no longer continue in that vein, mocked all the congressional puffery surrounding Cox's resignation. The House was "practically bathed in tears over the cruel wrong done to their colleague," the *Journal* asserted. "Moans and sobs filled the Chamber," it asserted, as congressmen wallowed "waist-deep in lachrymial brine." It was all a bit ridiculous.[27]

The papers did, however, have good things to say about Durr's part in Cox's removal. The New York daily *P.M.* called the resignation a "personal triumph for FCC Commissioner Clifford J. Durr, who risked his official position to force the issue against the powerful Georgian." The *Christian Science Monitor* spoke admiringly of the way he had "taken his courage in his own hands" in originally petitioning the House for Cox's disqualification. The *Nation* said the resignation was due to the courage of two men, Meyer and Durr. The *Birmingham Herald,* in an editorial called "Dogged Durr," spoke of his "record for sound Americanism," which was "as clean as a hound's tooth." The hero of the hour was quietly satisfied with what had happened and was amused by Cox's resignation speech, which he described as being "as dramatic as the Duke of Windsor's 'The Woman I Love.' " He had not enjoyed the fight much and was glad that it was over. "I don't like fights or even arguments," he confided to his sister Lucy. "I get butterflys in my stomach and my mouth gets dry and I begin to wish I was the kind who didn't give a damn (Don't pass that on to Mother without censoring)," he said. But he would always "give a damn" about certain things, and thus there would be further fights in the future about the abuse of power and the denial of basic constitutional guarantees.[28]

Cox was gone, but the investigation of the FCC continued. The new chairman, Rep. Clarence Lea of California, with some initial prodding from the *Washington Post,* quickly announced new rules of procedure which effectively removed the potentiality for further abuses of power such as those engaged in by Cox and Garey. Garey in fact soon resigned as the committee's counsel, the FCC was permitted to refute all charges against it, and the investigation limped to an inconclusive end in 1944, a waste of public money and time. Congress, however, had the last word, slashing the commission's budget by 25 percent.[29]

Still, it could have been much worse. That it was not so was due to the courage of Clifford J. Durr's convictions. His lone fight against the abuse of congressional investigatory powers and his refusal to sit back and allow Cox and Garey to ride roughshod over established procedures were the main reasons for the congressman's downfall. Eugene Meyer recognized this. Writing to Durr on October 1, 1943, Meyer praised him for his courage. "You are to be credited," he said, "for having fought well in a just cause in a way highly to be commended by your fellow citizens." Durr felt vindicated by what had happened, that "a basic principle of good government" had at last been upheld, but any euphoria was tempered by the assumption that there would be other such struggles in the future. He was not wrong. As formidable an opponent as Cox had been, the next public officer with whom Durr was to cross swords on a civil liberties matter was even more powerful. It was the director of the FBI, J. Edgar Hoover.[30]

In July 1946 the commission received an application from a group based in Hollywood, California, calling itself the Hollywood Community Radio Group Inc. for a license to operate a commercial station in Hollywood aiming to produce quality programs. The majority of the directors, of whom the best known was certainly the screen actor John Garfield, were either connected with the movie industry, mainly as writers, or were faculty members at the University of California at Los Angeles. A number had been active in Franklin Roosevelt's successful reelection campaigns of 1940 and 1944. As there were no competing applications for the vacant radio frequency in Hollywood, approval of the application seemed routine.[31]

FBI director Hoover, however, was following the course of the application closely. On October 1 he contacted FCC chairman Paul A. Porter to tell Porter that he and his staff, having scrutinized the list of officers and directors, had come up with something which Porter should know. "In view of the reported attempts on the part of the Communist Party to gain control of radio stations throughout the country," the FBI director wrote, "I thought that you would be interested to know that an examination of the list reflects that the majority of these individuals are members of the Communist Party or have affiliated themselves with the activities of the Communist movement."[32]

The commission, rather at a loss as to how to deal with this unsolicited information, took its time in responding. Eventually Acting Chairman Charles R. Denny replied, asking Hoover to let the FCC have any material he considered relevant as soon as possible, as hearings on the group's application were very shortly to begin. The FBI director needed no urging. On December 18, in a letter marked "personal and confidential" and delivered by special messenger, he provided Denny, now FCC chairman, with investigative reports on the officers, directors, and, for good measure, the stockholders of Hollywood Community Radio Group Inc. "None of the data furnished herewith should be placed in the records," he warned, "as it is submitted to you for your confidential information."[33]

The reports were detailed, at times colorful—but scarcely conclusive. Based entirely on the allegations of unidentified sources, they cataloged associations and statements, including support for the Soviet Union, America's wartime ally, but scarcely demonstrated Communist party membership. A few examples will suffice to demonstrate their flavor. The president of the group, broadcaster Alvin Wilder, had allegedly met with the executive board of the National Council of American Soviet Friendship, whose secretary was a personal friend of his. Moreover, in 1943 he had indicated to one source that he thought there was a very large native fascist element in the United States, which was attempting to disrupt the growing friendship between America and the Soviet Union currently being fostered by the war. People who listened to fascist propaganda should rather "get down on their knees and be thankful for what Russia has done in the war," he allegedly stated—a view, incidentally, echoed privately by more than one Allied statesman at the time. John Garfield had allegedly entertained officials of the Soviet Consulate in his home and been entertained by them. In 1942 he spoke at a National Council of American Soviet Friendship rally, concluding his remarks, the source reported, "with a dramatic shake of hands to the Red Army and Soviet leaders." In 1943 he attended a reception at Hollywood's famed Mocambo Cafe for a Soviet film director; he had entertained Tito's troops in Yugoslavia; and in 1945 he was present at a dinner honoring Paul Robeson. Franklin Fearing, a director and a professor at UCLA, had in 1938 been a sponsor of the Medical Bureau of the North American Committee to Aid Spanish Democracy; he had sponsored the first anniversary meeting of the American Youth for Democracy, "a Communist inspired and controlled youth group"; and according to one source, he regularly went to see Russian films. Abraham Polonsky, a writer, was president of the Paramount

Studios branch of the Screen Writers Guild, which was "alleged to be heavily infiltrated by Communists."

There were some well-known names among the group's stockholders. Paul Henreid, the actor, was a member of the National Council of American Soviet Friendship; Larry Adler, the harmonicist, allegedly associated with known Communists and was extremely active in front organizations; and Linus Pauling, the famous UCLA chemist, spoke regularly at meetings at which Communists attended. Also a stockholder was Robert W. Kenny, at the time attorney general for the state of California. "He has long been active in Communist front organizations," ran the report, was a state sponsor for American Youth for Democracy, and had received support from the Political Action Committee of the CIO in his various election campaigns.[34]

The FCC members simply did not know what to do with this material. Without doubt it showed that the Hollywood Community Radio Group Inc. was overwhelmingly made up of people who had a long history of support for leftist groups and causes, whose sympathies for the Soviet Union had survived the onset of the Cold War, who had been on the left wing of the New Deal spectrum, and who were often associated with the militant arm of the industrial labor movement, the CIO. However, there was no evidence of a Communist conspiracy in these unsourced, largely undocumented reports, and certainly no reason to deny the group a radio license. On the other hand, no one wanted to offend J. Edgar Hoover. He had powerful friends in Congress, and to have him ranged against the FCC could have the most serious effect on its funding.[35]

Accordingly the commissioners decided to make their own investigation of the Hollywood group. Raymond Lewis, an FCC investigator, spent some time in Los Angeles in January and February 1947, trying to get information on them that could be used in a hearing. First he saw the assistant chief of police in Los Angeles, who noted that "one of his closest personal friends" was listed as a stockholder, but he had nothing at all in his files about them. A Sergeant Kinsey, the person responsible for investigating subversive activities for the Los Angeles County sheriff's office, could not help either. He knew some of the names on the FBI list and noted that most of the people there seemed to be "liberal-minded"; but, as he said, that was no crime. "I am liberal minded myself," he confessed. Lewis had more luck at the Beverly Hills Republican Club. There he met with the actor Adolph Menjou, who had written to the FCC opposing the granting of a license to the group, and George Murphy, the song-and-dance man who was then president of the Screen Actors Guild and later became a United States senator. Both these men claimed to have plenty of evidence linking the Hollywood Community Radio Group with the Communist party, and this they promised to present at a hearing on the application scheduled for March 10.[36]

The hearing went ahead, but neither Menjou nor Murphy turned up. When asked why, Menjou said he had changed his mind. He really did not have the hard evidence of Communist activity he had previously claimed to possess, and while "he and his associates considered certain members of the Hollywood Community Radio Group subversive," proving it was another matter, as they had all cleverly disguised their involvements. This left the FCC in a dilemma. Desperately afraid of offending Hoover, the commissioners nevertheless had no reason to deny the group its license. Chairman Denny therefore decided on a policy of inaction. The commission simply took no further action on the application.[37]

To Durr, such behavior seemed pusillanimous in the extreme, and he eventually resolved to take the matter into his own hands. On October 26 he was guest speaker at the annual dinner of the National Association of Educational Broadcasters, held in Chicago. There, departing from his prepared text, he launched into an attack on HUAC, currently in the middle of its highly publicized investigation of Communism in the film industry. Yet, he said, at least HUAC conducted its business in the open and was thus subject to some public scrutiny. "The hidden activities of our military organizations and of the FBI are far more dangerous," he alleged, because they took place in secret, far from public view. Moreover, broadcasters were unlikely to remain safe from investigation. Referring indirectly to the Hollywood Community Radio Group matter, he went on to reveal that the FBI was already "furnishing to the commission unsolicited reports on individuals connected with radio and I can assure you that if you should be told the kind of things contained in many of these reports you would dismiss the information as baseless gossip."[38]

Because he was speaking to a small and specialized group, his speech received no media attention. Not until November 19 was it mentioned in the press. Then Marquis Childs, the syndicated columnist, referred to it in a column called "Freedom of Conscience," in which he deplored the climate of fear developing in the United States, out of which "something very like a witch hunt is developing." This, he warned, could destroy "the heritage of free thought that is at the base of our free society." Citing Durr's reference to unsolicited FBI reports as evidence of this constriction of liberty, he described Durr's remarks as "an extraordinary statement from a responsible public official." He must, he said, have made it "out of a deep sense of conscience after much soul-searching." Indeed, he did.[39]

Childs's column was widely syndicated and occasioned considerable interest. FBI director Hoover was quick to respond and sounded quite hurt about it all. From time to time, he said, he did send items of interest to various federal agencies, including the FCC; indeed, he would have been criticized had he not done so. He was, after all, only trying to help. However, in that the other commissioners had not repudiated Durr's unfair remarks, it must be presumed that they agreed with them. Accordingly, he would supply no more information to the FCC.[40]

If his fellow commissioners had been slow to repudiate Durr before, they rushed to do so now. On December 1, Acting Chairman Paul A. Walker released to the press a letter he had sent to Hoover in which he stated unequivocally that Durr had not been speaking for his colleagues when he attacked the FBI. Durr had not even discussed the matter with them, and they certainly did not share his views. On the contrary, they had asked him "to express its confidence" in the bureau and to advise Hoover that they wished to continue receiving any reports he considered to be of interest to them. Durr, yet again, was totally without support.[41]

On the same day, he released his own position paper. It was much longer than Walker's letter and was a restatement of his position on basic civil liberties. While the commission should welcome, he agreed, any information that helped it discharge its duties, its decisions had to be based "on substantiated, relevant facts, and not upon gossip or rumor." Besides, the commission could not deny a license to anyone except after a public hearing and "upon the basis of the record made in such a hearing." The FBI information, therefore, could not possibly be considered as relevant, given its confidentiality, and it would be "wholly improper for anyone to attempt to influence it to make its decisions other than on the basis of the record." Moreover, evidence had to be given "under oath by qualified witnesses," who themselves could be subjected to cross-examination. That was "not only law but elementary justice."[42]

The FBI evidence against the Hollywood Community Radio Group was simply not appropriate. It was presented anonymously, it was often hearsay, and it usually concerned the social, economic, or political views of certain individuals. Yet the Supreme Court had ruled that such views were not a relevant factor in an application for a broadcast license. Durr could, therefore, see no value in continuing to receive such reports. Moreover, in "times of heightened political and social tensions," he thought there was "a particularly grave obligation on those in positions to pass judgement to be doubly sure of the basis upon which their judgements rest." Nowhere in the FBI reports was there any indication that the members of the group had broken any laws; it was solely their beliefs which were queried. That was no basis on which to make such a judgment.[43]

Durr was of course bitterly attacked from the right for his action. Sen. Homer Capehart, the ultraconservative Indiana Republican, could scarcely contain his rage in protesting "the brazen effort of Clifford J. Durr to sabotage the FBI in its lawful duty and responsibility to uncover Communists and other disloyal persons." Asserting that "Communists and their New Deal fellow travellers," of which Durr was probably one, were "being harbored" in the federal bureaucracy, "where they can sabotage our Nation's policies," he called for a thorough congressional investigation of the "smelly . . . Durr affair."[44]

There was, however, considerable support for him in the liberal press. Jennings Perry, in a column called "Durr's Derring," described him as a "tall, quiet mannered American from Alabama who grew up with Thomas Jefferson, Tom Paine, George Mason and his own natural sense of fairness and decency." Durr had taken on the might of J. Edgar Hoover, said Perry, because he believed there was no room for the "okrana," the "thought police," in the United States. "I like his morals and his spunk," he concluded; "I like his sanity." I. F. Stone bitterly excoriated the FCC for choosing to "disown Durr and truckle to Hoover." Then, scores of people, including Justice Felix Frankfurter, wrote in support of his stand. Although his colleagues had repudiated him, he was certainly not alone. He wrote to his anxious mother, assuring her that he had weathered the storm; he was neither in jail nor out of a job, and he was in good spirits. But, he warned, "there will probably be more."[45]

Indeed there would be. The Hollywood Community Radio Group Inc. affair and its aftermath was simply an example of a much wider problem. It was but one small instance of what Marquis Childs had warned about—the climate of fear and suspicion engulfing the United States, the "witch hunt mentality" which was abroad, and the attacks on the "heritage of free thought," the very bases of American liberties, which it engendered in the name of patriotism. Clifford Durr stood resolutely against such attacks and, in so doing, was to come into direct conflict with the president of the United States himself.[46]

Between 1947 and 1955 the United States was gripped by what David Caute has described as probably the greatest challenge it had ever experienced to its liberal and democratic values. The course of postwar foreign policy, as the hoped-for era of peace following the defeat of Nazi Germany and imperialist Japan gave way to a new and disturbing form of struggle soon known as the Cold War, with the Soviet Union now the enemy, was accompanied by a severe domestic crisis. The failure to defeat Communism or the Soviet Union, would, Americans came to believe, directly threaten both American liberties and her position of global moral leadership. Properly wielded, however, by committed men, American power was omnipotent. Soviet gains could come about only through American mistakes or through treachery.[47]

One result of this thinking was what Athan Theoharis has termed "an obsessive national fear of subversion," with the real threat to American security seen as coming from disloyal federal employees who were willing to compromise their country's honor and security in the name of their Marxist ideology and their allegiance to an alien power. It became imperative then, to search out such pockets of disloyalty and to excise them root and branch. There were men who cynically rode this spirit to national power. Sen. Joseph McCarthy of Wisconsin used the mood to such effect that his name now characterizes the climate of the time. Men such as he pursued domestic traitors with a zeal and a determination which was not to be checked by such niceties as constitutional guarantees of freedom of speech and of association or the guarantee against self-incrimination.[48]

The federal government, too, both contributed to the national mood and was swept along by it. The most obvious example of this was the decision of President Truman, on March 22, 1947, by Executive Order 9835, to establish a federal loyalty program, a program not simply, as Theoharis points out, to "punish overt acts of disloyalty" but to preclude future subversion. "Accordingly," he writes, "the standard for dismissal for disloyalty became: reasonable grounds exist for the belief that the person involved is disloyal to the Government of the United States," and all federal employees, whether employed in classified positions or not, could be investigated. Moreover, the grounds for establishing disloyalty were broad past actions—beliefs or even associations could well be considered sufficient evidence for dismissal. Department and agency heads were responsible for administering the program within their particular bailiwicks, with a Loyalty Review Board to make a final review of their decisions if required. A product of the climate of fear and mistrust, President Truman's loyalty program "subordinated individual rights," as Theoharis observes, "to internal security, and internal security itself to internal suspicion."[49]

Not all historians have written about the loyalty program with quite the degree of outrage displayed by Theoharis, who admittedly has probably devoted more scholarly endeavor to the investigation of its workings than anyone else. Earl Latham, for example, emphasizes that domestic political pressures, and particularly the constant attacks from the Republican right, rather than Cold War hysteria forced a reluctant President Truman to promulgate Executive Order 9835. Moreover, while also stressing that the recent past had indicated some grounds for believing that pockets of disloyalty did exist within the federal bureaucracy, he considers that the loyalty program's more draconian provisions were often tempered by cautious administration. Nevertheless even Latham concedes the program did invest in departments the potential to remove summarily and without a hearing any person whose continued employment was deemed "not in the national interest." Alan D. Harper, like Latham, is much more inclined than Theoharis to accept that the president's intentions in establishing the loyalty program were not all negative. In particular, he believes that one of Truman's basic aims was to protect federal employees against "unfounded charges of disloyalty," given the developing climate of opinion, a reasonable action. Yet he too concedes that the program's aims were lost in its implementation. Too often, he writes, local loyalty boards were staffed "by social conservatives of narrow vision who frequently treated any deviation from the status quo as indicative of disloyal tendencies." Harper noted that Seth Richardson, the Loyalty Review Board's first chairman, was "not one to strive seriously for some balance between accuser and accused." As such, the loyalty program was bitterly opposed by Clifford J. Durr.[50]

Durr's opposition to the president's loyalty program took three main forms. He refused to cooperate in its implementation within the FCC; he attacked it publicly whenever he could; and he decided to leave government service rather than compromise with the changed climate of opinion. In April 1947 the FCC produced its procedures for implementing the loyalty review program. Durr would not have any part of them. Instead, he issued a long statement dissenting from their provisions and, in so doing, stated the basic position he was to repeat time and time again over the next few years.

He was, he said, strongly opposed in principle to Truman's executive order and therefore could not, "in good conscience, give approval to rules designed to put it into effect." He was convinced that the "evils of the Order far outweigh any possible good that can come from it," containing within it "such potentialities of injustice, oppression and cruelty" that it would cause alienation rather than "the promotion of loyalty among federal employees." Its basic concern was not with wrongful behavior, which the courts already had ample power to litigate, but with attitudes and associations, "with ideas rather than with deeds." Yet loyalty could not be measured, for it "is a condition of the mind and emotions." There are no objective tests for its determination, so those sitting in judgment will inevitably let their "personal opinions and tastes" be their guide. "Any attempt to punish men for their state of mind or to force their mental processes by intimidation rather than to persuade them by reason is as futile as it is wrong," he argued. A government could punish and reward; it could command obedience—but not loyalty. Loyalty, it seemed to him, had to be earned.[51]

Of course, intimidation could result in the temporary suppression of ideas, but it would not destroy them. "The only effective weapon against bad ideas," he warned, "is good ideas plus the demonstration of good ideas in action." For this reason, he was convinced that the executive order would endanger rather than safeguard national security, in that it would aid in the creation of a climate of fear "that the government cannot be trusted because of enemies in its own ranks." It would work against national security, too, by impairing the morale, and therefore the efficiency, of federal employees. It would drive good men out of public service and dissuade others from entering it. It would tend "to force all political, economic, and social thinking into orthodox patterns at a time when new and unorthodox ideas" were desperately needed. It created an atmosphere "hostile to reason."[52]

Moreover, the order ran contrary to some of the most basic tenets of American democracy and justice. "It treated rumor and gossip as evidence," sheltering it from the test of examination. "In the name of security," it raised "talebearers and informers to a new level of human dignity." Yet it denied their victims "the procedural safeguards guaranteed by our Constitution to the most vicious criminals—including spies, saboteurs, and traitors," by ignoring the principle that innocence should be presumed till guilt was proven, that everyone accused should have the right to a fair and public trial, that they should know both the "nature and cause" of the accusations against them and the names of those who accused them. Rather, it indicted people simply for their associations and convicted them "on speculations as to their state of mind."[53]

These were the main general themes Durr developed in the course of a tightly argued dissent which covered thirteen typed pages. He also mercilessly dissected the specific rules proposed by the FCC, exposing the arbitrariness, the contradictions, and the injustices built into them. But in his concluding paragraphs he returned to matters of general principle. The loyalty program was a new departure in the annals of American government, he claimed, challenging principles which all Americans "have been taught since school days to regard as fundamental." Its procedures could only be compared to the Alien and Sedition Laws, of which Americans had repented long ago. Yet the Alien and Sedition Laws did at least provide for trials in duly constituted courts under constitutional safeguards. The loyalty program did not. Rather, it ignored the rule of law and tried to control actions and beliefs by "methods outside of the law." Thus it was an even greater danger to "our kind of government" than those far off acts of the 1790s.[54]

"Our form of government," he concluded, "rests on a basis of substantive and procedural laws, the cornerstone of which is the Constitution." Any "warping or weakening" of this base endangered the whole structure of government. This was what, in his opinion, the loyalty program was doing, disregarding and perverting these fundamental laws. It was truly "subversive activity, of a most effective and dangerous kind," and he would oppose it with every fiber of his being.[55]

This uncompromising declaration of opposition, an opposition based on the firmest adherence to principle, Durr was to repeat regularly, usually from the public platform, in the months ahead. A few days after he wrote his statement, he addressed the annual luncheon of the Associated Church Press and the National Religious Publicity Council, in New York. He called his speech "Freedom and Fear" and in it restated much of what he had said in his dissenting views. After attacking the loyalty program for its assault on civil liberties, he concluded by reminding the audience that the basis of democratic government lay in "the belief that there must be a free and unrestrained flow of information and of ideas in order that men may make a free choice." We must insist, he said, "that those who use the words of freedom mean what they say and say what they mean."[56]

"Freedom and Fear" was widely reported and frequently reprinted, as were many other speeches he gave during 1947 and 1948, in which he invariably stressed the same themes. In "Where We Stand Today," for example, delivered to the National Citizens Conference on Civil Liberties in April 1948, he simply repeated much of the dissent's language, as well as its argument. "Fear and democracy have already embarked upon an all-out war for supremacy," he asserted. Democratic government, Durr went on to say, was "based upon faith in people—in their innate intelligence and decency—upon a belief in their ability to shape out a good destiny for themselves between the hammer and anvil of conflicting ideas, provided they are given full freedom to know and discuss, to inquire and to explore, to experiment and to compare, to associate and to exchange their views one with another, and to protest when the occasion arises. This was the gamble which the founders of our government made with destiny. It was not the gamble of fearful men. It will not be won by fearful men." In "Science and the Bill of Rights" he excoriated the "scorched earth policy" America was adopting toward her democratic institutions "for fear they may be taken from us by an alien foe" and poured contempt on "kleig-lighted courts of legislative judges, where conviction precedes trial." The danger was not from without but from within. Durr had become, in short, the most outspoken critic of Truman's loyalty program within the administration, and some wondered how long he would be permitted to stay there.[57]

Privately, Durr had already decided to leave. He would finish his seven-year term but would then go, he told William Rice of the University of Wisconsin Law School in June 1947, after Rice had asked if he was interested in a teaching position. He simply did not want to continue working for the government in the present climate of fear and suspicion. He said the same thing in a letter to his friend Harold McCarty in August. He did not want another term under present conditions, even if one were offered him. He was frustrated, he was deeply alienated by the loyalty program, and he was well aware that the commission could not "be very much better than the political atmosphere in which it functions." Besides, he was sure he would be in "even more trouble" before his term was completed. The president might not even give him the option of reappointment.[58]

Durr had a lot of support, however, from branches of the radio industry, from the press, from the general public, and even from within the ranks of Congress itself. As the time to make a decision on his reappointment drew closer, his supporters made their presence felt. President Truman was bombarded with letters pressing for his reappointment. The National Association of Educational Broadcasters urged he be retained, for he was "one of the few commissioners in FCC history who has been able to see the woods for the trees." The American Civil Liberties Union, though not normally supporting candidates for public office, decided to make an exception for Durr because of "the exceptional job he has done in the public interest." Mrs. Marion L. Stern, representing "thirty five women all interested in the future of radio," urged likewise, and there were hundreds more. He had strong press backing, and even the industry reportedly wanted him, in that he provided some balance on the FCC, and industry members had come to respect his honesty, even if they did not care for his politics. Within the Senate, Lister Hill and John Sparkman were waging an aggressive campaign on his behalf, and other senators had pledged support as well. Ironically, one of the first to declare in his favor was the junior senator from Wisconsin, Joseph R. McCarthy, who had written as early as May 1947, praising his stand on various issues and offering to help in any way he could to secure his reappointment—but then, this was before McCarthy had discovered the potentialities for political advancement in the issues Durr had begun to oppose so vehemently. President Truman got the message and, despite Durr's outspoken criticism of the loyalty program, decided to offer him another seven-year term.[59]

Durr, however, could not be persuaded; his principles and his sense of alienation were too strong. He advised the president in April 1948 that he did not want to be reappointed and stuck to his position during a personal interview on April 22, during which Truman tried hard to get him to change his mind. The president, in announcing Durr's decision to retire, said that political differences were not the reason for the decision but rather that he was leaving out of financial considerations. He needed more money. That was far from the truth, and Truman knew it. At their meeting, Durr had made it quite clear that he was quitting the commission because he could not in good conscience remain in an administration that was committed to the loyalty program. He was, he said, quite unconvinced by the president's excuse that he had been forced to institute it in order to take the anti-Communism ball away from J. Parnell Thomas, the new chairman of HUAC, and the rest of his committee. It was still wrong.[60]

Thus ended fifteen years of principled service in the public interest. Durr was departing the FCC because of his fundamental antipathy to certain developments in American public life which he believed ran counter to basic constitutional guarantees and to long-established principles of public behavior. His fight for civil liberties had dominated his last two years of public service. He was now to carry it over into the private arena.

7

Civil Liberties Lawyer

There is no doubt that, had Clifford Durr been able to choose a career for himself at the conclusion of his period of government service, it would have been that of a college professor. He knew he could always fall back on the practice of law, he told his brother James, but he did not want to. As an FCC commissioner he had frequently spoken on college campuses; he enjoyed the milieu, and he enjoyed being around young people. Moreover, he had had frequent feelers from law schools—Wisconsin, Chicago, and Yale had all shown interest at various stages of his public career—and he intended now to follow up these feelers. The most attractive position, however, seemed to be one at Princeton, teaching graduate courses in public law within the Department of Politics. When that particular inquiry came, he replied immediately expressing the strongest interest. Clearly, he had expected little difficulty in securing an academic appointment.[1]

One by one, however, the various academic avenues were closed. The last to go was the Princeton position, which, the departmental chairman wrote, could not now be filled for financial reasons. Durr was bitterly disappointed. "It looks as if all my academic prospects are fading away," he wrote in June, "and I may be forced into the practice of law, irrespective of my own preference." A month later, no longer on the FCC, he was still undecided as to what to do, but increasingly resigned to returning to law practice. The adjustment to private life was not proving particularly easy.[2]

Still, it was able to be postponed for a while. Quite unexpectedly, Cliff had the chance to go on an overseas trip and, what was most exciting, to take Virginia with him, under the aegis of the One World Award Committee. This body had been set up as a memorial to Wendell Willkie, to commemorate his internationalist ideas. Each year it made a travel award to someone who in the committee's judgment best represented the idea of one world. Previous winners included the film director John Huston and the conductor Arturo Toscanini. In 1948 the recipient was to be Fiorello La Guardia, former mayor of New York and Republican congressman and presently head of the United Nations Relief and Rehabilitation Administration, but he was terminally ill with cancer and could not travel. Indeed, he died before he could even accept the award. In his place, the committee decided to send a group of Americans on a shorter trip. They would dedicate memorials to La Guardia, and they would attend a conference of the World Intellectuals for Peace, in Wrocław, Poland, as guests of the Polish government. Clifford Durr was one of those chosen, and Virginia was able to go as well. There was just enough money, and Ann, now twenty-one, could take care of Lucy and Tilla for the month they were to be away, while Lulah could go to her grandmother.[3]

They left for Europe on August 14 on board the SS *Batory*, a Polish vessel. Other delegates to the conference included the broadcasters Norman Corwin and Saul Carson, the liberal attorney John Rogge, and Otto Nathan, the great friend of Albert Einstein's. The voyage was relaxing and enjoyable. There were many Poles on board, and Durr talked to them at length about the horrors of their wartime experiences, of the German occupation, and of the extermination camps. They were quick to point out that occupation by the Russians had not been much fun either, but there was one crucial difference. The Russians were rough, and their justice was often summary, but they did not kill for the sake of killing. There was no policy of extermination. That people could emphasize this distinction made a deep impression on Durr. It made him realize how little Americans understood, or even knew, about the extent of the suffering in Europe during the war.[4]

This perspective was reinforced upon arrival in Poland. As with his 1946 visit to the Soviet Union, he was staggered at the extent of the devastation still existing more than three years after the war in Europe had ended. Warsaw in particular deeply moved him. He walked among the ruins of the ghetto, "which the Germans left as a monument to their insanity," and found the prospect that the remains of human beings still lay unburied amid the wreckage almost too much to bear. "There is no iron curtain around the ruins of Warsaw," he wrote. "They can be seen—and also felt." He was also moved, however, by the courage of the Poles and their determination to rebuild their shattered cities, both in Warsaw and in the conference site of Wrocław, which he described as "rising out of the ashes of the old German city of Breslau." Their spirit, he thought, was quite remarkable.[5]

Durr talked to as many of the Polish people as he could and was overwhelmed by their desperate desire for peace, which he understood, and by their fear of the United States, which he, too, began to comprehend and which reinforced his doubts about the course of postwar foreign policy. It was difficult, he acknowledged, "for an American, convinced of the peaceful intentions of his own country to understand that the Poles fear the United States as the greatest source of danger of another War." But the extent of the devastation helped, for it was the Germans who were responsible for it, and now United States policy was to rearm Germany as a bulwark against the Soviet Union. The Poles could not understand why the United States "would want to rebuild the country that was responsible for Warsaw," and he was inclined to agree with them. Their fear of the United States, he was convinced, was not "just a synthetic product made in Moscow" but very real, even if Moscow did "fan the flames." Americans were so convinced of their peaceful intentions that it was quite an unpleasant jolt to be made aware that there were others not equally convinced. This was the most abiding lesson of the trip for him.[6]

The peace conference itself was not particularly memorable. The Russian delegates were rude and stridently anti-American, while the British led by Julian Huxley, whose "rudeness and arrogance" left a lasting impression, were dismissive and supercilious. Virginia had a row with Ilya Ehrenburg, the Stalinist writer, and Cliff missed as many sessions as he decently could in order to explore the city and meet the people, for it was outside the conference hall that the really important things were to be heard and seen, he believed.[7]

After Poland, there were short stops in Prague, Rome, and Paris. Virginia fell in love with Rome in particular, but Cliff was not so sure. The city seemed "as interesting and pleasant as ever," and all seemed well on the surface, but he had purposely explored some of Rome's less affluent districts, and the obvious poverty and want had very much disturbed him. Besides, the Catholic church was back securely in power, and good Protestant that he was, he could not feel totally at ease with that. "We are helping keep it there," he said, "and there are a lot of Italian people who don't like it." Paris they found similarly bright and cheerful, but, again, discontent simmered un-

Virginia with Henry Wallace and an unknown supporter at a Progressive party rally in 1948 (Courtesy of the Durr family)

derneath. They went to a political rally led by the Communist party and were mocked for their liberal perspectives. American liberals would have no part to play in the coming world revolution, taunted one of the speakers. The trip then had been thoroughly enjoyable, particularly for Virginia, who had never been abroad before, but it had also provided some disturbing insights into the way Americans and American policy were perceived in Europe. It reinforced Cliff's real doubts as to its wisdom and to its possibilities of success.[8]

The Durrs arrived home on September 13, still with no prospects of academic work for Cliff. There was nothing to do but to open a law office in Washington, and this he did the following month, at 1625 K Street, North West. He shared rooms and a secretary with Nathan David, a former FCC employee, though they were not partners in any formal sense. It was not what he wanted to do, but he was determined to make the best of it. As he wrote to Milo Perkins, "The adjustment to private life is going to be painful, but I suppose

I will find that there are still lots of things to do once I get underway." He was, however, as he told Wayne Coy, missing the FCC very much indeed.[9]

He got his first client the very first day he went to his new office. His name was Roy Patterson, and his case so typified the type of work Durr was to do over the next two years that it is worth discussing in some detail. In the first place, Patterson had no money and no job, so Durr's chances of payment were somewhat remote. Yet this was not a consideration for him, nor did it ever become so. "To take a case of this kind was simply part of the responsibility of being a lawyer," he considered. To refuse it solely on financial grounds would have been unethical. Throughout his years of practicing law, he held to this position. It was one of the reasons he made little money out of the profession.[10]

Patterson was a Department of Labor statistician who had recently been reviewed in accordance with the department's loyalty procedures and found to be disloyal. Accordingly he was dismissed. He had come to Durr, therefore, to ask him to handle his appeal. As Durr read the various documents connected with the case, they confirmed all that he had feared and warned about over the past two years. Patterson had an excellent employment history—there was ample evidence of that. Moreover, he was a genuine war hero, having been decorated for valor in combat. He had also been severely wounded and left permanently disabled. However, during the 1930s he had joined two or three peace groups which, respectable enough at the time, now, with the circumstances of the game so drastically changed, were seen as Communist fronts. Even more seriously, he admitted to membership of the Washington Book Shop, a cooperative to which, coincidentally, Virginia also had belonged. This was an avowedly Marxist store, which sold a range of left-wing literature as well as more standard literary fare. Though Patterson said that he went there mainly because the books were cheaper than elsewhere and that it had an excellent record collection, to the Labor Department's Review Board it seemed to indicate subversive tendencies of a most serious kind.[11]

Furthermore, Patterson had compounded his precarious position by admitting that he had also liked visiting the store because it was one of the few places in Washington where it was possible to have a cup of coffee and a chat with Negroes. Patterson had come from a small town in Texas and had grown up with racial views similar to those of most Southerners. These he had progressively shed, to the point that he wanted to meet blacks, to get to know them as human beings. So he had often visited the Washington Book Shop for that purpose as well. At this, the chairman of the review board, a Southerner, became most agitated. "How does it happen that a man born and raised in Texas would think it was a good idea to be a member of an organization where you could sit down and drink coffee with Negroes," he asked, in a tone, according to Durr (who did not attend the original hearing but was present at the appeal), which indicated that he, at least, considered such behavior to be obvious proof of disloyalty of the most pernicious variety. The board's finding was just that. Patterson was considered to be disloyal and lost his job.[12]

Given the nature of the evidence against Patterson, Durr fully expected to win the appeal. He did not, as a department appeals board confirmed the original decision. Durr then resolved to take it to the Loyalty Review Board itself and, in order to secure some publicity for the case, demanded a public hearing. Loyalty reviews were normally held in private, ostensibly to protect those being investigated, but in this case Durr thought exposure might draw the public's attention to the injustices which underpinned the whole procedure. His request was denied; nevertheless, the publicity which surrounded it may have had some effect. The Loyalty Review Board reversed the original decision and ordered Patterson's reinstatement.[13]

Though pleased at the case's eventual outcome, Durr was appalled at the whole proceedings. The case, after all, had all the ingredients of what he had warned against. Patterson had committed no crime, and there was not the slightest suggestion that he had committed any overt act of disloyalty. On the contrary, he had confirmed his patriotism, his love of country, on the battlefields of Europe. He had lost his job simply because of his ideas and his associations. He had belonged to groups, perfectly respectable at the time, which were now considered suspect, and he held views on race which may have conformed to the provision of the Fourteenth Amendment to the Constitution, but not to the prejudices of the chairman of his initial review board. Little wonder that, despite the eventual outcome, Durr's first loyalty case depressed him profoundly.[14]

It had two other related effects. Durr had expected to do quite a lot of legal work for broadcasters, and even for the radio networks, using the expertise acquired during his FCC years. Indeed, he had been promised such business. It never came—the publicity surrounding the Patterson case saw to that. However, it did bring him business of another sort. There were hundreds of people like Patterson, people now in desperate trouble because of associations and ideas, often made or held in the vastly different climate of the 1930s, often subsequently repudiated, but which still had the capacity to wreck their lives. Few lawyers would defend them, and when it became known that Durr was one who would,they sought him out or were sent to him. There were lawyers, successful lawyers, former New Dealers like the firm of Arnold, Fortas, and Porter (Thurman Arnold, Abe Fortas, and Paul Porter, all friends and former colleagues of Cliff's), who made a great fuss of defending the civil liberties of people falsely accused of being Communists. However, according to the Durrs, they had no interest in those of folk who had actually been so or had even associated with Communists. These people they sent on to Clifford Durr. Thus he never lacked for business, though it was not exactly of the most prestigious or lucrative kind.[15]

Two other cases provide examples of the type of work he did—and of the arbitrary nature of the loyalty review process. One concerned a young woman, employed by a federal department, which Durr never named, the daughter of Russian Jews who had come to the United States early in the century, like so many at the time, fleeing a pogrom. She now stood accused of disloyalty because of her "sympathetic association with people believed to be Communists." This association she freely admitted, for the people involved were her parents. She denied, however, that they were Communists or even had the slightest idea what Communism was. Once a year, however, they went to a Communist-sponsored rally commemorating the overthrow of the czar, because, given their early experiences, they believed that any group which had stood against the czar had to have its good points. The young woman said she would not disassociate herself from her parents, who had loved her and had sacrificed for her. For this, her loyalty was under suspicion.[16]

Of course Durr took her case. Once the chairman of the particular department's review board understood the facts of the situation, he quickly brought proceedings to a halt. As far as he was concerned, he said, the woman was completely loyal. Sadly, as Durr said, "The result of this hearing was not usual. The girl just happened to have a decent person as chairman of the loyalty board." Again, it exposed the arbitrary nature of the whole process.[17]

The second example highlighted the dubious quality of the evidence that was used to sustain accusations of disloyalty. His client in this case was a middle-aged black woman, Mrs. Anna Canfield Holcomb, who worked as a branch superintendent in the Air Force library. She was accused of disloyalty on two counts: one, that she had allegedly shown undue interest in Communism by collecting large amounts of Communist party literature, and the second, that she had been overheard arranging a Communist party cell meeting. She had been suspended from her job, pending a loyalty hearing. The woman was completely bewildered by the charges and could give no reasons as to their origin until Durr prompted her recollection that, as part of a public speaking course she was taking at American University, she had been assigned to prepare for discussion a topic on Communism. In the course of so doing, Mrs. Holcomb had collected a number of newspaper clippings and a published speech of J. Edgar Hoover's entitled "Communism in America." These she had had on her desk at work, as she went straight to her class from the library.[18]

This accounted for the first charge, but that of arranging party cell meetings continued to baffle her. The only thing that she could possibly think of was that, in her position as chairman of a neighborhood community group, she had infrequently used her office phone to arrange group meetings. If so, the only people who could have overheard her calls were the two women, both her subordinates, who worked on either side of her. When Durr asked about them and found out that they were both white and from the South, he guessed he knew the names of her accusers and the real reason for the accusation.[19]

The problem was, how could he prove it? Under loyalty review procedures, the names of those who provided information to the FBI were never even revealed, let alone their having to present themselves for cross-examination. Nevertheless, Durr decided to force the issue. He telephoned the lawyer handling the affair for the Air Force, told him that he knew who the witnesses against his client were, told him why he believed they had made the accusations, and though fully understanding that he had no power to subpoena witnesses, nevertheless considered that the two women should be made to appear at the hearing. As they were both Air Force civilian employees, he believed sufficient pressure could be applied on them, if the lawyer was of a mind to do so.[20]

Surprisingly, the Air Force lawyer, whom Durr later described as "a decent sort," came to agree. After verifying with the FBI that Durr had in fact guessed correctly as to the identity of his client's accusers, he arranged that the two women would appear at the hearing and that they could be cross-examined. "It is strange," Durr mused years later as he thought about the case, "but it was from the Air Force that I came closest to getting due process in a loyalty hearing."[21]

The lawyer was as good as his word. The two women duly appeared, furious that the FBI's promise of confidentiality appeared to have been breached, and Durr was permitted to question them. He quickly destroyed their evidence. In the first place, they revealed that it was the Hoover speech that they had seen on Mrs. Holcomb's desk which had prompted the accusation of collecting Communist literature. Second, after ascertaining that they had approached the FBI voluntarily with their story, he forced them to admit that they both resented bitterly the fact that Durr's client had been promoted over them. The charges against her, accordingly, were dropped, and Mrs. Holcomb was immediately reinstated. Again, Durr had won his case, but again, it gave him but fleeting pleasure, for it had demonstrated on what flimsy and false evidence people's careers could be jeopardized or even ruined under the loyalty program. Once again, his foreboding had been amply realized.[22]

Not all the civil liberties cases Durr took, however, concerned loyalty review hearings. He also appeared as counsel for a number of people summoned to testify before the House Committee on Un-American Activities, which, in the current climate of fear, had grown more powerful than ever. The most well publicized of these was his appearance in 1949 for Frank F. Oppenheimer, brother of J. Robert Oppenheimer, principal architect of the atom bomb and currently head of Princeton University's Institute of Advanced Studies, and Frank Oppenheimer's wife, Jacquenette. They had both been subpoenaed by HUAC to testify at hearings into possible Communist infiltration of Berkeley's university radiation laboratory, where much of the preliminary research which culminated in the Manhattan Project had been undertaken. Frank Oppenheimer, now a professor of physics at the University of Minnesota, had once worked in the laboratory and, later with his famous brother, at Oak Ridge, Tennessee, and at Los Alamos itself. He had also once been a member of the Communist party, something which the *Washington Times Herald* had brought to light as early as 1947, and which he had at the time dismissed as a "complete fabrication."[23]

It was Robert Oppenheimer, whom Durr knew slightly, who asked Durr to represent his brother and his wife. When he met the two of them, they impressed him as "very decent but deeply disturbed young people," and he readily agreed to act on their behalf. Both freely admitted party membership for about three years, from 1937. Oppenheimer made no attempt to keep his association a secret—in fact, "he was well-known as a Communist Party member and a Campus Red at Berkeley," he said. He had eventually left the party in 1940, not as a result of any violent disagreement over policy or principle but simply because he had become bored with it. For this reason, while he was willing to tell HUAC anything that it wanted to know about himself, he would not reveal the names of his party associates at the time. He did not want to get them into the same sort of situation as he now found himself.[24]

Durr explained to him that his was a difficult position to take. He could not answer questions about himself and then resort to the Fifth Amendment to avoid any probing as to his associates, as the amendment's purpose was to guard against self-incrimination. One either had to invoke it generally or not use it at all. For Oppenheimer to proceed as he planned was to court the risk of a contempt of Congress citation, and possible imprisonment. That, the physicist replied, was a risk he would have to take. His associates in the party had not been evil people but, rather, idealists like his wife and himself. Besides, membership had been very much part of a past life. He was not going to force them to relive it, and under public scrutiny.[25]

The Oppenheimers appeared before HUAC on June 14, 1949, amid wide publicity. Prior to their hearing, they issued a press release stating unequivocally that they had both joined the party in 1937, "seeking an answer to the problems of unemployment and want in the wealthiest and most productive country in the world." They did not find it there and left three years later, long before the establishment of the Manhattan Project. While in the party, neither of them did or was asked to do "anything inconsistent with the behavior of any loyal American concerned with the welfare of his fellow man," nor had they made any commitments or contacts "inconsistent with complete loyalty to this country and its government." While at the Berkeley Radiation Laboratory, at Oak Ridge, and at Los Alamos, Oppenheimer stated unequivocally that he had never engaged in espionage nor "turned over secret information to any unauthorized person." Had he had any knowledge of anyone else being engaged in espionage, he would have immediately reported it to the proper authority. In the case of the Manhattan Project, the "proper authority" would clearly have been its director, Gen. L. R. Groves. Oppenheimer, therefore, released a letter Groves had written to him in 1945, shortly after the Japanese had surrendered, in which he lauded his contribution to the development of the atomic bomb. "Your skill and judgement in the field of science are beyond praise," Groves said.[26]

At the hearing both the Oppenheimers talked freely about their past party membership but declined to answer any question about friends and associates, despite heavy pressure to do so. They made no attempt to plead the Fifth Amendment and were thus clearly in contempt of Congress. As it turned out, HUAC did not pursue the matter, but the Oppenheimers suffered severely in other ways. Given his name and the sensitivity of his former duties, the press gave wide publicity to his appearance and his admission of past party membership. As a courtesy, before coming to Washington, he had left his resignation with his department head, who had assured him that it would not be considered. Within an hour of the press publicity, however, it was accepted. There was an unsuccessful campaign to have him reinstated, and he and his family were forced to retreat to a ranch he owned in southern Colorado, his career as an academic scientist in tatters. Nor could he pursue his work abroad. The prestigious Tatra Institute in Bombay, India, invited him there in 1950 to carry out cosmic ray research, but he was denied a passport. Guilty of no crime, his loyalty unimpeached, such was the climate of the times that his professional and, inevitably, his personal life was ruined, and his considerable skills lost to American science. Little wonder that the outcome caused Clifford Durr both anger and despair.[27]

Oppenheimer was but the most famous of a number of young scientists whom Durr represented during the HUAC probe of the Berkeley Radiation Laboratory. In her recent study of the effect of the McCarthy period on America's universities, Ellen Schrecker has talked about the difficulty people, once summoned before HUAC, had in finding counsel willing to represent them, particularly if, as was the case with the Oppenheimers, they had at one stage been close to the Communist party. They usually, Schrecker writes, "ended up relying on the small handful of attorneys whose ties to the Communist Party or commitment to civil liberties overrode their desire for a normal, if not lucrative practice." She identified Durr as one such lawyer, who came to specialize in loyalty program or civil liberties cases. Often, as has been stated, their clients were passed on to them by other, more respectable, legal firms, unwilling to risk their reputation by doing the work themselves. Such was the case of David Bohm, another physicist whom Abe Fortas had sent to Durr.[28]

Bohm, in 1948 an assistant professor of physics at Princeton University, had worked throughout the war at the Berkeley Radiation Laboratory but was never at Los Alamos. He had also been, briefly, a member of the Communist party. At their first interview, Durr counseled him to take the Fifth Amendment, but Bohm was reluctant to do this, preferring if possible to base his refusal to answer questions on past associations and beliefs on the First Amendment guarantees for freedom of association, assembly, and speech. HUAC members, however, refused to accept this position, and Bohm in the end was forced to take the Fifth Amendment on questions relating to his past political associations. Durr, however, insisted that the First Amendment plea be read into the record. "We have assigned three grounds for the refusal to testify," he stated. "One is the right against self-incrimination; one is the rights under the first amendment; and the third is that the response might tend to degrade, impair a man's reputation, bar him from the normal opportunity of practicing his profession and obtaining employment." Richard M. Nixon was particularly incensed at the citing of the First Amendment, when the committee recognized only the Fifth, but Durr insisted, nevertheless, that all grounds be recorded.[29]

Bohm appeared twice before the committee, answering very few questions. As a result he was suspended from his Princeton job and was not even allowed to appear on campus. Embittered, not least by J. Robert Oppenheimer's lukewarm support for him, he too left the country, working briefly in Brazil and Israel, before accepting a position in the University of London's physics department. His, too, was another brilliant mind lost to American science as the result of the exposure of past associations.[30]

Although the bulk of Durr's appearances before HUAC had to do with its probe of the Berkeley Radiation Laboratory, he made appearances in other connections. Perhaps the most publicized of these concerned his acting for Mrs. Rose Anderson, in what *Nation* satirically billed "The Subversive Drugstore" case in June 1949. Since 1932 Mrs. Anderson had owned a drugstore, the Investment Pharmacy, at 15th and K, North West, in Washington D.C. She had built it into one of the most successful of such businesses in the capital and had received several local awards, including one for having the cleanest soda fountains in the city. Her employees, some of whom were black (she was among the first drugstore owners to integrate their staff), tended to remain with her for long periods of time because of the superior working conditions she provided. It is true that Mrs. Anderson, who had migrated from Belorussia at the age of fifteen, held leftish political views. She had joined Henry Wallace's Progressive party and had contributed to his 1948 presidential campaign. In that connection she had met Virginia Durr, herself a Progressive party member and at the time its candidate for senator from Virginia. However, it was as a successful small businesswoman that she was best known in the District of Columbia.[31]

That changed in June 1949, when HUAC subpoenaed her to appear before it, to testify in connection with its probe into Communism in the District of Columbia. Her appearance was brief. Counseled by Durr, she repeatedly pleaded the Fifth Amendment when asked about past membership in the Communist party, but the attendant publicity ruined her livelihood. Unofficial pickets paraded outside the store each day, asking intending patrons why they planned to put money in the "Red Jew's Pocket," her employees were harassed, neighboring employers warned their employees against visiting her store, and her business fell away to nothing. Mrs. Anderson herself stayed away from the store to try to deflect the publicity, but to no avail. Eventually, she sold the store to her former manager, with Clifford Durr doing the necessary legal work. The day the sign "Under New Management" appeared, business started to pick up and was soon back to normal.[32]

Clifford Durr was never much of a joiner; rather, he professed a dislike of clubs and other such organizations. One organization for which he did make an exception, however, was the National Lawyers Guild. Not only did he join it in 1949, he became at the same time its president. He joined it in order to have a vehicle for continuing the fight against the loyalty program, HUAC investigations, and the abuse of power by the FBI, a fight to which his experiences as a Washington lawyer had given even more urgency. It brought him again in direct conflict with J. Edgar Hoover and also resulted in the FBI's putting him under continuous surveillance as a suspected "concealed communist."[33]

Jerold S. Auerbach has written of the National Lawyers Guild that it "marked the first serious challenge to the hegemony of the American Bar Association." Formed in 1939, it attracted to its ranks many of the young and often leftist lawyers that the New Deal had brought to Washington, as well as a host of lawyers working outside government, and often from minority groups, who shared similar political and social aspirations or even went beyond them. Frankly critical of both the values and structure of the American bar, the National Lawyers Guild spoke to those lawyers who were committed to the liberal agenda and the issues it stressed—civil liberties, minority rights, and the rights of organized labor.[34]

From its foundation, the guild was politicized between New Deal liberals, who wished to reform the existing structure, and radical lawyers, some within the Communist party, who wanted to change it. Maintaining an uneasy existence during the Second World War, it became a prime target for the forces of the right in the turbulent years of liberal retreat, loyalty oaths, HUAC investigations, and, eventually, Sen. Joseph McCarthy. Its membership declined drastically, but for those liberal and radical lawyers, writes Percival Bailey, "who chose not to cut their losses in the intensifying Cold War," it remained as the "last outpost of the pre-war liberal radical alliance."[35]

Clifford Durr had not actually joined the guild before 1949, though he had developed close ties with many of its members and was in broad sympathy with its aims. In 1948, not long before leaving the FCC, he had delivered one of his most trenchant criticisms of the loyalty program, "The Voice in Democracy," at the guild's annual convention. The NLG was currently in the vanguard of those organizations opposing the loyalty program and as such was under pressure from the FBI. There was difficulty finding someone to succeed the retiring president, Robert W. Kenny, and Durr's close friend Yale law professor Thomas Emerson persuaded Durr to take the position for a year, given that the guild's platform of action, which called among other things for an end to the loyalty program and the abolition of HUAC, dealt with issues so dear to his heart.[36]

As Kenneth O'Reilly has pointed out, it was during Durr's presidency that the FBI's running feud with the NLG exploded, and the issue was the bureau's activities as revealed in the trial for espionage of Judith Coplon. Coplon, a Department of Justice employee, was accused of stealing FBI secrets for a Soviet agent. During the trial, it became startlingly evident that much of the evidence the FBI had against her had been gathered illegally, particularly through the tapping of her office and apartment phones and the phone in her parents' house.These illegal taps had continued after her arrest. Moreover, other documents produced at the time confirmed the highly political nature of FBI investigations. The bureau had for years been keeping extensive files on prominent liberals who had committed no crime nor evinced disloyal tendencies. They were under surveillance solely because of their political opinions.[37]

Durr, accordingly, decided that the guild had to act decisively. In a long letter to the president, he said that even the newspaper accounts of the Coplon trial disclosed "practices and policies of the FBI that strike at the very roots of our civil liberties." Among these were the collecting of "detailed information of the lawful political activities and opinions of American citizens," especially those holding "views anywhere left of center"; the recording of "all manner of gossip, rumor and hearsay, without checking it"; the tapping of telephones without permission, "in direct violation of Federal Law"; the use of professional and amateur informers; and the hounding and harassment of law-abiding citizens. The American people, said Durr, were entitled to full information "on the extent to which the FBI has developed into a dangerous political secret police." On behalf of the guild, he called on the president to appoint a "Committee of outstanding citizens" to undertake a "comprehensive investigation" of the FBI's methods and to make recommendations toward getting the bureau back on track toward "a sound and democratic program."[38]

Truman thanked Durr for his views and promised to take them under consideration. He had, of course, not the slightest intention of doing so and announced this on June 29. The NLG therefore decided to institute its own probe of the Coplon evidence, with Durr announcing the formation of a special committee including himself, O. John Rogge, Thomas Emerson, and guild secretary Robert J. Silberstein to do the job. They went at it with a will and by November had completed a rough draft. The FBI, however, was ahead of them. Hoover had ordered a thorough investigation made of the guild, the phones in its offices and in Durr's home were tapped, and Hoover warned the president that the projected report, a draft of which he had seen, would be no more than a left-wing diatribe and could thus be safely ignored.[39]

The Lawyers Guild submitted its final report to the president on January 17, 1950. A long and scholarly document, complete with several appendixes, it carefully reviewed the Coplon trial transcript and other related evidence, took account of Hoover's statements on this and other matters, pointed to inconsistencies between these and the realities of bureau behavior, and concluded that the "practices and policies of the FBI violate our laws, infringe our liberties, and threaten our democracy." Calling on Truman to ensure that in the future the agency should no longer break federal laws in the course of its investigations and should investigate only when there was reason to believe a crime has been committed and not simply because of "dissident views and associations," and again calling for a thorough review of "the programs, practices and policies of the FBI," the report asserted in its final sentence that "the liberties of the American people are not safe" as long as the bureau continued "on its present path."[40]

The guild report was comprehensively ignored. The FBI knew exactly what Durr's plans were and kept HUAC members fully informed of them. The day before the report's release, Rep. Richard Nixon, a member who had already used the position to achieve national prominence, launched a blistering attack on the NLG and called for an immediate HUAC investigation of it, a call which, predictably, was immediately taken up. The FBI stepped up its harassment of the discredited organization, the HUAC investigation concluded that it was the "legal bulwark of the Communist Party," and membership dropped drastically, perhaps by as much as 80 percent. If the aim of the FBI was to destroy the National Lawyers Guild, then clearly it had succeeded. It provided dramatic evidence of the power of J. Edgar Hoover at this time, and of his determination to break those agencies and individuals who attacked his policies. By attempting to ensure, as Bailey has written, "an independent and searching inquiry into FBI illegality and violations of the democratic process," the guild under Durr had instead ensured its own demise.[41]

It also ensured that henceforth Clifford Durr would come under close FBI scrutiny. There is no evidence in his FBI report that, after the original investigation in 1942, either Cliff or Virginia had been placed under further bureau surveillance before he assumed the NLG presidency. There was indeed some suggestion that he should have been investigated following his October 1947 speech criticizing Hoover's policies, but the FBI decided not to do so for the moment, as it "could easily be construed by him and publicized as persecution in view of his attack on the Bureau." There were no such qualms after 1950, however. Durr was placed under continuous surveillance and remained so for the next decade. Periodic investigations continued until 1965. His speeches and other public utterances were collected and analyzed; his movements were closely monitored, even to details concerning the transfer of his furniture from Denver to Montgomery in 1951; and his correspondence and that of his family was intercepted and read, some even being filched from his desk. Various professional informers, notably Louis Budenz, routinely testified that Durr had been "under Communist discipline" in the 1930s and 1940s. Budenz, in fact, attested that he had attended several party meetings with Durr in New York City. Some informants were less certain than Budenz, however. One Montgomery resident who knew the Durrs reported in 1956 that, though Cliff was in possession of a book by Corliss Lamont—impressive evidence of subversive intent—on the other hand, he had heard him defending "Christianity at a dinner party," and this had confused him a little. The FBI even attempted to influence people in contact with the Durrs. When the governor of Alabama, Gordon Persons, worriedly inquired of its Mobile office in 1952 whether or not he should name Durr as his representative to a regional conference on educational television, he was strongly advised by bureau representatives not to do so. Not until 1965 did this essentially petty harassment cease. Thus, one of the results of Clifford Durr's outspoken criticism of the politicization of the FBI, of its use to spy on domestic dissenters in defiance of law and constitutional guarantees, was that he himself became a victim of the procedures he opposed so vehemently.[42]

Though the attack on the FBI was the most important aspect of Durr's period as NLG chairman, there were other matters on which he acted on the guild's behalf. He prepared a lengthy statement opposing the Mundt-Ferguson Bills, which would have required "Communist political and Communist front" organizations to register with the attorney general as such, and appeared before a subcommittee of the Senate Committee of the Judiciary in order to defend his position that the proposed legislation fundamentally contravened the Bill of Rights. He prepared a memorandum for the Senate Committee on Foreign Relations and argued that the North Atlantic Treaty, which established NATO, was contrary to the United Nations Charter and thus should be opposed. Though Durr did not enjoy the NLG experience in all its aspects and, Virginia recalled, some members of the guild were impatient at his reluctance to embroil it in the twists and turns of Eastern European politics, yet he was glad to have had an institutional base from which to oppose the excesses of the loyalty program and of the FBI. Fittingly his keynote address at the guild's 1950 convention, as he left office, was an uncompromising attack on the trends of the times, on Senator McCarthy, who was just starting to make headlines, and on the moral duty to stand firmly against these. "The danger to our liberties, it seems to me," he said, "lies not in evil men, for they are few." Rather, it lay with the "normally decent men" who were silent when they wanted to say, "These things which are being done are wrong and I will stand against them." Durr was, manifestly, not such a man.[43]

Despite his busy, if not lucrative, law practice and his work with the National Lawyers Guild, Clifford Durr also found time to write during this period, and his subject was invariably the contemporary erosion of civil liberties. Some of the articles he produced were solicited. Freda Kirchwey, of the *Nation*, asked him to write one on congressional committees, for example. He replied that he was more alarmed by the activities of the FBI and other intelligence agencies than by the committees, for at least those who appeared before such committees knew why they were there. If she still wanted it, he would try something along those lines. She did, and the article duly appeared, using the Roy Patterson loyalty hearing to show how such people were utterly powerless to prove their innocence, given that they could not be told the names of their accusers or even the basis of the allegations against them.[44]

Sometimes he revised earlier speeches for publication. "The Loyalty Order's Challenge to the Constitution," published in the *University of Chicago Law Review*, was one such. It was an expanded version of a speech he had made to a civil liberties conference early in 1948, called "Where We Stand Today." In it he repeated his unfavorable comparison of the loyalty program with the Alien and Sedition Acts.[45]

Sometimes, however, Durr's writing took rather original forms. It was at this time that he first attempted to retell his favorite biblical stories with a civil liberties twist, a not unsurprising approach, given his strong Christian faith. The first of these was "Jesus a Free Speech Victim: Trial by Terror Two Thousand Years Ago," written in early 1949. In it Jesus is pictured as a troublemaker, a dissident, someone who had committed no crime but whose ideas were unpopular with those in power and whose associates were "questionable characters . . . of doubtful social standing." The Pharisees and Sadducees became a Palestinian HUAC, men who had no tolerance for dissent, who used "secret agents and confidential informants," who brought Jesus to trial "not for his actions, but his beliefs and associates," who at his trial inquired closely into his private attitudes, who "questioned his loyalty," and who eventually secured his conviction through the aid of false witnesses. Pilate is shown to be a normally decent man whose instincts were good but who betrayed the public trust reposited on him by acting expediently—a Trumanesque figure, in fact. He knew what the right was—he just did not follow it. The point need not be labored. Durr saw close parallels between what had happened to Jesus nearly two thousand years ago and what was happening at present to people like himself. Yet the "right" had eventually triumphed then; surely it would do so again.[46]

Durr tried hard to get "Jesus a Free Speech Victim" published. The *New York Times,* the *New Republic,* and the *Nation* all turned it down as unsuitable, and while the *Churchman,* a religious periodical, initially accepted it, they in the end decided not to use it because certain Jewish readers to whom the editor had shown the galleys considered it to be anti-Semitic. Durr eventually delivered it as a sermon in Denver, Colorado, in 1951. Not until 1960 was it finally printed, and then with a rush. His friend Aubrey Williams brought it out privately; the *Churchman,* atoning for its prior failure, published it in two parts; and the National Emergency Civil Liberties Committee, headed by Virginia's friend Corliss Lamont, also published it that year as a pamphlet. It was republished by them in 1982 and remains in print, easily the most enduring of his biblical updatings.[47]

There were to be others. He once reinterpreted the story of Paul's trial, picturing the apostle as a member of an old and respected family who "went back on his raising" and became a subversive, thus throwing away a promising career. As with Jesus, Durr showed that it was Paul's ideas, not his deeds, that had got him into trouble. Fortunately the judge, Gallio, was an honorable man. He attacked the prosecution for "charging a man with nothing more than advocating unorthodox religious views," and Paul regained his freedom. Again, the parallels with contemporary America and with his own situation were obvious, as indeed they were meant to be. In "Ahab, the Vineyard, and the Syrians: An Old Story Retold," Naboth is falsely accused of blasphemy by two "professional witnesses," which was the Hebrew equivalent of "saying he was an atheistic communist," and done to death. These two stories, together with "Jesus a Free Speech Victim," were eventually published in booklet form by the American Humanist Association. They represent a serious attempt by a deeply committed Christian to draw meaning from the Scriptures applicable to what he considered to be the yawning crisis in contemporary American life.[48]

Durr continued to speak as often as he could, all the freer to do so for having left public service. Occasionally he was still invited to talk about broadcasting, but most often, as with his writing, he talked about the loyalty program, about the FBI, and about the current assault on civil liberties. It was what he wanted to do. He could not "speak dispassionately about Executive Order 9835," he told a Yale University audience late in 1948, because he had seen its cruelty and must therefore warn against it whenever he was able. Speaking to the New York City Teachers Union in 1949, he took as his subject the Declaration of Independence, asserting that, in the present climate of fear, it should doubtless be considered a "dangerous and highly inflammatory" document. He appeared on television and radio debates, with topics such as "Should the FBI Methods of Investigation Be Made Public?" and "Whether New Laws Are Needed to Combat Communism." In the program "American Town Meeting," held in Johnstown, Pennsylvania, in April 1950, he was able to confront the Loyalty Review Board's chairman, Seth Richardson. The subject was "How Best Can We Insure the Loyalty of U.S. Citizens and Officials." Disagreeing completely with Richardson's contention that the loyalty program had in fact improved the morale of government employees, Durr talked of reputations being placed "at the mercy of tattlers, busy bodies and gossips." Loyalty could not be ensured by fear, he concluded, but by keeping the United States "the kind of country" that inspired and deserved loyalty. "We cannot protect our freedom by destroying it," he warned. If Durr occasionally sounded repetitious, it was by design. His public life in these years had become a single-minded defense of civil liberties in an atmosphere where they were continually threatened.[49]

As if he did not have enough to do, Durr also taught part-time at Princeton University for the spring term in 1949. George Graham, chairman of the politics department, who had once wanted to hire him full-time, offered him the chance to teach a course on public law, which would meet on Friday afternoons and Saturday mornings. Despite the increased pressure and the havoc it wreaked on his weekends, Durr decided to accept. The extra money was welcome, and he hoped, too, that it might lead to something more permanent.[50] On the whole he enjoyed the experience, despite the pressure of the preparation and the constriction it placed on what little free time he had. It was harder than he had expected, though, and at times he worried about his lack of background and his style. "When I talk from personal experience they liven up," he told his mother, "but when I give them theory from books they look a little bored." Nevertheless he got through the term well enough and would have been happy to do it again. There was, however, no renewal. Whether the fact that one alumnus had complained bitterly to Graham that a man so clearly subversive should be teaching in his department had anything to do with it, or whether the reason was much more routine, arising from budget priorities or even questions of Durr's competence, is not known. But certainly, the hoped-for offer from Princeton never came.[51]

By the end of 1949, it had become clear that the law practice was not working out financially and that something had to be done. His clients were "good people," he told his mother, "college professors, atomic scientists, and lesser government employees whose reputations and jobs were at stake." He was proud to represent them—the problem was that often they could not pay him, or if they did, the money came in so slowly that he was having real trouble meeting the financial demands of a growing family, something he hated. When his daughter Ann was forced to apply for a scholarship to complete her college education, which did not bother her in the slightest, he was desperately upset and considered himself a failure. His mother offered a loan, but that was really a stopgap solution. It would be cleaner to give up the practice and look for something else to do. Besides, he was heartily sick of the Washington atmosphere of fear, suspicion, and conformity and wanted to be out of it. Things were just not working out in Washington, he told George Graham, and he was "in search of greener pastures."[52] The question was, Where would these be found—for a fifty-year old man with a growing family and a reputation as a dissident in a conformist era?

8

Colorado Interlude

For Clifford Durr, the location of the "greener pastures" he sought was obvious—back home in Alabama. He had, Virginia wrote Ann, been thinking "more and more longingly of Alabama," of getting back "to where he has some roots." He had shown real interest, for example, in his brother James's suggestion that he consider becoming dean of the Law School at The University of Alabama—and now he had a real opportunity to return home. His former assistant at the FCC, Red James, had opened a law office in Montgomery with Cliff's nephew, Nesbitt Elmore, and they both wanted him to join them. It seemed a fine answer to the family's problems.[1]

Cliff certainly wanted to go. Accordingly Seminary Hill was put on the market and very quickly sold, itself a traumatic experience, as it had been a beloved family home for so long. Cliff would still have preferred to teach somewhere, but the job with Red James was a good second best. And so they prepared to return home.[2]

The only problem was, Virginia did not want to do so and made no secret of the fact. She was "frankly terrified of going to Alabama," she told her daughter Ann, because she thought the social pattern there "utterly evil." This was certainly part of the reason for her reluctance. More than her husband, she understood what Southerners were like on the race issue. She had had to confront them frequently during her work with the SCHW's Anti Poll-Tax Committee. She knew about their intransigence, their viciousness when attacked, and she feared it. She was, she later wrote, "more afraid of the race issue than I was of the Communist issue." She also dreaded returning to Cliff's family, partly because they were so far apart on race (Cliff found disagreement with them to be very painful) and partly because of conflict between herself and Cliff's mother. Her own political activities were incomprehensible to Mrs. Durr, and the latter thoroughly disapproved of them. Moreover, the family, she believed, tended to blame her for Cliff's current difficulties, as if she were responsible for the positions he took. For these reasons, then, she faced the prospect of a return home with the deepest reluctance and urged Cliff to explore any available alternative.[3]

There was one such. James G. Patton, president of the National Farmers Union, had suggested that Durr might be interested in working for his organization. The NFU was the smallest and most liberal of America's three farm organizations, the other two being the American Farm Bureau and the National Grange. Indeed, the historian George Tindall once aptly described it as "carrying the populist spirit into the twentieth century." Strongest now in the Midwest and with its headquarters in Denver, Colorado, it had taken liberal stands on the major issues of the day, including that dearest to Durr's heart, the loyalty program, which it opposed. Durr had had previous dealings with Patton, whom he liked personally and whose liberalism he found congenial. Moreover, his friend Aubrey Williams had worked for a time as its director of organization and was currently president of the Alabama state branch of the NFU. For these reasons, given Virginia's reluctance to return to Alabama, he decided to follow up Patton's suggestion.[4]

What Patton offered was this: Durr would move to Denver and work for the National Farmers Union Service Corporation, headed by Mr. C. E. Huff. The corporation handled the union's large insurance interests and other investments, and Durr was to spend half his time on its business. The rest of the week would be his own, time in which to write, to do private legal work, or to teach. After visiting Denver and discussing the fine details with Patton and Huff, he decided to accept. The prospects looked good, he told his mother, as both Denver University and the University of Colorado wanted him to teach some courses there. He was "pretty enthusiastic about the move," and since they had to vacate Seminary Hill imminently, they planned to leave Washington right away and, after a short visit to Alabama, drive straight out to Colorado. Virginia, predictably, was ecstatic. "The thought of living in Denver sounds like heaven," she told Ann.[5]

They arrived in Denver on July 15, after a trip which took them through the Southwest and which they all enjoyed, despite its length. Tilla in particular was fascinated by the changing landscape. Fortunately, they had a place to stay for the summer, as Barney Whatley, a former law partner of Hugo Black's, had offered them the use of his home. House hunting began immediately, and in light of Denver's high rents, they quickly decided it would be cheaper to buy. Fortunately there was a place close to the Whatley's for sale, and though Cliff did not like going into debt so soon after arrival, they decided to take it because they all liked the neighborhood and the girls had already made friends there. Though the landscape was "more unfamiliar than England or Scotland" to Cliff, he was sure they would soon get used to it. When daughter Ann, now through college and working in Chicago, at Hull House, visited the family in October, she found everyone well and happy, moved into their new home, and busily adjusting to the new city. Their "political behavior" had "been beyond reproach," Cliff wrote his friend Tex Goldschmidt. Virginia spent her time cooking and cleaning, and he spent his either at work or fixing up the new house. The move was working out really well.[6]

There were, however, two ominous clouds on the horizon, one political and one personal. Cliff's radical reputation pursued him to Denver and into the Farmers Union. Indeed, his joining the organization coincided with the beginning of a sustained attack on it by the Farm Bureau and its political allies. On September 7, 1950, Sen. Styles Bridges, the New Hampshire Republican, spoke in the Senate on "The Communist Invasion of Agriculture," during which he denounced Communist attempts to take over farm associations. They had had no success with either the Farm Bureau or the Grange, he was glad to report, but it was a different matter with the Farmers Union. Its leadership, in fact, had attempted to turn it into a Communist front, with impressive results. His evidence was simply to list the alleged Communists and their sympathizers who worked for the NFU, one of whom, not surprisingly, was Clifford Durr. Durr, he said, "yields to few people, if any, in his list of Communist associations," and yet here he was, recently hired by the NFU.[7]

Patton angrily refuted Bridges's charges, and Durr himself wrote the senator, denouncing "the attack made on me personally in your devious effort to discredit the Farmers Union" and accusing him of compounding "falsehood and cowardice." Yet Durr was sickened by the attack. "I thought I would find security in the vastness of the Rockies," he wrote a friend at the time, "but apparently this was not to be." Besides, even as Patton rebuked Bridges, Durr had noticed a certain nervousness in his demeanor. He certainly did not want to be an embarrassment to the NFU, so soon after joining it.[8]

The personal problem concerned his back. Cliff Durr had suffered from back problems since the summer of 1919, when he was working on a farm and had injured it trying to keep up with the black laborers in shifting cotton bales. It had plagued him intermittently thereafter, keeping him in bed periodically for several days at a time, and was the reason for his slight stoop. He had tried various remedies and contrivances; Jesse Jones, a fellow sufferer, had once sent him to his osteopath, while at times he resorted to wearing a back brace, yet the condition persisted. Any untoward activity or strain could set it off, and the drive to Colorado had done this. He had arrived there with his back "stiff and sore," and it refused to heal. Something had to be done.[9]

Accordingly, Durr saw a specialist who told him of a surgical procedure for conditions such as his in which the disks in the lower spine were fused. It was extremely painful, and there was an element of risk involved, thus he preferred not to do it unless it was absolutely necessary. He would, however, operate on Durr when "the time came." The time came rather sooner than expected. Cliff bent over in the bathroom one morning and could not straighten up again. There was no point in delaying surgery further. He had the operation in November and spent a month in the hospital in intense pain, the first week in a Stryker frame and the next three in a cast from neck to knee. He was then sent home, still in a cast, needing a nurse to come in each day to attend to his needs. The operation, as well as being dangerous, was also expensive and used up what remained of the profit from the sale of the Seminary Hill home. It was, then, scarcely the most auspicious start to a new life. Yet Ann, who visited them at Christmas with her fiancé, Walter Lyon, found her father "well and cheerful in spite of his cast." He was bored, she said, and still in pain but keen to get back to work and optimistic about soon doing so. He was unaware, of course, that the events which would foreshorten his stay in Denver were already in train.[10]

The background to the problem was Patton's decision, upon the outbreak of the Korean War, to reverse the union's position and bring it firmly behind the administration's foreign policy. There were a number of reasons for this, of which the "red-baiting" attacks of people like Styles Bridges was one. Having done this, Patton also decided to sue the Utah Farm Bureau for libel over its charges that the NFU was Communist dominated. Both these policy changes were unknown to Durr, preoccupied as he was with his convalescence. Nor was Virginia aware of them. Had she been so, she might not have treated so casually a postcard she received in the mail while Cliff was in the hospital. The card was from Linus Pauling and Phillip Morrison, the Cornell University chemist and peace activist, representing a group of scientists concerned that the Korean War could widen into a nuclear conflict. It asked recipients to indicate whether or not they supported the Americans' bombing above the Yalu River, the border between Korea and Red China, and to sign and return it. Virginia certainly did not support widening the war and said so, posted the card, and promptly forgot about it.[11]

Unfortunately, signing the card elevated her, unwittingly, to the position of sponsor of a group called the American Peace Crusade. Its aim was to mobilize public opinion to force the withdrawal of American troops from Korea, and its immediate task was to organize a "peace pilgrimage" to Washington on March 1 in support of this action. A pamphlet entitled "Let the People Speak for Peace" was accordingly produced explaining the pilgrimage and listing Virginia, along with such prominent leftists as Jerome Davis, James Dombrowski, the actress Uta Hagen, Paul Robeson, Harry Bridges, as well as Pauling and Morrison, as cosponsors. Meanwhile, she remained blissfully unaware of what her signature had wrought.[12]

But not for long. Cliff had been back at work scarcely a week—still in a cast and on crutches—when, on February 21 the *Denver Post,* under the headline "Wife of General Counsel of Farmers' Union Insurance Corporation Signs Red Petition," stated that Virginia was cosponsor of the American Peace Crusade, which, the paper alleged, was a "Red-dominated" affair. There had, of course, been no attempt to check with Virginia before publication. The whole thing took her completely by surprise.[13]

Reaction from the Farmers Union was immediate. The *Post* had been one of the union's most trenchant critics, insisting that it rid itself of Communist influences. Moreover, the libel suit against the Utah Farm Bureau, on which, ironically, Durr had just begun to work, was in full swing. Consequently Huff was furious. He called Virginia and told her either she had to repudiate the American Peace Crusade entirely and state publicly that she had been duped into joining in the first place, or Cliff's job would be over. Staggered, she simply did not know what to do. She was willing to resign from the Peace Crusade, but to repudiate it publicly meant turning her back not only on a cause she supported but on people she both knew and respected. Moreover, Cliff was most unwilling for her to compromise her principles on the issue.[14]

One of their few Denver friends, Rudy Gilbert, a Unitarian minister, arranged a meeting with Patton to try to work the problem out, but to no avail. In fact Patton was even more adamant than Huff that severing connections with the Peace Crusade would not be enough. Only a signed repudiation of the organization and its leaders would do, to be published in the *Denver Post.* When she refused, though again stating that she would have nothing further to do with the crusade, he lost his temper and called her a "rigid, leftist intellectual who would sacrifice her husband and children for her own pride," until Cliff could stand no more and told him to be quiet. Patton stalked out of the house in a fury, and Cliff's brief period in the Farmers Union's employ was over. Here they were, almost completely on their own, Cliff still on crutches, with no money and no job. It was one of the bleakest periods of their married life.[15]

Durr did have some support within the Farmers Union. Aubrey Williams made a special trip to Denver to try to get the decision reversed. Eventually Patton agreed to reinstate Durr, on the condition that Virginia, as she had been willing to do, withdrew her support for the American Peace Crusade. By this time, however, it was too late. Durr said he could not go back now, since the basis of trust between all concerned had been destroyed, and neither Williams nor anyone else could restore it. "I could not stay here," he said; "if I were to agree to go back, it would not be three months until something else would come along that would force me out." Privately, Williams agreed with him. Saddened and disappointed, Williams wrote to Patton accusing him of "giving way to fear" in acceding to "the violation of Cliff Durr's right of opinion." Patton had, he charged, failed to live up either to his own ideals or those of Franklin Roosevelt, as he, too, prepared to sever his ties with the Farmers Union.[16]

Friends from all over the country wrote offering sympathy and support. Dallas Smythe, who worked with Durr on the Blue Book, said he was shocked and would make inquiries about a job for him at the University of Illinois, where he now was. Eugene Cotton of the Chicago law firm of Cotton, Fruchtman, and Watt offered him office space with them. Karl Heiser, one of his Washington loyalty case clients, regretted that the "virus," so rampant in the capital, had reached as far as the Farmers Union. A former Princeton student, who said that he regarded his contact with Durr "as among the most stimulating of my college career," just wanted to let him know that there were still some people, "not important enough to get axed themselves, who can distinguish between decent people and SOB's, between loyalty and mere conformity," and who stood "ready to be of help if it is possible."[17]

Such support was morale boosting, yet Durr remained bewildered and bitter. His cynicism poured out in a long letter to Hugh Wilson of the Princeton politics department. "I followed the rabbit into the rabbit hole," he said in an obscure reference to Lewis Carroll, "drank just the right amount out of the right bottle to become just the right size and walked into the palace of the Red Queen"—who chopped his head off. Yet he felt headlessness was now a desirable condition, because one could no longer think, "and that is what causes all the confusion." When he had his head, he said, it had never occurred to him that he could get fired by the Farmers Union on a loyalty charge. Yet, here it was; it had happened without his even trying "and even though I have spent two-thirds of my time with the Farmers Union under the handicap of a full body cast that kept me immobile." How ironic, too, that he had become disloyal the very day he started working on the lawsuit "against nasty people who were saying that the Farmers Union was disloyal."[18]

Durr was angry, though, at the pressure put on Virginia to "denounce peace and everybody who said he or she is for peace," but as for himself he had seen "too much of the behavior of frightened people in the past few years" to be too surprised at what had happened. What he would do now, he did not know. The house was on the market; they would leave Denver as soon as possible and might go back to Alabama. He was obviously going to have to keep his head down for a while, hard as it would be "to keep quiet and pretend I don't believe any more in the things I have been fighting for since the Goodwin [Watson] case, nearly ten years ago." Yet he would have to. His current circumstances left him no choice. "It seems to me," he concluded sadly, "that we have got to save some of the seed corn of decency out of the debacle as there won't be any for replanting when and if the season gets right again." But for him it was too late—he was out of the battle. His spirits had never been lower.[19]

His bitterest barbs, however, were reserved for the *Denver Post*, whose February 21 story, which he considered to be irresponsible, started off the unfortunate sequence of events. The editor, Edwin Hoyt, was inclined to doubt this. The problem, as he understood it, was caused by Durr's being attorney of record in the libel action against the Utah Farm Bureau, which had asserted that the NFU was Communist led. In this circumstance, to have his wife continue her association with the American Peace Crusade was analogous to his "suing someone for libel for having called me an habitual drunkard and in the middle of the action my wife announced her affiliation in support of a society of topers." The Farmers Union, in the circumstances, could not permit that.[20]

Durr did not accept this. He had lost his job, he said, not because of his or Virginia's political views but to placate the *Denver Post,* to try to forestall any future attacks on the Farmers Union. Moreover the *Post* story had been unfair; there had been no attempt to check with the Durrs before publication, nor was the reporter the slightest bit concerned with the sincerity of Virginia's motives in, or even the circumstances of, her sponsorship of the Peace Crusade. The journalist did not state categorically that the Durrs were Communists, "for that would have been false," yet, through innuendo, he clearly left that impression. "I am willing to live with the reputation I have made for myself through my own efforts and behavior," Cliff angrily protested, but he could not accept one manufactured for him "by reckless and unscrupulous reporting." Yet, the issues involved went deeper than the personal hurt done to the Durrs, the deprivation of livelihood that had occurred at a time when they were least able to sustain it. What Virginia and her fellow sponsors had done was simply exercise what had always been regarded as a basic American right. As a result, she had been forced to choose either "the surrender of her self-respect and intellectual integrity" or the termination of Cliff's job. "Neither she nor I," he wrote, "had any difficulty in reaching our decision." The newspaper, he believed, had to accept the major responsibility for what had happened.[21]

That was doubtless true, and perhaps, too, Virginia should have thought a little more about the consequences before she signed the initial card. Yet Cliff Durr was surely right when he pointed out to Hoyt that there had been no crime committed here, no overt act of disloyalty—simply the exercise of normal American civil rights. But these were not normal times, and once again Clifford Durr had become their victim.

The question of where they were to go took on a new urgency, as, no doubt partly because of the strain. Cliff's back collapsed again, and he was forced to return to the hospital for a time. He desperately needed rest. Mrs. Durr wrote from Montgomery suggesting they come and stay with her until Cliff was fit enough to work again, and there really was no alternative but to accept. The return to Alabama, which Virginia dreaded and which the move to Colorado had been meant to avoid, was now about to become fact. She could not feel totally glad, she wrote Ann, but Cliff was clearly so pleased to be going home that she herself felt better about it. Besides, she had learned a valuable lesson in Denver. "The struggle is the same everywhere," she now knew, and she would never again put pressure on her husband to do something "he did not want to do." The Denver episode, too, had reinforced something she should have known already about Cliff, but perhaps had forgotten. It did not matter where he was, "he will do good just by being"; she had never been prouder of him than she was at this time. Besides, she was now sure that they would never have felt at home in Colorado. "It is not our country and these are not our people," she told her daughter.[22]

She said the same thing in a warm letter to her mother-in-law, accepting her offer of a haven. They had been treated outrageously, she told her, "but at least we did get a new back for Cliff." Until his setback he had been freer of pain than he had been for years. She was looking forward with absolute joy to leaving Colorado. She and Tilla, in particular, had not fitted in there, in that "dry and barren" place with "more bad manners than I ever ran up against in my life." Virginia was so looking forward to leaving the "thin dry air and the dry barren earth behind" and to "hear the sound of rain again and feel the dampness on the ground." That would be very pleasant indeed. Besides, the one important matter was to get Cliff well again, and he would be able to get the rest he needed back with a family who loved him and cared about him. Lucy, who had been wildly popular with the Denver teenage set, had some regrets at leaving, but everyone else was eager to be away, even though, as Virginia told Clark Foreman, she knew she would have "to eat a lot of my stiff-necked pride with the hot rolls." Yet Alabama no longer seemed so bad after the Colorado experience. If she had to "live under Fascism," she quipped, "I want it to be where it rains."[23]

Besides, there were some pleasant things to be done before leaving. They visited the Oppenheimers on their ranch, where they had a marvelous time. Lucy had stayed behind with the Whatleys in order to attend a prom, and Tilla, with no big sister to compete with and with horses to ride and territory to explore, found it all especially wonderful. Then it was back to pack and to prepare to move. Virginia and the girls drove to Chicago, where they picked up Ann and then continued on to Washington. Cliff had flown ahead, since car travel was still out for him.[24]

The reason for the Washington stopover was that Ann and Walter were to be married there on May 19. Virginia and Cliff both felt guilty that, with all their recent troubles, they had not thought as much about the wedding as they should have done, nor had they the resources to make it a lavish affair. They need not have worried—it was a lovely, happy event. The Unitarian church where it was held was full of flowers; their one Colorado friend, Rudy Gilbert, performed the ceremony; and Cliff was, after all, able to walk down the aisle to give away his daughter, radiant in a gown she herself had made. It was good, too, to see their Washington friends again, who clearly did not feel that they were pariahs in any way. It was the tonic they needed after what had been a desperately hard period in their lives. The family left for Alabama soon after the ceremony, in better spirits than they had been for months.[25]

9

Montgomery and New Orleans

The city that the Durrs returned to was a city in transition. Capital of the state, proud of its reputation as the "cradle of the Confederacy," it was still pictured as the epitome of an unreconstructed Southern community. In 1950, as it had done for nearly a century, the flag of the old Confederacy flew proudly above the state capitol. Yet the city was changing, for the war had brought industrial growth, and this had continued—indeed, it had accelerated—in the postwar boom. It also brought people, both white and black, although the white percentage of the population increased the more rapidly. By 1950, the ratio of white to black was 60 percent to 40 percent. In 1955, when the city population reached 120,000, it was 63 percent white and 37 percent black.[1]

Even more important was the presence of large military installations on the outskirts of the city and their growing importance to Montgomery's economic life. By 1955, nearly 20 percent of its families depended on the two large air bases, Maxwell Field and Gunter, for their livelihoods, and in that sense Montgomery had been "nationalized" by the war and its Cold War aftermath. Yet much remained the same. The postwar boom and the rapid influx of population had not altered the city's living patterns. Montgomery was still one of the South's most segregated of cities.[2]

Cliff Durr did not see much of Montgomery for a while. In fact, his first three months home in Alabama were spent on his back in Birmingham, where specialists could monitor him, under the loving care of his sister Lucy. Even when he finally made it to his mother's house, he was still forced to spend much of his time in bed. He loved being back with his family though, and everyone was, as Virginia put it, "very nice" to them. They did not understand many of his ideas, of course, and those that they did comprehend they did not approve of. This was especially true of his mother, in her eighty-sixth year when they returned home. She was, said Virginia, "the most typical Southern lady of the old school you can possibly imagine." She certainly did not like Virginia's political ideas at all, yet she had no hesitation in opening her home to the whole family when they were in such need. As Virginia wrote later, "Her love for her son and her loyalty to her son overcame all the disapproval she may have felt about his ideas." The rest of the family was the same. It was a good homecoming.[3]

At first things went reasonably well. The relationship between Cliff's mother and Virginia seemed to him better than it had ever been. "The respect and affection between the two strong women, I would have thought impossible a few years back," he told Ann in December. Moreover, now that he could get about a bit, he was able to get a sense of Alabama "and have about decided it is a pretty good place." Indeed, in his euphoria about his home state, he sounded again like he had more than thirty years before, when he was the young Confederate at Oxford. "Still," he warned Ann, "maybe things would change when he had to make a living."[4]

That he started to do early in 1952, at first on a part-time basis. His back was still not good, he wrote Rudy Gilbert in January; nevertheless, his doctor had agreed to his doing some legal work on behalf of the State Public Service Commission. He was improving all the time, however, and was "hoping to hang up my shingle in another few weeks." He had resumed his association with the First Presbyterian Church, Virginia had taken a secretarial course during his illness and planned to work as his secretary once he had opened his office, the family was well, and he was loving being home—and being spoiled by all. To another Colorado acquaintance he wrote that, after all that time away from Alabama, they were "at last beginning to feel at home again" and, indeed, in their "enthusiasm for the land and its people," were starting to sound like "unreconstructed Rebels," if not Dixiecrats. It all seemed to be working out well.[5]

He was able to resume full-time work in March when he formally opened a law office in Montgomery, sharing a suite with Red James and having Virginia as secretary. His plan was to specialize in civil law, and at first he refused to take criminal cases. The family had given him the Durr Drug Company work, which provided a solid base on which to build, and Aubrey Williams, who published the *Southern Farmer* out of Montgomery, had also retained him. Moreover, he had made a conscious decision not to involve himself or his practice in national issues. When Beanie Baldwin wrote offering him some work on behalf of the now-struggling Progressive party, he refused. "I have got to make my choice between practising law down here and getting back into the old fight at a national level," he told him. He could not do both, and he believed that in time he could be more useful in Alabama, which was why he was trying hard to become part of the Montgomery community. He was leading a city library discussion group on the topic "Our American Heritage," he told Hugh Wilson, and if he tried to focus on contemporary issues occasionally, he did so most cautiously and indirectly. Conscious of the fact that he had made his choice to live in a community becoming increasingly hostile to the positions he had taken, he knew he had to tread very warily. Besides, such an "abdication" had its compensations. "We find the peaceful life of the Confederacy a welcome relief from the confusion and bickering of Washington," he told John K. Galbraith. It was surprising how pleasant life could be, "if one takes a firm stand in opposition to the boll-weevil, and in favour of white face cattle and crimson clover" and avoided "the petty issues of domestic and international politics." There was some nostalgia for the "scenes of a few years back," but on the whole he was pleased with his new life—or professed to be.[6]

Virginia was not quite so enthusiastic. She missed very much having a house of her own, and though she recognized and appreciated the kindness of her mother-in-law, nevertheless the situation was not without its tension, the more so as Mrs. Durr's health began to fail and she became "obsessed with the thought of death." Moreover, she was already feeling the "spells of claustrophobia," the "lack of any sympathetic political companionship," the feeling of being "out of touch with the living world," which was to distress her so much in the years to come. She missed being "in communion," as she had been for so many years, with people "that believed and worked for a solution to the ills of the world." She had taken that environment completely for granted, and now that it had been cut off, she felt quite bereft. Moreover, she could not speak publicly or take a position on anything of importance—their dependent situation simply did not permit it. Even though she felt acutely the "sullen repressed resentment of the Negroes" around her, there was simply nothing she could do, except feel guilty—and this she did continually. Cliff did not seem as affected as she, she thought, but then "perhaps he doesn't expect as much as I do."[7]

Nevertheless, there was the law practice, which in a sense they shared. If they could build that up, perhaps they could do some good through it. This was very slow work. There was soon plenty of business, but it was almost all of the small-claims variety and, as such, scarcely profitable. The Durr Drug Company work took care of basic office expenditure, but Cliff was still a long way from making a decent living out of the practice. In 1953 he did attract some larger suits, the biggest being one in which he represented some truckers operating on a leasehold basis who claimed to have been "substantially horn-swoggled for loads hauled" by the company for whom they worked. This gave him some interesting insights into the trucking business, which he described as running on "little more than debts and benzedrine tablets," and there was the prospect of a substantial fee at the end of it all, but the end was far from being in sight. He had also started to represent people in claims against loan sharks, again potentially a source of income, but in the meantime producing nothing but hard work. He described his practice to George Graham in September 1953 as busy, but having "not yet reached the lucrative stage." The description was apt. He could not yet afford to move his family from his mother's house to one of their own.[8]

Still, he remained optimistic about the prospects of eventual success and the correctness of the decision to move back to Alabama, even though he, too, was becoming a little frustrated at not being able to involve himself in the vital issues of the day. "For my part, I can give no account of battles won or even fought," he told Rudy Gilbert. "Virginia and I both go our way quietly and continue the process of integrating into the local community." There was nothing much they could do until that had been achieved. To this end, he had started to teach Sunday school at First Presbyterian and was enjoying it immensely. Besides, he remained convinced that the South was changing for the better, albeit slowly. It remained good to be home.[9]

By the end of 1953, Virginia, on the other hand, had lost any illusions, either about the prospects of Southern change or their chances of ever being part of the Montgomery community. "I think we are going to be doomed to the same isolation that Aubrey [Williams] lives in," she wrote in despair to Clark Foreman. "We have gone outside the tribe and broken the taboos and they won't take us back in unless we do penance and confess our sins," and she just did not believe they could ever fit in. It was hard on her, this sense of utter isolation, and it was becoming hard on the girls, as of course was their continued financial dependency on Cliff's family. She believed that the failure to make a living was hitting Cliff hardest of all, though he rarely spoke about it. He had come home "determined to live and die in Dixie," she said, and it was hard for him to come to terms with the realization that "all the personal affection and uncles and cousins and relatives of all sorts and descriptions still does not add up to a law practice." Cliff had always thought that character and "personal relations and personal affection" were stronger than economic interests or political ideals in determining who one did and did not do business with, and she feared that he was learning the converse the hard way. Still, he was determined to stay, and she knew how hard a blow leaving would be for him so, despite her own increasingly desperate desire to go; she nevertheless hoped that the business would pick up.[10]

If it did, even marginally, then at least one of the sources of tension would be relieved because they could then afford a place of their own. Occasionally Virginia would let Ann know just what it was like, though she tried to keep it from Cliff. The problem was there were not two but three strong-willed women in the house—Mrs. Durr, Virginia, and Little Auntie—and only one man, Cliff. His brother James could see clearly the tensions engendered by having "one man among so many women" and advised everyone to be as patient as possible. Nevertheless, the situation was becoming extremely difficult. It was affecting everyone, including Cliff, and even he had come to realize the urgency of getting a place of their own.[11]

Into this situation, in March 1954, a further ingredient was injected. The hunt for domestic Communists, against which Cliff had fought for so long, caught up with them both in Montgomery. One March morning they arrived at the law office to find their friend Aubrey Williams sitting on the step waiting for them. He had been served a subpoena summoning him to New Orleans to appear before the Subcommittee on Internal Security, Committee on the Judiciary United States Senate, on March 16, 1954, "there to testify what you may know" about the Southern Conference Education Fund. He knew quite a lot because he was president of SCEF, and he had come to ask Cliff to be his counsel at the hearing. Cliff was reluctant to do so, not because he did not want to, but because the strains and tensions of the past two years had left him with a slight angina problem, and his doctor warned him sternly against involving himself in a case guaranteed to put him under considerable stress. For that reason alone, he was unable to give Williams a definite answer.[12]

His mind was made up for him, however, when Virginia received a similar subpoena a few days later. For Cliff, the prospect of staying in Montgomery with Virginia in New Orleans would be far more of a strain on him than his being there, and he determined to go, too, as Aubrey's lawyer. At first there was thought of his representing Virginia as well, but he was dissuaded from this idea by John Kohn, a well-respected, thoroughly conservative Montgomery lawyer who was a lifelong friend of Cliff's and who agreed to represent her. Virginia still worried about the effect the hearing might have on him, the struggling law practice, and on general family dynamics, but she knew there was no stopping him. "Don't tell Daddy he shouldn't do it," she implored Ann, "because he is committed now."[13]

The organization about which they were to testify, the Southern Conference Educational Fund, was all that was left of the old Southern Conference for Human Welfare, of which Virginia had once been such a committed member. "Established with such high hopes in 1938," as one historian has written, it "had passed the peak of its influence by 1946." Initially it was a coalition of various interest groups, "educators, unionists, businessmen and blacks, united principally by their adherence to the principles of New Deal liberalism" and their commitment to applying these to Southern situations, but it soon became more specifically an organization geared to electoral politics and in particular the abolition of the poll tax, the cause for which Virginia had worked, at first under SCHW aegis, for so long. It drew the bulk of its financial support from the CIO, and when this was withdrawn in 1946, the SCHW had little hope of survival.[14]

In January 1946, in order to preserve its tax-exempt status, the SCHW decided to divide its educational and political functions. SCEF was created to direct all educational activities, while the SCHW became solely a political-action organization. The SCHW eventually folded in 1948, not before it had been red-baited by HUAC, but SCEF survived under the leadership of Aubrey Williams and SCHW's former administrator, James A. Dombrowski. Together they turned it into the most militant voice against the segregated South to be heard in the region. Virginia Durr had been one of SCEF's original contributors and supporters but had ended her association with it in 1950, when they moved to Colorado. Nor had she rekindled the connection upon their return to Montgomery, except insofar as they were friends of Aubrey Williams and saw a lot of him. Cliff had never been a member either of SCHW or its successor.[15]

Up till 1954, the search for domestic Communists had left the South largely untouched, as Senator McCarthy and his committee, HUAC, and other like bodies concentrated their activities either on the "traitorous" corridors of power in Washington, D.C., or on locations such as Hollywood or New York, where the headlines were likely to be of maximum benefit. In 1954, however, with the Supreme Court gearing up to rule against segregation in public education, and with their way of life under attack in many other quarters, Southerners were flocking to the barricades. There were some Southern politicians who saw that the domestic subversion issue, the loyalty issue, might be used to slow the pace of social change in their region by branding those individuals and groups who advocated it as agents of the Communist conspiracy. One such politician was Sen. James Eastland of Mississippi, a key member of the Senate's Subcommittee on Internal Security.[16]

The Subcommittee on Internal Security was created in 1950 under the provisions of the Internal Security Act, with the conservative Nevada Democrat Patrick McCarran as its first chairman. When the 1952 Eisenhower landslide gave Republicans control of the Senate for the first time in more than twenty years, it was reconstituted under the chairmanship of Indiana's William E. Jenner, a committed McCarthyite, and charged with the broad task of investigating "communism in government." Eastland, however, remained a powerful member, and it was he who was mainly responsible for its move south in 1954 in order to discredit groups and individuals prominent in the fight against segregation. As the most uncompromising critic of the region's treatment of blacks, SCEF was sure to be in the firing line, while Virginia's relationship to Hugo Black, a man especially hated by segregationists as a traitor to his region and his race, added impetus to the probe.[17]

Williams was outraged at the very idea of the investigation and bombarded his friends and acquaintances in Washington with letters and telegrams of protest. Virginia, likewise, was scarcely silent. The Durrs had maintained their friendship with Lyndon and Lady Bird Johnson, and it was to Senator Johnson that she turned. She phoned him late one night to see what he could do, and the minority leader agreed to help. He could not stop the hearing, he said—he no longer had that power—but he would try to see to it that no Democrat accompanied Eastland, whose show it was, to New Orleans. He thought Aubrey and Virginia should be able to handle the Mississippi senator easily enough. Next she contacted George Bender, a conservative Ohio Republican with considerable influence in the party. He had worked with Virginia in the fight against that poll tax and promised that he would try to get the Republican members of the committee to stay at home as well. Actually, he need not have bothered, as the Republicans had never intended to come. When Eastland, as the subcommittee's ranking Democrat, announced the forthcoming hearings on March 8, he had stated explicitly that he would be accompanied to New Orleans only by his Democratic colleagues, McCarran and John L. McClellan of Arkansas. Besides Williams and Virginia Durr, James Dombrowski, Myles Horton of the Highlander Folk School, and Prof. Alva Taylor, all of whom had had SCEF connections, had been subpoenaed, as well as two residents of Miami, Leo Sheiner and Max Shlafrock, whom none of the others knew personally.[18]

Lyndon Johnson was as good as his word. When Eastland arrived in New Orleans on March 17, he was without his two colleagues. Ominously, however, he did have with him Paul Crouch, one of the most important of the FBI's paid informers. Crouch, a former Communist organizer in the South and in other areas, had been a key witness at a number of important Smith Act trials and at several internal security and loyalty hearings, including that of Frank Oppenheimer's much more famous brother Robert. It was Crouch's memorandum "Communist Infiltration in the American Armed Forces" that had provided the spark for the Army-McCarthy hearings currently getting underway. His presence showed that Eastland was extremely serious about the investigation.[19]

The hearing began the next day and was dominated by Crouch, who, having identified himself as a former Communist party organizer, proceeded to describe how he was one of the three people who had originally planned SCHW and that it was a vehicle to promote Communism in the South. The purpose of its lineal descendant, SCEF, was the same, he claimed. He duly identified Sheiner, who took the Fifth Amendment, as a party member. Shlafrock in a brief appearance consistently took the Fifth as well, and the day ended with Dombrowski on the stand, also accused by Crouch and another professional witness, John Butler, of being very close to the Communist party if not of maintaining actual membership. It had been an unpleasant time for all three witnesses. They had been badgered by both Eastland and committee counsel Richard Arens, but the day's testimony produced no dramatic headlines, no startling revelations. Indeed, the national press carried no accounts at all of the day's events, and only the New Orleans *Times Picayune* gave them extended coverage. This was soon, however, to change rather dramatically.[20]

After a brief reappearance by Dombrowski, Virginia took the stand when the hearings reconvened the next day. Kohn would not even allow her to identify herself, counseling her to remain silent while he advised Eastland that, for a number of reasons but specifically excluding the Fifth Amendment, his client would answer no questions at all. She did wish to make a statement as to why she had chosen to take this course. This was refused, and the questioning began. Virginia denied that she was, or ever had been, a member of the Communist party, agreed that Clifford Durr was her husband, and then "stood mute," refusing to answer any more of the questions put to her. Eastland, at a loss, warned her that she was clearly in contempt of the subcommittee and then brought back Paul Crouch.[21]

Crouch did have something to say. He had known both the Durrs in Washington during the New Deal years, he said, and Virginia had been under party discipline throughout that time. The Durr home, he claimed, "was a frequent meeting place for the people connected with top Soviet espionage and infiltration of the United States Government." Moreover, she had used her friendship with Mrs. Roosevelt and her kinship with Justice Black to introduce top Communists into the White House circle during the New Deal years, men like Joseph Gelders, a cofounder of SCHW, and thus given them legitimacy. Mrs. Roosevelt, not knowing that Gelders was "one of the top Soviet Communist Agents in America," had yielded to his pressure and addressed the first SCHW meeting. For this and for many similar events, Virginia Durr was responsible. She had, said Crouch, "plotted with the Communist leaders to exploit her relationship as sister-in-law of a Justice of the Supreme Court in the interests of the World Communist conspiracy and interest of overthrowing our Government."[22]

When Mrs. Durr was excused from the stand, she promptly and ostentatiously began to powder her nose, to the delight of the press photographers. Their journalist colleagues were more concerned with making something of the startling news that Virginia had introduced Soviet agents into the White House circle. Her husband,

Clifford, sat silent, outraged because, of course, he had heard it all before, in Washington in 1949 and 1950.[23]

Soon, however, it was to be his turn. Aubrey Williams was called to the stand, but before he had begun to testify, Durr listed a series of objections to the whole course of the investigation, which were promptly disallowed. Williams was then asked a series of questions about SCEF, all of which he answered fully, though he refused to provide a list of its contributors. He denied ever having met Crouch before, ever having been a member of the Communist party, or ever having knowingly associated with Communists. That was not what Butler and Crouch said when they were recalled. Both claimed to have met Williams from time to time in the 1930s and 1940s, and always in conjunction with their Communist party work. Butler in fact testified that he had attended a closed party meeting with him, which caused the furious Williams to leap to his feet, demanding that he repeat the allegation outside the privileged location of the hearing. "I'll sue him the minute he does," he roared. Durr then asked, no doubt with tongue in cheek, if there could be a recess called "so that Mr. Williams and Mr. Butler could go outside." Not surprisingly, the request was denied.[24]

After Crouch had similarly identified Williams as "a secret member of the Communist Party," Durr was given permission to cross-examine him, a surprising development, in that counsel had not been allowed to question previous government witnesses. Perhaps even Eastland, who, though he disliked Williams, did know enough about his WPA and NYA career to realize the absurdity of the charges. Perhaps, too, the fact that Williams still had powerful friends in the Senate may have influenced his decision to permit cross-examination. Whatever the reason, Durr had a field day. In a series of probing questions he elicited considerable detail on Crouch's past activities as a Communist. More to the point, he was able to show that Crouch's recollections of past meetings and conversations, on which the government had set such store at this and earlier hearings, seemed quite imprecise. He could not, for example, remember just when he had left the Communist party, he could not explain why it took him so long to go to the FBI after doing so, nor could he remember much detail about his allegedly frequent meetings with Williams. Moreover, it became clear that his job with the United States Immigration and Naturalization Service was simply a front for his real functions, that of full-time informer and witness.[25]

Crouch showed such signs of stress and tension under Durr's merciless cross-examination that committee counsel Arens felt moved to intervene to protect him. It was a bad mistake in judgment. Arens asked Crouch if he thought Durr himself was a Communist. He was not sure if he was still one, the informer replied, but he certainly had been one once. The whole committee room erupted in derisory laughter, in which even Eastland joined. "I am going to strike that," he said. To Durr, however, it was no laughing matter. "His testimony is under oath," he shouted at Eastland; "let's leave it in, under oath." Reluctantly, the chairman was forced to comply.[26]

What followed was as remarkable as it was unscheduled. After the questioning of Williams was concluded, Cliff insisted that Crouch answer questions about the statement that he, Durr, was also a Communist. "Let's get it all out right here on the record," he insisted. Crouch was rather vague as to times and places but did state that he had seen Durr in New York City at meetings with "national Communist leaders like Earl Browder, William Z. Foster, Jack Stachel, Henry Winston, Gene Dennis," and other like luminaries. This was about all he could remember, however. He had forgotten exactly where the meetings were held, when they took place, and if he had ever actually spoken to Durr at any time. He was sure, however, that Joe Gelders had assured him that Durr was "a reliable comrade," who would ensure that certain material be transmitted to Justice Black.[27]

Durr then insisted that he be placed under oath. Once Eastland had complied, he angrily stated that Crouch's testimony as to having seen him at party meetings was "a complete and absolute falsehood." He was not a member of the Communist party, he said, and had never been one, nor had he any intention of being one in the future. "I have never taken the Communist discipline," he said, "and this statement is completely and absolutely false." Either Crouch was lying or he was, he said, in which case a perjury indictment should follow the hearing.[28]

Arens, somewhat desperate at the unexpected turn of events, tried to discredit Durr by citing Durr's association with the National Lawyers Guild, his relationship with Joseph Gelders, and his attendance at the World Congress of Intellectuals for Peace in Wrocław six years earlier, all of which he linked with the world Communist conspiracy, but he could not redress the damage that had been done. One of the FBI's most important informers had himself been grilled and had not shown up particularly well under scrutiny. That would have probably been sufficient of itself to attract some national attention, let alone the allegations that Virginia had introduced Communists to the White House and that two top New Deal officials, Williams and Durr, had been secret party members. The major newspapers all devoted space to the hearings, usually accompanied by the photograph of Virginia powdering her nose.[29]

The final day of the hearings also had its share of drama, though not to the previous day's level. It was the turn of Myles Horton, director of the Highlander Folk School, whom Durr also represented, to testify. When it became clear that it was not his SCEF association but Highlander's activities in which Eastland was primarily interested, the quick-tempered Horton refused to answer questions and instead tried to make a statement of principle. He was refused permission to do so, proceeded anyway, and was dragged from the hearing room, shouting imprecations at the chairman. The hearing then rather swiftly came to an end. In his concluding remarks, Eastland gave notice that there would be more of them. They were, he said, "part of a general investigation over the South of the Communist Party," and the next venue for further probing would be Birmingham, Alabama.[30]

There was more drama to come, however, again with Durr as the central figure. As the committee room began to clear, Cliff and Crouch found themselves face to face. At that moment, all his accumulated tensions—the strain of the hearing and of listening to his wife so traduced, the strain of their domestic arrangements in Montgomery, indeed the strain of the last six years, of constantly battling against the erosion of American liberties—welled up inside Durr, and he lost control. Vaulting the jury rail, he lunged at the startled informer. "You dirty dog," he reportedly cried. "I'll kill you for lying about my wife." Federal marshals closed in and quickly bundled the government witness away, while Durr's friends made him sit down on a bench for a while. After fifteen minutes or so he said he was fine, but a doctor who had been summoned thought otherwise. The outburst had put serious strain on his heart, he said, and Cliff was duly dispatched to a hospital for a week. The incident provided further good copy and photographs for the nation's newspapers. It was also dramatic indication of the effect the hearing had had on the principal players.[31]

Senator Eastland held a press conference just after the Durr-Crouch confrontation. He seemed somewhat shaken by what had occurred and emphasized that Crouch had not convinced him that either the Durrs or Williams were Communists. The journalists who had covered the hearings went further than that. When polled by the *Montgomery Advertiser* as to which of the people they had seen on display in the past three days was the greatest threat to American ideals, half thought Eastland was; of the remainder, most went for Crouch, and none for the Durrs or for Williams. Most Southern newspapers echoed this view, even those obviously unsympathetic to SCEF. Even the *New Orleans Times Picayune* was forced to conclude that the hearing had been "messy" and a discredit to all concerned. The *Montgomery Advertiser* called on Southern senators to do something about Eastland. "There is a matter of Southern honor involved here. A Southern gentleman and lady have been publicly branded with the most opprobrious term of the hour. They have denied it under oath. . . . This is the type of character lynching which Southern Senators should deeply resent."[32]

As well as a considerable amount of press approval for their position and sympathy for the way they had been treated, the Durrs were buoyed by the hundreds of letters of support they received in the hearing's wake. Many were from old friends or former clients from Washington days, outraged, like Hubert Wilson, "that one so deserving of the highest honors this country could award should be exposed to such abuse," or Alan Barth, who, referring to the confrontation with Crouch, wished he had "socked the bastard." Jessica Mitford wrote from California, full of praise for Cliff for "challenging those filthy creatures in the way that he did." Clark Foreman welcomed him back to the battle. "When you decide to get back in the fight you certainly come in slugging," he exulted. Both Tilla and Lulah sent their support and love, something which must have especially delighted their parents. But there were also letters and telegrams from complete strangers, like Ruth E. Moore, who had read newspaper accounts of the proceedings and simply wanted to say how sorry she had felt at their ill-treatment. All this was intensely gratifying to the Durrs, to know that they were not alone.[33]

Nevertheless, they returned to Montgomery, after a brief break, with a considerable sense of trepidation. They were both worried about the effect of the publicity on the family, on the practice, and on their precarious social existence in the city. Both Cliff's mother and Little Auntie coped with it simply by not talking about the hearing at all, though they were full of concern over Cliff's collapse and the subsequent state of his health. "That's the way Southern women have so often met a difficult situation," Virginia reminisced years later. They just pretended it had not happened.[34]

It was the effect on his brother James, however, about which Cliff was most concerned. James, as president of the Durr Drug Company, had given him the company's business and had been under some pressure for having done so. Cliff had certainly not wanted to cause him further embarrassment. Consequently, when James told him that he had made a fool of himself in New Orleans, he became somewhat upset. It turned out, fortunately, that his brother had only been joking. If he really had wanted to kill a man, James twitted, a federal courtroom, full of United States marshals, was hardly the best place to make such a threat. "Get him in an alley or on the street and then kill him," was his tongue-in-cheek advice. James also arranged to cover his hospital expenses. Both Lucy and Tilla were teased at school for being the children of disloyal parents, and this was hard on them both, but especially the younger Tilla. Perhaps saddest of all, Cliff found that he no longer had a Sunday school class at First Presbyterian. Attendance had fallen right away, he was told, and the few remaining members of his group were to be placed in other classes. Nothing, Virginia recalled later, hurt him more than that. Nevertheless, at least on a personal level, both family and acquaintances in Montgomery had on the whole been "wonderfully kind and friendly" about the whole thing. This was all the more gratifying for being somewhat unexpected. There were grounds for hoping, Virginia wrote Decca in May, that the New Orleans experience would "not kill off the feeble beginnings of the law practice" after all.[35]

Unfortunately this was not quite the case. The ordeal of the hearings had so flattened him that it was more than two months before Durr could go back to the office. When he did so, it was to find that much of the bread-and-butter side of any practice, the "wills and deeds" side, was already slipping away. Their clients did not believe the Durrs were Communists—they knew them both too well for that. They just did not want to leave their legal work in the hands of a man who had been publicly labeled as such. The New Orleans hearing probably finished any chance Durr had of developing a lucrative practice in Montgomery.[36]

The experience of New Orleans marked something of a watershed in Clifford Durr's life in Montgomery. In the first place, it was the catalyst which got the family out of his mother's house and into an apartment of their own. Both the physician who treated him in New Orleans and his regular Montgomery specialist were quite blunt in stating that the crowded home environment, with its inevitable strains, was one of the factors affecting his own health. His outburst in New Orleans and its aftermath also served to "convince him thoroughly" of this. Yet the problem of money remained. His brother James, who was highly sympathetic to his situation, solved this by enabling him to draw in advance on his share of his father's inheritance, currently held in trust, and this relieved the financial burden a little. By the end of May they had moved into a modest little apartment on Felder Avenue, which, after the past two years, seemed to Virginia like a palace. It was a crucially important decision and gave them all some privacy at last.[37]

Second, the New Orleans experience seemed to have convinced Clifford that there was no point in holding his tongue, in avoiding controversy, in no longer fighting in public for the principles he had advocated so clearly for so long. He had deliberately kept out of the battle for three years, first because of his illness, then because of the need to establish himself in Montgomery, and, of course, to avoid hurting his family. It had not worked. The climate of the times had caught up with him. He had gone to New Orleans simply as a lawyer, as counsel to his friend Williams, yet he had ended up on the witness stand himself, accused by a government informer of something he had never done, his picture reproduced throughout the land. There was no point in staying silent when such things could happen. He told this to Lister Hill in July, when writing to him about the prospect of the subcommittee's report repeating Crouch's charges against him. If that happened, he warned, he would publicly demand again what he had first demanded in New Orleans—either he or Crouch should be indicted for perjury. "The issue is clear," he told Hill. "Either Crouch lied under oath or I did. If I am a perjurer, I should be in the penitentiary. If I am not, then Crouch should be removed from the possibility of continuing his attacks upon the reputations of American citizens under the auspices of the Congress of the United States and the protection of Congressional immunity."[38] Clifford Durr was decidedly back in the battle, something his opponents certainly recognized. Immediately after the New Orleans hearing, his FBI surveillance was increased, and this was not modified until May 1959.[39]

Neither Clifford Durr nor Crouch was ever indicted for perjury, nor did the Internal Security Subcommittee take its probe for Southern Communists any further than New Orleans. Crouch's veracity had been so discredited by his performance there that he never testified for the government again and died the next year, a broken, lonely man. Ironically, Clifford Durr wrote the kindest obituary

Crouch was to receive. In *I. F. Stones Weekly,* Durr called him "not the source of evil, but its mere conduit. Crouch did what he was hired to do. . . . He died a lonely and despised man by those who used him, but those who hired him remain in respectable and powerful positions. They used him, and when he was no longer any use to them, they threw him aside." It was a compassionate judgment.[40]

Durr's realization that there was little point in trying to avoid controversy because it was not going to avoid him came at a crucial time, not only in his own life, but in the postwar history of the American South. In May 1954, the Brown decision declared segregation in public schools to be unconstitutional. It did more than that, however. It laid down a clear warning to the white South that it was on borrowed time, that the final assault on segregation was soon to come. To those few white liberals like the Durrs, whose instinct was not to man the barricades but to fling open the gates, it hastened often painful choices, between family loyalty and public duty, between accommodation and social isolation, occasionally between life and death itself. As he resumed an involvement with the crucial issues of the day, Clifford Durr had to face some of these choices with a particular poignancy, as increasingly his law practice and the cause of the South's blacks became enmeshed.

10

The Civil Rights Revolution

Throughout his life, Clifford Durr was uneasy about designating the conflict between the aspirations of Southern blacks determined to break down the walls of segregation and Southern whites determined to maintain them as a problem in "civil rights." Rather than separate it out in this way and locate it in a particular region, he much preferred to consider it as an aspect of the struggle to secure basic civil liberties in America. "The big problem," he told his daughter Tilla in 1965, as he had done many times before, was "civil liberties" and not just "civil rights." If black Americans were allowed to exercise those liberties guaranteed them by the Constitution, then the turmoil currently engulfing the American South would be unnecessary. He consistently argued this line: if American civil liberties were upheld, there would be no need even to talk about civil rights. There were not two separate problems here. They were one and the same.[1]

Obviously he had come to this position partly out of intellectual and philosophical considerations, but it may also have reflected his own particular evolution on the question of Southern racism. Durr was brought up to hold traditional Southern values on race, as on most other issues. As a young man, he expressed fairly stereotypical Southern views, and though these moderated steadily throughout his period in Washington, he never invested the race issue with the importance that Virginia came to do. He was not a member of the SCHW, nor, in the various government positions he held, did he ever come in direct contact with the problems of race. Nevertheless, his upbringing had also taught him that a Southern gentleman "never took advantage of a black man"; to cheat one or "to take advantage" of their second-class status was deplorable. He was deeply shocked when he first started to practice law in Montgomery to find that not all the town's leading white citizens held to this view, that some of them exploited blacks by charging excessive interest rates or cheated them over the fine print in insurance policies. He would represent these poor people in court and do his best for them, despite little hope of payment. Jessica Mitford believed that his upbringing prevented Clifford Durr from ever being at ease with blacks socially, and that may have been true, but it certainly did not prevent him from feeling deeply that American liberties belonged equally to them as to him or from doing what he could to ensure this. This belief drew him, inevitably, into the struggle of Southern blacks to end segregation, a struggle which had its symbolic beginning in Montgomery. And yet, at the same time it set him apart a little from his fellow protagonists, for, unlike them, he never saw the fight as something unique, something particular, but rather as part of the continuing battle to prevent the further erosion of American civil liberties. For Durr, there was a direct connection between his fight against the loyalty program and his efforts to secure justice for Montgomery's blacks, a link which was not always equally obvious to his contemporaries.[2]

Clifford Durr had always represented black clients—but then most white lawyers did. A decision he took in 1955, however, was much less usual, and that was to work with a young Negro lawyer, Fred Gray, in a suit against a white man. Even Cliff recognized that in so doing he was stating a position, he was setting himself apart from family, friends, and community. "The case will set a precedent of some kind or another—at least for Montgomery," he told Clark Foreman. "It involves the death of a twelve year old Negro boy, killed by a Jaguar car being driven by a white man at a speed of not less than 100 miles an hour." The boy's father had retained Gray, "a pretty keen young fellow" but quite inexperienced. Gray felt he "needed the help of a more seasoned lawyer" and asked Cliff to join him. He agreed. "It will be interesting," he commented, "to see how a Black Belt jury will react to the Negro-white legal combination."[3]

Virginia was amazed, admiring, and somewhat apprehensive at her husband's decision. "Cliff is so astonishing," she wrote Foreman. He would not commit himself verbally on the race issue at all, she said, and tried to prevent her from doing so. Nevertheless, he then acted in such a way "that his sentiments are clear to see." This was a turning point in his life in Montgomery, and he had acted quite without fear of the consequences. "He has lots more determination and courage . . . than I have" was her conclusion.[4]

This was not the only case in which Cliff and Gray cooperated in 1955. They worked together, too, when Claudette Colvin, a fifteen-year-old black high school student, refused to give up her bus seat to a white passenger and was charged with violating city and state segregation statutes. Given the importance of a similar case later in the year, that of Mrs. Rosa Parks, the Colvin case is worth discussing in some detail. Montgomery's black community had in recent years developed an increasingly powerful, increasingly politicized leadership. The most prominent of these were E. D. Nixon, a huge, outspoken Pullman porter, leader of the city's black Democrats and a longtime NAACP member; his NAACP colleague, Mrs. Rosa Parks; and Mrs. Jo Ann Robinson, an English teacher at Alabama State College, president of the Women's Political Council and, like Nixon, an articulate community activist. During the early 1950s, through the influence of a white moderate, Dave Birmingham, a member of the three-man Montgomery City Commission, the city's black leadership had a brief taste, if not of political power, at least of cooperation with the white power structure. This had ended, however. By 1955 Birmingham had lost his position, and the Brown decision had hardened white hearts against further concessions to blacks.[5]

Within this context the question of segregation on the city's public transport system became crucial. The WPC in particular had been complaining for years about the way the Montgomery City Lines, the municipal bus company, treated its black customers, and especially the city ordinance which required them to stand while seats designated "white" remained vacant. In early 1954, Mrs. Robinson suggested its replacement by a law which would permit whites to sit from front to back and blacks from back to front, a practice already in operation in a number of other Southern cities, until all seats were taken. Negroes, after all, comprised three-quarters of the city's bus-riding population. Without them, the system could not possibly operate. Surely, therefore, a reasonable solution to the problem could be found.[6]

The City Commission, in the wake of the Brown decision, stood firm against any talk of compromise. Some black leaders, therefore, including Mrs. Robinson, began to talk about an organized boycott of the bus company. Opinion in the black community was far from unanimous, however. But then on March 2, 1955, Claudette Colvin was arrested. She had refused a driver's demand that she give up her seat, well to the rear of the bus, to allow recently boarding whites to be seated. The fifteen-year-old student was, therefore, dragged from the bus by police officers and placed in custody.[7]

Colvin was not really an ordinary teenager. She was in fact an active member of the NAACP Youth Council and thus could be expected to cooperate if Robinson and Nixon decided to use her arrest as an opportunity to test the city's segregation laws in the courts. Initially this is what they decided to do. Fred Gray was immediately put in charge of the legal work, and he quickly turned to Cliff for assistance. Virginia, for her part, started to help Rosa Parks, who was adviser to the local NAACP Youth Council, to raise money for what was expected to be a protracted and expensive legal battle. "Send the money (if any) CASH," she instructed Decca (Jessica Mitford). She was thrilled, she confessed, at being back in the battle again, especially since she really had not yet adjusted to living in the South. "The only time I like it is when I am trying to change it—and that little bit does give me great satisfaction and it seems to give my Negro friends satisfaction too," she confessed. Meanwhile, the black leadership began to talk again of a boycott of the city's buses to accompany the Colvin trial.[8]

The boycott, however, did not eventuate, nor did the legal challenge to the city's segregation statutes. Almost immediately problems developed. First, Colvin had resisted the officers called to take her from the bus and had thus been charged with assault and battery as well as violation of segregation statutes. More important, it was learned that she was several months pregnant. Both Robinson and Nixon, therefore, decided that she would be "neither an ideal candidate for symbolizing the abuse heaped upon black passengers nor a good litigant for a test suit certain to generate great pressures and publicity." Colvin was accordingly convicted of both charges, but on appeal only the assault count was confirmed, the prosecutor choosing not to pursue the second charge. She was released on indefinite probation in her parents' care. Durr assisted Gray with preparing her defense both at her original trial and at the appeal.[9]

Nevertheless, the Colvin case did highlight the growing tension between Montgomery's black community and the City Commission over their treatment on the city's buses. Many blacks, infuriated at her conviction, refused to ride the buses in protest, though most drifted back after a few days. Complaints poured into the bus company. A delegation of black leaders, including Nixon and Robinson, met with bus company officials and the city commissioners to try to reach agreement on front-to-back, back-to-front seating, but the whites would give no ground at all. There matters rested, hardly resolved. As Virginia wrote to Jessica Mitford, the Colvin case had "created tremendous interest in the Negro community and made them all fighting mad and may help give them the courage to put up a real fight on the bus segregation issue." She certainly hoped so.[10]

Late in the afternoon of December 1, 1955, Rosa Parks left her job at the Montgomery Fair department store and, after doing a little shopping, boarded a Cleveland Avenue bus to go home. The only seat she could find on the crowded bus was in the row directly behind those always reserved for whites only. As more passengers boarded the bus, the whites-only seats filled up, until one white male was left standing. The driver, accordingly, directed those in the seats immediately behind to vacate them, including Mrs. Parks. All of them did so—except Rosa Parks. She had made her gesture; she was not going to move. The bus driver immediately phoned for the police. She was removed from the bus, taken to the city jail, and there charged with violating Montgomery's segregation ordinances. In terms of what was to follow, it was one of the most significant actions in the whole history of the American South.[11]

Like Claudette Colvin, Rosa Parks was not quite typical of Montgomery's black citizens. She had been an active member of the NAACP since 1943 and had worked with E. D. Nixon on a number of voter-registration drives. She had acted as a counselor to Claudette Colvin's NAACP Youth Council and had raised funds for her defense. Just prior to her arrest, she had attended an interracial conference at the Highlander Folk School. She was also well known to Cliff and Virginia Durr. Ann often sent her used dresses down to the family, and Virginia needed a competent seamstress to help her alter them for the younger girls' use. Someone recommended Mrs. Parks. She was thus often in the Durr home. They both got to like her, and Virginia arranged for her to attend the Highlander Folk School, getting Aubrey Williams to put up the money.[12]

Word of Mrs. Parks's arrest spread quickly through Montgomery's black community. When E. D. Nixon heard it, he called the police station to ask the nature of the charges against her but was told nothing. With no intention of letting the matter drop, and knowing that Fred Gray was out of town, Nixon called Clifford Durr and asked him to try to find out what was happening. Durr agreed to do this, and after doing so, told Nixon the nature of the charges and reported that Mrs. Parks could be released on one-hundred-dollars bond.

Nixon said he would arrange that, and the three of them—Nixon, Clifford, and Virginia—went down to the city jail. There the desk officer, naturally, gave Durr the bond papers to sign. No, he said, he was not a property owner and thus ineligible to do so, but Mr. Nixon was. Mrs. Parks was duly released. They went back to her house, where Durr, having heard her description of the arrest, explained that this could be the test case that the NAACP had been waiting for—if she had the strength to go all the way with it. After some consideration, she decided that she had.[13]

Robinson, Nixon, and others also soon decided that this was the incident for which they had been waiting. Quickly they began to plan a boycott of the city's buses for the following Monday, the day of Mrs. Parks's trial. This boycott, as is well known, eventually lasted not for a day but for more than a year, ending only when the United States Supreme Court declared segregation on Montgomery's public transport to be unconstitutional. During that year, the contours of American history began to alter significantly. The Montgomery bus boycott, for good reason, is generally taken to mark the start of the civil rights revolution in the United States, that swelling campaign to do away with segregation in the Southern states which had its legislative peaks in the Civil Rights Act of 1964 and the Voting Rights Act of 1965. Certainly, the young minister who was chosen to head the boycott, Rev. Martin Luther King, Jr., went on to become the most important black leader of this century, the very embodiment of the notion that change can come in a nonrevolutionary way, using the political process, reinforced by mobilizing the people in peaceful demonstrations of protest. The story of the boycott and of King's subsequent rise to national greatness has been told well and told often, most recently in David Garrow's Pulitzer Prize-winning biography. There is no need to repeat it here. What, however, was Clifford Durr's role in this stirring sequence of events?[14]

Typically, when writing about it himself, Clifford Durr was inclined to downplay his significance. It was Fred Gray, and later the NAACP lawyers, who were sent to the city, appeared in court, argued the cases, and lodged the appeals. To them, Durr said, belonged the credit for the success of the legal side of the boycott. All Durr had done was provide some help in the beginning, until Gray got back to town, and then gave him a little advice thereafter. That was an exercise in understatement. As Virginia told Clark Foreman, his involvement was much deeper than that. "Young Gray calls him up every day on something," she wrote, but Cliff, recognizing that "this is a Negro movement and has to be one," wanted "no recognition or claim to fame" as a result of his work for the boycott. This attitude of self-denial, she admitted, arose not solely out of altruism. He also recognized that, if it became known in the white community that he was assisting Gray and the other black lawyers, his fragile practice would be ruined. It was a risky business. Yet he continued to work behind the scenes for no financial reward, except for some funds raised by their Northern liberal friends, duly alerted by Virginia, because she believed it to be the right thing to do. Moreover, said Virginia, even he admitted that he had "been a lot of use," and that made him feel that the risks were worth it.[15]

Just how much use was he? Fred Gray provided an answer in 1973. Responding to an inquiry, he said that Durr had "made substantial contributions in connection with the bus boycott movement. He assisted me personally in connection with drafting pleadings, briefs and other documents in connection with not only the suit itself . . . but he substantially helped in connection with all the litigation we were involved in." Gray's recollection was that "the work was gratis." Durr's role was "a behind the scenes one," he said, "but without which it would have been almost impossible for the movement to have survived." Such a statement from the lawyer principally acknowledged as having borne the brunt of the boycott's legal responsibilities indicates how important Durr was to its success, regardless of his own demurral.[16]

Though Durr was probably able to keep the extent of his involvement in the bus boycott movement to himself, he did not attempt to disguise his sympathy for its aims. As such, he and Virginia found an increased amount of tension and isolation from the city's white community. Indeed, Jo Ann Robinson claimed that they became "martyrs to the boycott" and found themselves publicly scorned and socially ostracized. This may well have been true, although the sense of being able to accomplish something at last was clearly some compensation.[17] It was the effect on the girls, especially Tilla, that seemed the most immediate cause for anxiety. Lucy seemed to be relatively unaffected by the gathering tension; "the boys" said Virginia, evidently "find her charms more attractive than her repulsive ideas." Besides, through various devices she had got together the money to go to Radcliffe in the fall of 1955. She was able to earn her board and keep there, while tuition was covered by a small legacy. Thus she had left Montgomery by the time of the boycott. Lulah had some nasty experiences but was still too young to understand the import of what was happening around her. It was Tilla who suffered most from having dissidents as parents.[18]

Tilla was much more vulnerable than Lucy and had not adjusted well to life in Montgomery. As the racial tension increased, things got steadily worse. She had to listen to constant jibes about her parents and her Uncle Hugo, not only from her classmates but from her teachers as well. Little wonder that she felt so friendless and alone. The boycott made life simply intolerable for her. Virginia described her situation as being rather like that of a young Jewish girl in a Nazi school, where even the teachers were openly opposed. She was desperately unhappy, and both Cliff and Virginia reluctantly decided that, if she was to have the "good time and the normal life of a teenager" that she deserved, it would have to be away from Montgomery. They looked around, therefore, for a boarding school they could afford—or rather, where a small legacy which Tilla had received could be stretched sufficiently to meet the fees and where she could also qualify for a scholarship. They were fortunate enough to find one in the Cambridge School in Weston, Massachusetts. Tilla was able to go there in April 1956 for the last six weeks of the term, with good expectations of getting a scholarship for the following year. Virginia and Cliff were vastly relieved. "Now that Tilla is rescued," Virginia wrote Clark Foreman, and they no longer had the "awful weight" of her unhappiness to bear, they felt far less affected by their own ostracism.[19]

Moreover, although helping with the bus boycott had made them both feel much better about their situation and had given Cliff, in particular, a sense of being "a functioning person" again, it had not helped the law practice at all. They lost business steadily; again, as after New Orleans, the legal bread-and-butter of wills, deeds, and so forth simply dried up. As a result of his work with the boycott, there would be in the future regular contributions to the Durrs from such liberal philanthropists as Corliss Lamont. There would need to be. Durr's support for the cause of Montgomery's blacks effectively ruined what slim chances he had had of making a decent living as a lawyer in the city. When Lucy married a young historian, Sheldon Hackney, in 1957, she had to pay for the wedding herself—from checks received as gifts. Her parents had nothing with which to help her.[20]

Lucy's wedding was a happy affair, yet there were incidents which illustrated how difficult it was for the Durrs to feel remotely comfortable in white Montgomery society. First, there were problems with the church. The secretary called Cliff's sister-in-law, with whom Virginia was not particularly friendly, and asked if it was the intention to ask Negroes to the wedding, since Virginia was "so well known as an integrationist." If so, they would have to sit in the balcony, away from the rest of the guests. They had intended to ask the family servants, of course, who had expected to sit there, but also Fred Gray, who had not. The Durrs had in fact recently been to his wedding, as honored guests. He did not in the end come to Lucy's. Then, there was the question of Jessica Mitford's attendance. Lucy had asked her cousin Josephine Black to be a bridesmaid, and she had accepted. However, when Hugo Black learned that Decca, by now well known as a Communist party member, was to be present, he said that neither he nor Josephine would attend. There was a family council of war—the decision to invite Decca was affirmed, and neither of the Blacks was present. The wedding, of course, was a huge success, yet these two incidents revealed just how difficult it was for them, as social and political liberals, to exist in the growing climate of conservatism.[21]

Clifford Durr probably continued to feel the social and political ostracism less than did his wife. He was, after all, home where he wanted to be, and he was determined to stay if he could. He loved the Alabama landscape, he loved revisiting his childhood haunts, and he especially loved being back with his family. The fact that they had come to differ so widely on basic issues did not really affect the closeness of the relationship. Cliff and his brother James were particularly good friends, while he remained absolutely devoted to his mother and was devastated by her death in 1959. Virginia understood all this. "He feels at home here, whatever its ills," she admitted, but there was also something else behind his determination to remain, "something too deep for him to ever express." It had, she said, something to do with the way he had always stuck "by other people when they are in trouble," as he had stuck by her. In the same way, he believed he had to "stick by the people down here," if he possibly could. Besides, as Cliff himself once said, despite all the evidence to the contrary, he still believed "we have got more decency here than in most of the country"—or so his "old Confederate spirit" told him. The South, in short, was his "patch," and he did not want to leave it.[22]

From time to time inevitably even he became despondent and thought about bailing out. In particular, the fact that he could not make a living, that he could not support his wife and children by his own efforts but was dependent on his family and on the benefaction of a few rich liberal friends, that he could not even pay for his daughters' education, deeply distressed him. "No amount of belief or faith can take the sting out of not being able to make a living," Virginia admitted. It came at great cost to one's pride. In such moods, Cliff would think seriously about leaving and sometimes would even write letters of inquiry to universities, seeking teaching jobs. Nothing ever came of these, however; no one wanted him. As Virginia said, "it sometimes seems like a dream that we were once respected, honored and sought after members of society." It was probably just as well. If Cliff at times felt a failure in Montgomery, it would have been a far greater confession of failure to have left.[23]

Besides, their social isolation was never complete. Cliff belonged to two men's dining and debating clubs, the Forum and the Unity clubs, and was an active member of both. In 1955, for example, he led a Unity club discussion, "In Defense of the Fifth," in which he used the story of Melitus, who informed on Socrates, to justify providing guarantees against compulsory self-incrimination. In 1956 he supported Adlai Stevenson in an Eisenhower versus Stevenson debate at the Forum Club. In 1958 he took the negative in a debate on the proposition "That the Fourteenth Amendment Is Invalid," again at the Forum Club, during which he questioned some firmly held Southern traditions, such as the obligatory hatred of Thaddeus Stevens. He also pointed out that, though the Fourteenth Amendment had undeniably radical origins, it had subsequently "become a most conservative document," used much more by businessmen than minorities. He also, in the course of his remarks, stoutly defended the Brown decision. Durr's continued involvement in activities such as these showed that, despite his identification with unpopular causes and beliefs, he had not become an absolute pariah in the Montgomery community.[24]

Moreover, there were white friends in whose company they could relax, could talk about the past and the present, and could say exactly what they thought without holding back. There were Aubrey and Anita Williams, of course, friends from New Deal days. They saw a lot of them and their family. There was federal judge Richard Rives, Montgomery born and bred, who upheld the law fearlessly and faced the ostracism and hatred of his former colleagues at the Alabama bar for so doing. There was Ray Jenkins, one of the city's leading newspapermen. All these were people with whom the Durrs could be relaxed and who thought more or less like them. They were, it is true, few in number, but they were strong in their support. Given that Cliff needed few friends, that he was manifestly not at home in large gatherings and had a considerable liking for his own company, he probably found this situation quite satisfactory. Virginia, with her much more gregarious nature and her love for social occasions, admittedly did not.[25]

Perhaps the time they felt most ostracized in the community occurred in 1960 and resulted from an article based on their lives published in the *New Yorker.* Early in 1960 they were interviewed by Nat Hentoff, currently in the city, as had been numerous other journalists, for stories about the mood of the South were very much in vogue at that time. There was a clear misunderstanding—the Durrs thought they were talking off-the-record entirely, while Hentoff believed he had simply assured them that he would protect their identities. The result was a disaster, for the Durrs took the opportunity of what they believed to be a private conversation to unburden themselves, to talk extremely frankly about the problems of being a liberal in the South. They spoke of dealing with one's family, of coping with one's friends, and made a number of highly critical comments about Montgomery's white citizenry, especially the clergy, and the way they had turned over political and moral leadership to a few extremists. They deplored the breakdown of communication between the races, and even within the white community itself, that had occurred as a result.[26]

Hentoff's article appeared in July 1960. Entitled "A Conversation in Alabama," it certainly gave the Durrs new names—Joseph and Alice Winters, and their pretty, blonde daughter Mary (Tilla was home at the time)—but they were instantly recognizable nonetheless. Mr. Winters, for example, was portrayed as a civil rights lawyer with a high-strung wife. The family lived on what he made from a struggling law practice, plus borrowing from his family. Their remarks on the craven nature of the city's white leadership were fully reported, as were those on their own sense of isolation and rejection and on their fears for the future of the South. "I am worried about my folks," Mr. Winters was reported as saying, "about what we are doing to ourselves, backing down on everything that we profess to believe in."[27]

The citizens of Montgomery certainly knew who the Winters were and were quick to let them know what they thought of their views. There were anonymous phone calls, with the invitation to leave town if they did not like it; there was tension in the family and unpleasantness in the street. Grover Hall, editor of the *Montgomery Advertiser*, in a letter to the editor of the *New Yorker*, which he also ran as an editorial, attacked both Hentoff—a "bearded jazz music critic"—and Durr. Claiming Cliff was "as hipped on race mixing as the cranks who oppose fluoride in the water," he argued that to have pilloried the city on his "emotional, unsupported testimony was outrageous," something on which even Durr's "friends and fellow radicals" agreed. Durr replied, complaining that Hall had put "Mr. Winters' pipe" into his mouth and called him Durr. He was not responsible for Mr. Winters's views, he said, but would gladly state his own on a range of issues, if Hall wanted them. There would be few who would have believed him. The incident cost both of the Durrs a considerable amount of what credibility they had remaining with Montgomery's white citizenry.[28]

Virginia was furious and let Hentoff know it. He had left them "exposed to the full weight of the wrath of the community," she told him, accusing him of betraying confidences which they would never have told him had they not been assured they were speaking off-the-record, and to someone who had "posed as a trusted friend." His behavior, she continued bitterly, was rather typical of the "Northern hit and run liberal," who came south briefly, interviewed a few people, and then, from the safety of New York, exposed them "to the full blows of our enemies." Moreover, she said, he had missed the whole point of their continuing to live in Montgomery. They liked the people; "they are our own people," in a way that he, Hentoff, could never be. He had simply ridden roughshod over them, showing "no concern whatever for our lives, our livelihood, our friends, our families or our community." To Clark Foreman she poured out her bitterness at the writer's behavior, at the same time expressing her own ineluctable Southernness. They had taken him in, she said; they had liked him, and he had promised that everything they said would be off-the-record. Now look what had happened—everyone was mad at them, even their friends, and their "little store of goodwill is sadly diminished." Those "God Damned Yankee liberals," she cried—"I think they are simply stinkers."[29]

The Hentoff article certainly did nothing for Cliff's practice, but it had been going downhill for years as a money-making concern. Increasingly his work was of two kinds. He defended black people, usually poor, often falsely accused, and often subjected to police brutality; and he acted on behalf of people, white and black, who were facing criminal charges as a result of their activities in what was

Cliff and Civil Rights leaders at Chapel Hill, North Carolina, 1961 (Courtesy of the Alabama State Department of Archives and History)

becoming commonly known as the "civil rights revolution." Clifford Durr had never been "consciously bent" on improving the lot of black people as such. He was not a "damn bit interested," he said, in their legal and constitutional rights as blacks, as a special group—but rather, in their rights as people. His whole life's experience had taught him "that our legal and constitutional safeguards are not selective. They've got to protect everybody or in time they won't protect any of us." Thus, when he fought to protect the rights of an indigent black man suffering from police harassment, he always believed he was also protecting his own civil liberties. Thus, he continually made his point that the "civil rights revolution" was but a facet, or a regional variant, of the larger and enduring civil liberties struggle. This is what differentiated him from other liberals in that region, from his friends like Aubrey Williams and James Dombrowski, and even from his own wife. They consciously came to see themselves as specifically "racial liberals," people who invested the civil rights movement with a particular significance and who saw it as the key which would unlock the door of widespread Southern change. Cliff Durr, while in no sense minimizing the importance of what was happening around him, nevertheless refused to allow "civil rights" that degree of specificity, preferring always to link it with the broader civil liberties perspective. In so doing, incidentally, he tended to remove it, at least partly, from its distinctive regional setting, giving it instead a more national context.[30]

A few examples from his case files provide a flavor of the work he came to do. The case of Rufus Horne was one which Durr handled in 1958. Horne, a black Detroit resident and a visitor to Montgomery, had been at a nightclub till around 3 A.M. on the morning of December 3, 1958. He then set out to drive a woman acquaintance home. They were both hungry and decided to pick up some hamburgers at a roadside diner. Horne, though not from the South, was sufficiently attuned to Southern ways to inquire carefully if blacks could purchase orders to go and was assured that there was no problem. Accordingly, he placed and duly received his order, which he paid for out of a $20 bill, receiving $18 change. He had, he said, a considerable amount of money on him, having cashed a veteran's disability check for $263 at Sears Roebuck that very afternoon.[31]

According to Horne's story, he returned to his car and was preparing to drive off when a police car pulled up beside him. Two officers were in it, one of whom dragged him from the car, while the other assaulted him, saying, "Nigger, what are you doing going into that white place?" He was searched, the large amount of cash he was carrying was duly discovered and confiscated, and he was taken to the police station. He was warned to keep quiet about the money or it would be much the worse for him, charged with driving while under the influence and resisting arrest, and then jailed.[32]

Durr was asked to help him and quickly moved to do so. Bail was arranged, and his belongings were duly returned to him, including the $18 change he had received from the diner. The larger amount, however, was not there, and predictably the arresting officers denied that it had ever existed. Horne, being from Detroit, was not about to take this without protest. He provided the chief of police with a written statement alleging theft, his claim receiving at least some credence because of Sears Roebuck's affirmation that a check for $263 had indeed been cashed there.[33]

When Horne came to trial, Durr asked for and received a continuance. He had no doubt that the man had been robbed, and he was also probably not guilty of anything. On the other hand, the police evidence against him was growing daily. Seven officers were now listed on the arrest report, and a third charge had been preferred against him, that of disorderly conduct in the diner. This was on the basis of a complaint from a white waitress, whom Horne did not recall seeing and whose statement was incorrectly dated. Nevertheless, Durr believed that it was in the best interests of his client for him not to fight the case. If he lost he would certainly go to jail, and he had already antagonized the Montgomery police department sufficiently to ensure that it would not be a pleasant experience. Accordingly, he arranged for the two most serious charges to be dropped. Horne pleaded guilty, reluctantly, to that of driving under the influence. He paid a small fine and duly departed to Detroit, not exactly enamored of Southern justice and still minus his money. For Durr, however, there was some comfort in the fact that he had kept his client out of jail, though cases like this—and he handled many such—left him sad, not only for the black victims of such injustice, but for the white South as well. "Looking at the whole picture," he once commented after a succession of like cases, "I find myself more concerned about what we white Southerners are doing to ourselves and to the South than what we are doing to the negroes."[34]

At about the same time as Durr was defending Rufus Horne, he was trying to get justice for Willie Howard, another black, in what was a rather different case but one that was again typical of the type of work he came to do. Howard had lost both legs in an industrial accident in 1954 and had been eventually paid $9,200 for total disability, this being the appropriate amount for such settlements under Alabama's workmen's compensation law. The check he had received, however, was for a sum considerably less than this. The state, it transpired, had deducted Howard's medical expenses from the settlement claim, though this was in direct contravention of its own legislation, which provided for the payment of medical and hospital expenses on top of the settled sum. Howard was clearly owed money, and Durr eventually got it for him. It took a lot of legal work, however, for which the small payment he eventually received was scarcely adequate compensation.[35]

A case that Durr won on appeal, thus preventing the jailing of a young black, was that of *Caesar Davis* v. *City of Montgomery*, in 1961. Davis, a janitor for the State Health Department, had been charged with making a series of phone calls to a white divorcée, Ruby Boldring, inviting her to meet him "in the dark place on Oak St." The evidence against him was scarcely strong—his car was allegedly seen in her street just after the calls, a workmate claimed that he was oversexed, and Mrs. Boldring recognized his voice on the phone when the police made him call her later, some hours after his arrest. The arrest was made possible only through the identification of his car through its license plate, the number of which Mrs. Boldring had allegedly taken down through her window before fainting at the shock of having been propositioned by a black man in this way. Davis was able to account for his doings on the night in question, and if he were to be believed, could not possibly have been anywhere near Mrs. Boldring's neighborhood. But he was not believed, nor was Durr allowed even to cross-examine the city's chief witness, Mrs. Boldring. Instead Davis was quickly convicted and sentenced to sixty days' imprisonment with hard labor. Given the nature of the offense—a black man propositioning a white woman—and the feelings such matters invariably engendered, Durr held real fears for his client's safety if he were ever to go to jail. Durr himself had had his life threatened simply for defending Davis. Accordingly, he immediately filed notice of appeal.[36]

At the appeal, Durr was able to bring out in evidence what he had not been permitted to do at the original trial, namely, that Mrs. Boldring had a history of mental illness and was currently under outpatient psychiatric care. He was also able to show that she had herself been frequently convicted of making obscene and annoying phone calls, often alleging miscegenation. Indeed, she was twice convicted of such offenses in the time between the first trial and the hearing of the appeal. Because of this and because of some mistakes in procedure made by the original judge, Davis's conviction was quashed. Again, Durr had saved a client from jail, and again he had devoted a tremendous amount of time and effort to the case. Yet all he ever received in payment was forty dollars.[37]

Perhaps the case of this type which occupied Durr the longest was that of *Bessie May Prince* v. *B. G. Bryant*. Mrs. Prince was one of several people present at the house of Elizabeth Brown on the night of August 21, 1959, playing poker and watching a televised football game. Two police officers, claiming to have been attracted by "loud cursing, talking and music," allegedly witnessing through the window the drinking of corn liquor and admittedly acting without a search warrant, entered the house and placed the group there under arrest. Mrs. Prince, who opened the door to them, was charged with disorderly conduct for trying to prevent their entry.[38]

Mrs. Prince, whose husband worked for the Durr Drug Company, told a somewhat different tale. There was no liquor being drunk, she said, nor was there much noise. She had opened the door to the police when asked and had immediately been viciously assaulted and kicked in the ribs and back. One of the police officers, she alleged, had shouted as he did so, "I am going to teach this nigger woman how to open the door when I say open." She was in terrible pain but was denied medical attention. Instead she was placed in the patrol wagon with her companions and taken to jail, where she spent the night in the cells. Medical evidence, while obviously not corroborating the facts of her account, was at least consistent with her story. She had suffered severe, though not permanent, kidney damage.[39]

Mrs. Prince was duly convicted in the recorders court. Durr appealed and took the case all the way to the Alabama State Supreme Court, where her conviction was finally reversed. Then, acting on Durr's advice, she sued one of the original arresting officers, B. G. Bryant, with assault and battery and false arrest and imprisonment, claiming eighteen thousand dollars damages. Again the case moved through the Alabama court system, and once again it was the supreme court, reversing an earlier jury verdict which refused to award her damages, which rendered the vital decision. In the end, Mrs. Prince, faced with the prospect of a further court action, decided to drop her demands for damages, provided her full court costs were met. This was duly agreed to, more than four years after the original arrest had taken place. It did represent a victory of sorts, and it would not have occurred had it not been for Clifford Durr's persistence and his considerable legal skills. If he lost most of these cases in the lower courts, time and time again the verdicts were reversed on appeal.[40]

Such cases, of course, did not make him any money. They did not attract the business of Montgomery's more affluent Negroes, who continued to go either to the better-known white lawyers or to the Negro attorneys who had set up practice in the city in the wake of Fred Gray's success. Cliff was left with the cases they would not touch, either because they estimated the chances of being paid to be low or because the cases involved charges against the police force. Ciiff always took them, however, which improved neither his relationship with the police force nor the town generally. "People are now needlessly insulting," Virginia wrote despairingly in 1961, and even Cliff was "tired and discouraged" and was beginning to feel that "all his efforts" had been in vain, that "the Southerners are not going to reform themselves." She was desperately unhappy living among people who disliked her, and even Lulah was now experiencing some ostracism. Eventually friends and a timely legacy made it possible for her also to be sent away to school. In this situation, Durr's persistence in taking the cases of poor black people, with no hope of adequate payment for the work involved, simply because of his conviction that to deny justice to one particular group was to place at risk its availability to all, takes on a heroic cast.[41]

It was certainly Durr's involvement with the legal side of the civil rights revolution and especially his defense of people involved in the peaceful demonstrations to bring social change to the South, now becoming a fact of Southern life, that brought him most obloquy from Montgomery's citizens. Two examples of such cases will illustrate their nature. One involved a Fred and Anna Gach. They were a young Southern couple—he a Korean war veteran, she a law graduate but currently working as a linotype operator—who lived in a small apartment just opposite the Greyhound bus station. In 1961 bus stations were in the news, for it was the time of the "freedom rides," as brave young students, black and white, under the direction of the Congress on Racial Equality (CORE), rode the interstate buses and attempted to integrate the bus terminals in the cities and towns through which they traveled. Their explicit aim was to create a crisis. They expected to be attacked at the bus terminals—as James Farmer, one of their leaders said later, "We were counting on the bigots of the South to do our work for us"—and thus national attention would be drawn to the continuation of segregation in interstate travel. The resulting press coverage, they hoped, would force the government into action.[42]

When the riders reached Montgomery on May 20, 1961, they found a crowd of angry whites there at the terminal to greet them and no police, local police commissioner L. B. Sullivan having decided to allow the mob ten minutes of free time before the local police, whose job it was to protect riders, arrived on the scene. As the riders left the bus, therefore, they were set upon and savagely beaten, often with clubs and chains. This was the scene that Fred and Anna Gach stumbled into as they left their apartment, heading for Sears Roebuck in order to pay an account.[43]

Neither of the Gaches was particularly political, and they were certainly not civil rights activists. Nevertheless, Fred could not walk by the sight of three white men beating a young black with baseball bats, while policemen, who meanwhile had shown up, looked on. He appealed to the police to stop the violence, and when they took no notice, the burly former paratrooper attempted to do so himself. Fortunately, Floyd Mann, the Alabama State police commissioner, arrived on the scene and threatened to shoot the rioters if they did not back off. Gach and Mann then took the young man into the bus terminal, where it soon became apparent that he was fortunately not too badly hurt. However, when the Gaches emerged, the frustrated mob turned on them. Feeling rather more certain of protection from the state troopers now present than from the local police, they tried to make their way to where the former were gathered. Local police intercepted them and told them to change direction. As the indicated path would have taken them right through the mob, understandably they argued the point. For that they were both arrested and taken to the city jail.[44]

Anna Gach was charged with disorderly conduct, in that she had cursed "in a plainly audible voice" and had used the words "Goddam, Sons of Bitches, Bastards, and other profane and offensive words and language." Her husband was also charged with using these same words and also with failure to obey a police officer in that he did not leave the scene of the violence when ordered to do so. Because they were new to Montgomery and had no one to contact, they spent some time in jail (which was a particularly shattering experience for Anna) before bond was posted, and they were directed to Clifford Durr. He agreed to represent them both, using money raised by supporters including James Dombrowski, Jessica Mitford, and her husband, Robert Truehaft, to help with their costs.[45]

Both Gaches were quickly found guilty in the police court and fined substantial amounts. Durr immediately lodged an appeal, requesting a jury trial. This duly took place, and though their convictions were not quashed, their fines were drastically reduced, which was, Durr said, the "best that could be hoped for by a Montgomery jury at the present time." He very much wanted to take the case further, believing he could have won a reversal of their convictions, but the Gaches were not similarly keen. Anna had found her brief jailing particularly harrowing and wished to take no further chances. Moreover, she had been forced to leave her job on the *Montgomery Advertiser* because of harassment by her workmates. The young couple soon left Alabama, with their lives, if not ruined, at least severely shaken by the consequences of what had been simply an instinctive action on Fred's part, so poisoned had the climate of opinion in the city become.[46]

The Gach trial occasioned considerable attention in Montgomery, and Durr's defense of the couple did not go unremarked. However, easily his most important civil rights case was *Nesmith* v. *Alford*, or the MacMurray College case, as it was often known, which, as Virginia once said, "dropped into our lap out of the Blue" in 1960. The details were these. On March 30, 1960, ten students from MacMurray College, a Methodist liberal arts school in Jacksonville, Illinois, arrived in Montgomery, accompanied by the chairman of the college's sociology department, Dr. Richard A. Nesmith, himself an ordained minister, his wife, and their two-year-old daughter. The students, all white and all sociology majors, were on the final leg of a Southern field trip, during which time they had visited a number of communities, looking at them from a sociological perspective. Such trips, it should be added, were compulsory for all of MacMurray's sociology majors.[47]

One of the topics the students were researching was that of nonviolent social change in the South. For this reason, they were interested in meeting with blacks who had been involved in the successful bus boycott four years before. A seminar was therefore arranged for the morning of March 31, and this proved to be so fruitful that it was decided to continue the discussion over lunch. Accordingly the group, blacks and whites, moved to the private dining room of the Regal Cafe, a black-owned and -operated establishment. Just as they were sitting down to eat, however, a policeman arrived, then another, then police photographers, then television reporters, and finally, the chief of police and police commissioner themselves. Moreover, a crowd began to gather across the street from the cafe. However, nothing was said to the by now thoroughly discomfited group—no warnings were issued until the commissioner finally gave the order for their arrest. The whole gathering was then loaded into paddy wagons and taken to jail.[48]

Dr. Nesmith was sure no law had been broken, for he already knew that the Montgomery segregation ordinance forbidding whites and blacks from gathering together had recently been repealed. Moreover, they were clearly not trespassers in the cafe but invited guests. He received no answer to his questions as to the nature of the charges against him, nor was he allowed a telephone call to alert the college as to what had happened and to arrange bail for them all. Instead, they were all placed in cells, and most disturbing of all, the Nesmith's little girl was taken from them and placed in the juvenile detention ward of the county jail.[49]

This was the situation Clifford Durr found when he went to the jail, having been urgently contacted by Ralph Abernathy, of the Montgomery Improvement Association. He believed Durr could do more for the students than Fred Gray, since they were all white. A lawyer from Jacksonville, representing the college, telephoned soon as well. Durr's first job was to try to arrange bail for the group, but he was successful only in arranging it for the Nesmiths, and the students were forced to remain in prison. Next came the task of retrieving Nesmith's little girl, and this became an increasingly frantic search, given the initial refusal of county officials to disclose her whereabouts. Only after the threat of serious legal action, including the pressing of kidnapping charges, was she eventually restored to her by now desperate parents.[50]

The MacMurray group was tried the next day. The charges against them did not make the reason for their arrests any clearer, as it was alleged of them all simply that they "did disturb the peace of others in violation of ordinance 11-60 of the Montgomery City Code." The prosecution conceded that the segregation ordinance had in fact been repealed and that the group had not been behaving offensively in any way but was simply sitting talking in the cafe. Moreover, Durr brought out in cross-examination that the decision to arrest them had been made only after a sufficiently large crowd had gathered. However, it transpired on further questioning that the crowd had been attracted not by the integrated group but by the presence of so many police vehicles, that it was peaceful, and that it was made up almost entirely of blacks. Nevertheless, the judge found them all guilty of disorderly conduct on the grounds that, despite their admittedly peaceful behavior, "for whites to eat with negroes was so offensive to Southern customs that a breach of the peace might have been committed if whites have learned of it." Thus the defendants were clearly guilty of conduct likely to provoke such a breach. Accordingly, he fined the Nesmiths one hundred each and the students fifty dollars each.[51]

Durr knew the decision was so wretchedly wrong in law that the group had the most solid grounds for appeal. But would they agree to do so? Eventually they did. The MacMurray College president posted bond on their behalf, and back they went to their classrooms until May 9, 1960. Durr decided on a trial before a judge and jury;

essentially the same evidence was presented; and the jury, in what was clearly a compromise verdict, found all of the defendants not guilty except Dr. Nesmith, whose fine of one hundred dollars was sustained. Durr immediately announced his intention to appeal to the state court of appeals on Nesmith's behalf, which a year later reversed his conviction.[52]

That was not the end of the matter, for Durr, as had become his practice, now raised with the group the prospect of filing suit for damages against the police officers concerned in an effort to establish the point that the capricious use of police power could and would be resisted. Eventually, the Nesmiths and two of the students decided to do this, filing suit in federal court against the police commissioner, the chief of police, and several other officers and alleging false arrest, malicious prosecution, and a denial of civil rights. Again, liberal support groups met their expenses. Predictably, the lower court jury voted in favor of the defendants, but in June 1963, the United States Court of Appeals for the Fifth Circuit held that their arrests had been illegal as a matter of law. The case was eventually settled with the defendants paying all the group's costs and expenses. Cliff Durr had finally made his point. "It is thrilling sometimes to come off the victor," wrote a jubilant Virginia to Clark Foreman.[53]

Of course, the case, perhaps the most important of his whole legal career, did not make Cliff much money. Wryly, he later recounted the story of dining with a wealthy Los Angeles lawyer who had successfully used the precedent of *Nesmith* v. *Alford* to win substantial damages for a client and a fee of $250,000 for himself. When Cliff told him that he had done all the work for a total of $1,500, the lawyer registered some discomfort, though not to the extent of offering to split his fee with him. Nevertheless, his real satisfaction came in other ways, in the reaffirmation of the principles he had devoted his public career to defending. In its judgment reversing Nesmith's conviction, the Alabama Court of Appeals had argued thus: "But liberty is at an end if a police officer may, without warrant, arrest not the person threatening violence, but those who are its likely victims; merely because the person arrested is engaged in conduct which though peaceful, legally and constitutionally protected, is deemed offensive and provocative to settled social customs and practice. When that day comes, freedom of the press, freedom of speech and freedom of religion will all be imperilled." If *Nesmith* v. *Alford* did, as Durr believed, ensure that the "rights of all citizens have become a little more secure," it was in large part due to his persistence, his considerable legal skills, and above all, his firm devotion to principle.[54]

Cliff's family may have been unhappy at his involvement with the MacMurray case. If so, they never once mentioned it to him. "It is that dead silence that is so hard to bear," said Virginia. He received, of course, the expected amount of criticism from around the town. He was, however, more worried by the effect this had on Lulah than by anything else and was greatly relieved when a scholarship was arranged so that she could attend the Windsor Mountain School, a private boarding school in Lenox, Massachusetts. There she roomed with Harry Belafonte's daughter, something that doubtless would have scandalized Little Auntie, whose namesake she was and whose legacy partly supported her. The knowledge that Lulah would no longer be affected made the increased ostracism a little easier to bear.[55]

In 1962, Virginia commented on a relatively new development in the Durrs' life. There seemed, she said, to be a never-ending stream of students passing through their household. In fact, this had been happening for some little time. Young people would arrive, sometimes civil rights workers looking for a safe haven, others simply seeing the South for themselves. Tom Hayden spent a night on their floor in 1961 before going to Albany, Georgia, and jail, and he was just one of many. They were assured of a place to sleep, a hot bath, and a good meal, all necessities, particularly those who came straight from Southern jails. There was such a group there, for example, on the night of May 21, 1961, when in an ugly riot after the arrival of the freedom riders, the Durrs' car, parked close to the church where Martin Luther King, Jr., was holding a rally, was overturned and burned. Jessica Mitford, herself staying with the Durrs at the time, had driven it there, and the mob took its revenge appropriately. Virginia loved these young visitors, and for a time Cliff did too, though eventually he tired of the continual invasion of his privacy. "At times," he once wrote Lucy and Sheldon in frustration, "after hauling away accumulations of coca cola bottles, cleaning up and burning masses of scattered newspapers and other trash and gathering up glasses and coffee cups left in their wake by young—and sometimes middle aged and even older—champions of justice, democracy, equality, peace and human dignity, whose time is too precious to be wasted on such trivial matters as cleaning up their own mess, I begin to feel, sometimes, that my own dignity has been affronted." But that came later, after six years of such visitations. At first, he, like Virginia, welcomed their presence.[56]

Perhaps the visitors he enjoyed most were those from England, often sent on by Decca. One of the first of these, Christopher Bacon, a former RAF pilot and Cambridge history graduate, brought Durr again in brief direct contact with the FBI. Bacon, an exchange student at Berkeley, had been arrested in May 1960 for demonstrating at a HUAC hearing, though charges against him were subsequently dropped. Nevertheless, when he went on a motor tour of the South and East in August with two friends, their car was followed everywhere by FBI agents. They called on the Durrs, as Decca had suggested they do, and eventually stayed there for a couple of days. During all this time the FBI agents sat resolutely outside the Durr house in the summer heat, refusing Cliff's invitation to come inside for a cup of coffee and a chat. Cliff found it all rather amusing but understood why it seemed rather less so to the young visitors. He warned them that anyone who visited the Durrs was likely to find themselves on an FBI list of some sort or another.[57]

Nevertheless, English visitors continued to appear. One that they particularly liked was Anthony Lester, a young Commonwealth Scholar at Harvard, where he was reading law, who stayed with the Durrs in 1961. He kept in touch with them on his return to England, and when he wrote in June 1963 with the "crazy idea" that Cliff come to England on a lecture tour, Cliff was thrilled. "I won't let my hopes build up too high," he responded, but he had certainly given him "something pleasant to think about." The offer fitted in, he confessed, with his own equally "crazy notion" of easing himself out of the practice of law, of retiring to a piece of property he had been given at Wetumpka, part of Grandfather Judkins's old farm, and reflecting on the experience of his public life.[58]

Lester took this to be an affirmative answer and proceeded to organize an English visit for Cliff, even to the extent of getting financial support from Louis Schweitzer, a wealthy New York philanthropist, so that Virginia could accompany him. It was to take place in February and March 1964. Cliff was to lecture at the London School of Economics, at Oxford and at Cambridge on the concerns of his public career—the titles of his speeches were "Racial Discrimination," "Dissent and Conformity," and "Civil Rights and Civil Liberties"—as well as taking part in a number of seminars and giving radio and television interviews on the contemporary South. Lester handled all the details as to transport, accommodation, and expenses with extraordinary efficiency, even advising Cliff on pronunciation. Durr, like most Southerners, said "Negro" as "Nigrah," and this, warned Lester, might be heard by English audiences as "nigger." They would be profoundly shaken, he said, "until they realise that Cliff is not a Klansman!"[59]

The tour duly eventuated. Cliff was extremely nervous about lecturing but found to his surprise, as he told his daughter Lucy, that he was quite good at it, at least if the enthusiastic reaction of his audiences was a valid guide. In the lectures, he reported to Louis Schweitzer on his return, he had talked about the legal implications both of McCarthyism and the present Negro movement, drawing on his own personal experiences as well as the "historical development of the law" in attempting to show "that Civil Rights and Civil Liberties were part and parcel of the same bundle and could not be separated without disastrous consequences to both." This was his familiar message. It was a message to which his audience had been receptive, and this had clearly been a tremendous fillip to his ego, battered as it had been by years of being an outsider in Montgomery. To be respected, to be made much of, to be listened to—this was an experience he had almost forgotten.[60]

On a personal level, too, the trip was a success. Tilla, currently an au pair in France, joined them for part of it, they renewed acquaintance with their English visitors, they loved the sights and sounds of England, and they reveled in the freedom they found. "Virginia, Tilla and I have fallen in love" with England, Cliff wrote his sister Lucy, and he, personally, could "never again think of the British as reserved and aloof." The whole experience of the trip belied that. Settling back to their Montgomery existence was extremely hard, after the "taste of freedom of speech" they both had had. In a gesture full of significance, Cliff finally took out formally the degrees he had qualified for at Oxford more than forty years before but to which he had never bothered to seek admittance. The trip had changed all that.[61]

It was also instrumental in helping Cliff decide how he wanted to spend the rest of his life. Not long after his return home he decided to close his law office. Part of the reason was financial; the return from the cases they took was now so minimal that Virginia described the practice as "like running a free legal aid bureau." Moreover, their own financial position, though still far from good, had at least improved slightly, largely as a result of the successive deaths of Cliff's mother in 1959 and Little Auntie in 1962 and the consequent distributions of assets. The other factor was of course the sheer enjoyment he had had from the English experience and his desire to repeat it whenever and wherever possible. He had learned at long last that he had something to say that people wanted to hear. There was an audience for him outside Montgomery, and he was going to reach it if he could.[62]

11

Retirement and Reflection

Cliff Durr closed up his law office on November 1, 1964, and almost immediately departed again for England, this time without Virginia. Once again, the trip was due to the good offices of Anthony Lester and other young English friends, who recommended to the administrator of the Wilton Park Conferences, Dr. G. C. Harcourt, that Durr be placed on the list of Americans invited to attend. These conferences, underwritten by the Foreign Office and billed as a British contribution to the formation of an informed international public opinion, were held regularly at Wiston House, in Steyning, Sussex. The theme for the sixty-seventh conference, to be held between November 8 and 21, 1964, was "East-West Relations," and Durr was invited to be one of the participants.[1]

He was somewhat surprised by the invitation, but as all his expenses were to be paid, he readily agreed to go. Moreover, he was able to arrange two lectures as well, one at the University of Sussex, where his theme was "A Southerner Looks at the South," and one at the University of Manchester. He enjoyed these more than the conference itself, which he found rather too stuffy and remote from life. He was afraid his "contributions to the high level discussion haven't seemed very scholarly so far," he wrote his sister Lucy. Still, the trip was pleasant enough, the only sour note being that through it he found out that the FBI was still interested in him. He was held up for some time at Heathrow Airport on arrival, and though no explanation was ever given for the delay, he suspected it was due to an FBI message about him to the British authorities. This proved to have been the case. Durr's FBI file revealed that Hoover had indeed alerted the British to the impending arrival of this "controversial individual," though conceding that neither he nor Virginia had been engaged in "any actual subversive activities in many years." The realization that he was probably still under surveillance did distress him.[2]

The theme of the University of Sussex lecture, "A Southerner Looks at the South," was the now-familiar one linking civil rights and civil liberties while at the same time pointing out that what Southerners claimed now to be "The Southern Tradition and Way of Life"—white supremacy—was in fact quite untraditional. "I have found some difficulty in joining my fellow Southerners in their fervent invocation" of what they termed ***the*** tradition, he confessed, because he was "unable to admit that the South which produced George Washington . . . and the authors of our Declaration of Independence, the Virginia Bill of Religious Liberties, the Bill of Rights of our Federal Constitution and much of the original Constitution itself, is now so bankrupt of tradition that it has left only the single tradition of white supremacy." But there was still much that was good about the South, he asserted, and despite the current dark times, it would, in the end, reassert itself. This was fairly typical of his speeches about his native region, a statement of dissent from current policies and practices, together with an obvious love for its "real" traditions and an optimism that these would again become the dominant ones.[3]

He scarcely had time to settle in before he was off on the lecture circuit again, this time to Canada. His old friend and colleague from FCC days, Dallas Smythe, was now a professor at the University of Saskatchewan and arranged for him to lecture there on "The Equality of Difference: The Southern Problem," as part of a general lecture series. While in Canada, Durr was also invited to talk at Queens University and the University of Montreal Law School. Then, on the way back home, he spoke in Portland, Oregon, before spending a week at Stanford University. There he participated in a lecture series entitled "The Legacy of the Civil War," along with the distinguished historians C. Vann Woodward and James Silver, and also spoke to the Stanford Law Forum on his experiences as defense counsel for poor blacks. The trip was exactly what he had hoped would eventuate after he had retired from the law, and he reveled in the excitement of it all.[4]

This was to be the pattern for the next two or three years—frequent visits away from Montgomery in order to give lectures and seminars, more often than not accompanied by Virginia. In 1966 he was at UCLA for a month as Regents Professor in the Department of Theater Arts, where he was able to lecture again about radio and communication generally, but mainly he talked of the contemporary South and its present agonies. One of the most important of these was his "Chancellor's lecture" at Washington University, in St. Louis, in November 1965. Taking as his theme "The Relevance of Morality," Durr drew on his life experiences to stress yet again his conviction that the current civil rights problem was but one aspect of a generalized erosion of American civil liberties. If he had gained a reputation as a defender of civil rights for Negroes, he said, it should be understood that that was "not because they are Negroes but because they are people and I fall into that same category." Relating the problems of Montgomery, Alabama, to those of Washington, D.C., he used the Goodwin Watson story as a means of illustrating the interconnectedness of the civil rights and civil liberties struggles. It was a long, intensely personal and very moving speech and was greeted with "prolonged applause." It was also typical of the speeches Durr gave on the issue.[5]

He was not always so applauded. Indeed, at Miles College, a black college in Birmingham where he had been invited in 1967 to talk to the freshmen about Arthur Miller's *The Crucible* and the context in which it was written, several students walked out noisily from his talk in protest at his Southern accent—in particular, at his pronunciation of "Negro" as "Nigrah." In his response to the college official who had written to apologize, Durr voiced his growing concern at what was happening to the spirit of racial amity which had characterized the first years of the civil rights revolution, as the strident rhetoric of "black power" became more insistently heard. He was not, he said, nearly so bothered by the rudeness of the students as by "the seeming acceptance and even recommendation by their elders of hate as a useful catharsis." There was nothing "more corrosive of the human mind and spirit" than hatred, and for the black movement to be moving in that direction was, he deeply believed, to invite disaster and destruction. This was not the only time the Durrs would face the rising anger and antiwhite rhetoric of young blacks. Invited to speak at Tuskegee in 1971 on his and Virginia's contributions to Southern change, Clifford never got a chance to say even a word, the students having literally shouted Virginia away from the rostrum, proclaiming, "We don't want to hear no white folks." Such experiences were deeply distressing for them both.[6]

Fortunately, they were far outnumbered by the most positive of times, nowhere more so than in Great Britain. They were able to go again at the end of 1967, once more through the good offices of Anthony Lester and other friends. Lester started it off, but the organization this time was done by Jonathan Steele, another Harkness Foundation scholar who had visited the Durr home in the early 1960s, now an editorialist for the *Guardian.* Durr was to lecture on civil rights and civil liberties at the Universities of Edinburgh, Exeter, Sussex and at the London School of Economics. This time, the Harkness Fellowship agreed to supplement the lecture fees with a Commonwealth Fellowship, something quite unusual, in recognition of the assistance Durr had provided to British Harkness fellows over the years. It was a wonderful gesture of the esteem in which these young Englishmen held him.[7]

Again the trip was a great success. They spent a considerable amount of time in Scotland, which they both fell in love with. They were royally treated by their old friends and made some fascinating new acquaintances, including the writer Philip Toynbee, whom they visited at Jessica Mitford's insistence. Cliff, by now an accomplished lecturer, delivered his various talks with practiced ease, and they were able to visit Paris again. It was strenuous, of course, but the stimulation they both got out of these visits and the sense of accomplishment that Cliff had made the fairly hectic pace thoroughly worth it. Truly, their hospitality to their young English visitors had been amply recompensed.[8]

The Durrs made only one further trip to England, in 1973, and this was a private affair. Tilla joined them, and they went to Germany and Austria as well. It was a tremendous success. Cliff, who had not been fully fit for years and who had spent much of 1972 in the hospital, coped much better than expected with the traveling. He "ate huge Scotch breakfasts, porridge and kippers," as his strength rapidly returned. Moreover, his spirits rose perceptibly, Virginia said, as "we were entertained by all of our student visitors." Their obvious continued respect for him was of the greatest importance in giving him a sense that he still had something worthwhile to contribute. Though an outsider to the citizens of Montgomery, in the wider world he was not generally held to be so. "All that cornbread we cast upon the waters," once wrote Virginia in gratitude, was returned to them many times over during their visits to Britain.[9]

At the time Cliff closed his law practice in 1964, there were some who hoped that the Durrs' old friend and new president, Lyndon B. Johnson, would make him a federal judge. Aubrey Williams from his deathbed implored the man to whom he had given his first government job to appoint Cliff to the Fifth United States Circuit Court of

Appeals. "Lyndon, I have ask [*sic*] you for very little. I ask you for this," was how his note concluded. An organized campaign among Montgomery's black community sought the same result. Even Virginia, briefly, thought that perhaps something might come of it. They had, after all, been recently invited to tea at the White House, with Aubrey and Anita Williams. Perhaps that could mean something?[10]

Cliff, however, had no such illusions. Quickly he wrote to the president, telling him how deeply he had been moved by Aubrey's sponsorship but assuring Johnson that he was not "unaware of the political realities of life" and knew he could not be confirmed. The idea, he said, was "Aubrey's and not mine" and argued that either Frank M. Johnson or Paul Johnston be appointed to the position. The president replied, thanking Cliff for his support and for his understanding that "Aubrey is sometimes a little naive on these things and makes problems simpler" than they really were. To Aubrey, Cliff wrote movingly, thanking him for his championship, "one of the finest things that ever happened to me." He would rather have that on the record than be a federal judge, he asserted. His sense of the reality of the situation was correct, and there is no reason to doubt the president's reply to Williams that he simply could not get Cliff confirmed. Yet he must have had a twinge of regret that, at a time when the president he could most reasonably have expected something from was in office, his uncompromising devotion to principle had effectively prevented him from being a serious contender for a position for which his legal skills otherwise qualified him.[11] The Durrs never lost contact with nor affection for the Johnsons, though as with many liberals there was a period of estrangement at the height of the Vietnam War. They both gave oral history interviews for the Lyndon Johnson Archives, in which they talked at length about their admiration and affection for the president and the sense of purpose they all shared during the New Deal. After his death they continued to see Lady Bird; in fact, one of the last trips they made before Cliff's own death was to visit her at the Johnson ranch.[12]

Though a federal judgeship was never a serious possibility, other awards and honors began to come Cliff's way. None pleased him more than the decision of the New York Civil Liberties Union in 1966 to award him its Florina Lasker Award for outstanding service to the cause of civil liberties. The panel which selected Durr included such distinguished Americans as the historian Arthur Schlesinger, Jr.; Louis Pollak, dean of the Yale Law School; Burke

Marshall, assistant attorney general with special responsibility for civil rights; and Gilbert Harrison, editor of the *New Republic.* The citation stated that, from the early days of the New Deal until his retirement, Durr had dedicated his public life "to the expansion of human rights." It spoke of his public service on the FCC and his dedication to helping "the penniless and the oppressed" blacks of his native Montgomery. He had, the citation concluded, "served as a guiding light to many young people who are today entering the national scene," as a living example of a dedicated public servant.[13]

The award was actually presented at a lunch at the Waldorf-Astoria Hotel in late February. Here, his old friend Charles Siepmann spoke of his life of service, first to the people's "right to know" while on the FCC, and later to the "poor and oppressed" of Alabama. Durr was, he said, "a simple man of great dignity, one of nature's gentlemen." There were other similar plaudits: the guests at the luncheon gave him a standing ovation, and the *Nation* commissioned broadcaster Saul Carson to write a guest editorial honoring Durr. Entitled "The Conscience of a Lawyer," the editorial discussed his public career, emphasizing in particular his achievements while on the FCC—the Blue Book, the AVCO dissent, the fight to preserve the networks from control by advertisers—and also his opposition to Truman's loyalty program ("he denounced McCarthyism even before the term was invented") and his work as a poor people's lawyer in Montgomery. "Clifford Durr would agree that he has tried to do his duty," concluded Carson, "but nothing he has ever said suggests that he feels he has done more than his personal integrity and professional skills required of him. It would not have occurred to him that there was anything unusual in that, and we are particularly happy, therefore, that the Civil Liberties Union has obliged him at last to see himself as his admiring contemporaries see him."[14]

Cliff was genuinely delighted by the Lasker Award, which he saw in part as a vindication of his conviction that "civil rights" was a part of the struggle for civil liberties. "I thought I had been charged off as obsolete long ago as 'Civil Rights' became fashionable and 'Civil Liberties' forgotten," he exulted to Charles Siepmann, who had first told him of the impending honor. He enjoyed the lunch, the plaudits of his colleagues, and the letters of congratulation and respect from those unable to attend. Probably nothing about the award gave him more pleasure, however, given the respect in which he held his brother-in-law Hugo Black, than the letter Black wrote to the *Nation* in response to its editorial. It was a veritable paean to Cliff.

Durr was "one of the best men" he had ever known, wrote Black, the "personification of gentleness, kindness and toleration." He spoke, too, of his courage and his unwillingness to compromise "with that which he believed to be evil and against the best wishes of his country" and discussed at length the reasons that Durr left the FCC and what they revealed about the man. The president had wanted him to continue, Black said, and had pledged to support his confirmation in the event of senatorial opposition, despite Durr's uncompromising opposition to the loyalty program. It was Durr who decided that to continue, feeling as he did about it, would be dishonest. Congressman William Fitts Ryan placed both the *Nation* editorial and Black's letter in the *Congressional Record,* together with some prefatory remarks in which he compared Cliff to Thoreau. It was all very gratifying.[15]

Clifford Durr would receive other honors and rewards in the future. The Southern Regional Council, for example, made both Virginia and him "Life Fellows" in 1973, and this was both surprising and pleasing, especially since the Durrs and the SRC had not always seen eye-to-eye in the past. Nevertheless, it was the Lasker Award and the circumstances surrounding it which pleased him most of all. It seemed in a way to be recognition of the particular perspectives he had come to hold, not only on civil liberties but on the concept of "public interest" as well.[16]

The fact, too, that he was finally regarded as someone whose recollections were worth preserving also gave Durr a sense of vindication. He reviewed his life for the Columbia University Oral History project and for the Southern Oral History collection at the University of North Carolina at Chapel Hill. He spoke of his relationship with Lyndon Johnson for the Johnson Archives and enjoyed it all hugely. Studs Terkel, the oral historian, spent three hours with him, recording his views on the New Deal, and, increasingly, postgraduate students began to seek him out, treating him as a source for projects ranging from the history of the FCC to the role of lawyers in New Deal Washington. In 1973 the director of the Archive of Contemporary History at the University of Wyoming wrote asking for his papers, as part of a drive to "collect the papers of those individuals who have played a prominent role in the twentieth century political, social, and economic scene." Durr publicly joked about his new role as a "historical exhibit," but in fact it pleased him immensely that people now seemed to find what he had done and what he had seen to be of some value. In particular, he was hopeful that someone might finally get straight the story of the DPC and was disappointed that his son-in-law Sheldon Hackney had not been able to interest a graduate student in the project, for increasingly, despite all his best intentions, it looked less and less likely that he would tell the story himself.[17]

This had not always seemed the case. Indeed, one of the reasons Cliff had decided to close down his law office was to give himself time to write. At first he was going to do a book on Aubrey Williams, at James Dombrowski's request, although, as he told him, he found writing a very difficult task. Then it was decided that perhaps he and Sheldon could do the book together, provided Anita Williams agreed, but nothing came of that. He returned from his lecture tour of Canada and the West Coast in 1965, as Virginia described it, "in a perfect glow" at the enthusiastic reception he had been given and determined to write his memoirs, to set down the sorts of recollections and personal experiences that seemed to make his lectures so lively and immediate. Over the next two years he began the task, though frequently interrupted by his busy lecture schedule.[18]

In 1968 Durr actually signed a contract with Houghton Mifflin to publish his autobiography. Negotiations had in fact begun in 1965, after a mutual friend who had heard his Stanford lectures alerted Anne Barrett of the firm's editorial department that he might have a book to write. Houghton Mifflin was looking for a "Southern" manuscript following the success of James Silver's *Mississippi—the Closed Society* and immediately wrote offering to publish a book written round his life experiences. Negotiations continued for two years, with nothing being concluded until his friend from FCC days, Ed Brecher, came to work with him on the project. Together they put his files in order, then Brecher sent to Anne Barrett a package of transcribed tapes and other writings by Durr, to see whether she still thought there was a book in Durr's reminiscences. After reading the material, she was more convinced than ever that there was, even if the best approach might be for him to tape his recollections and then have them edited. Brecher helped Durr overcome his real doubts about the autobiographical approach, and a contract was duly signed providing for a one-thousand-dollar advance immediately, a further two thousand dollars on delivery of half of a satisfactory manuscript, and a further two thousand dollars when the job was done.[19]

The book was never completed. Despite Anne Barrett's initially gentle, then increasingly firm, requests for progress reports, despite Durr's guilty insistence that he would get something to her soon, and despite all the help he was given, both by friends and by people who were paid to assist, the book never went past the first-draft stage. It remains still a vast collection of handwritten reminiscences and transcribed tapes, an important source collection for both biographer and historian, but very far from the manuscript both Durr and his publisher wanted it to be. There were a number of reasons for this. First, his uncertain health from 1966 on made the task of writing, already difficult for him, all the more physically daunting. Then, he did find it difficult to write about himself. Like his friend Aubrey Williams, who had similar trouble with his own memoirs, he much preferred to talk about other people. Finally, he simply had other interests which became more important to him, none more so than his piece of property—Pea Level—at Wetumpka in Elmore County, Grandfather Judkins's old place. When he told Charles Siepmann as early as 1965 that he was spending more and more of his time there, thinking up excuses for not getting on with the writing he should have been doing, he had touched on the main reason why his book was never finished. He was never sufficiently interested in it to make the necessary commitment.[20]

Though Durr had been spending time at the Pea Level since he had first acquired it in the mid-1950s and had built a cottage there where he and Virginia often spent weekends, it was not until after his retirement that they could seriously consider moving there permanently. Cliff of course wanted to do so as soon as possible, and by 1966 was spending more and more of each week there, improving the property, with hope of preparing for a permanent move. "I am anxious to stay put here at the Pea Level," he confided to his daughter Ann in 1966. Virginia, however, was not quite so sure that she would enjoy Elmore County on a permanent basis; besides, there was a difference between a weekend cottage and a permanent home. Virtually a new house would have to be built there before the move could be contemplated.[21]

By 1968, however, she had agreed to go, once the house had been rebuilt. They had spent the summer of 1967 there, and she had liked it sufficiently to resolve her doubts. In order to save money, the plan was for Cliff to do most of the new building himself, and this he did, though it took most of 1968, and he severely damaged his back in the course of it. Nevertheless, early in 1969 they moved permanently to the Pea Level. For Cliff it was an absolute joy to do so, and Virginia, sharing his happiness, knew it had been the right decision. "He hates

A family group at Lulah's wedding, 1970. Front: Cliff and Virginia. Back: Ann, Tilla, Lulah, and Lucy (Courtesy of Lucy Durr Colan. Photograph by Walter A. Lyon)

to leave it even for a day," she told Clark Foreman. It was "the culmination of a dream he has had for a long time and he adores it," she said. If she still had doubts, she kept them to herself, for she could see how reestablishing himself on the old family farm was helping make up for those long, empty years, when he tried so hard to fit back into the Montgomery community but could not quite do so.[22]

Increasingly, the Pea Level became the focus of Clifford Durr's world. He spent most of his time in the garden, growing all their own vegetables, making it beautiful with flowers and trees, and improving the property in every way. In 1971 Lulah, who had inherited some money, bought her father a tractor, which just delighted him. When the Durr Drug Company went public and they became for the first time in their married life quite well-to-do, Virginia had hoped that

Cliff, Virginia, and one of their grandchildren, at Pea Level (Courtesy of the Alabama State Department of Archives and History)

they might travel more, but Cliff was not at all keen. "The very idea of going anywhere out of town" made him sick, she once told Jim Dombrowski ruefully. Pea Level was his world now, and he had little interest in leaving it for long. Given the fulfillment he got from the property, which occupied so much of his time, it is scarcely sur-prising that his book remained uncompleted.[23]

A sure gauge to his love for the Pea Level and the peace he felt there were the long letters Durr wrote to his children, trying to bring to them, too, the feel of the place. He described to them in detail its sights and its sounds, the changes of seasons, the sun and the storms, the flowers and the trees, hoping to make them sense it as he did. "March has come in like a sopping wet, bad tempered lion," he told Ann in 1971; "Corn Creek has been roaring like a mighty cataract." When Lulah told him about the tractor, he was ecstatic. "With its spreading oaks and pines, its clear streams with their banks pink and white with mountain laurel," he wrote, slightly tongue-in-cheek, "its dogwoods and azaleas, its bowers of roses . . . the Pea Level is the most impressive estate south of Middleburg, Vg. At least it is on the way to being as soon as I get my hands on that tractor and break it into my way of thinking." Later that year he wrote at length to Tilla about the sheer beauty of watching the morning sun make patterns of light on the damp grass. If he lived his last years in what was, even for him, great serenity, much of the reason can be found in the joy his home brought to him.[24]

Nevertheless, the last years of his life were not totally inactive ones politically. He probably worked as hard in the 1964 Goldwater-Johnson election campaign as he had done in any previous presidential election. Goldwater's opposition to the 1964 Civil Rights Act had great appeal in the South, and in Alabama the state Democratic party was hopelessly split as a consequence, with the majority, supporters of the governor, George C. Wallace, favoring a scheme to keep Johnson off the ballot altogether. Durr, along with the senior members of the state's congressional delegation, fought hard though unsuccessfully to defeat the plan, an effort which secured him the personal thanks of Sen. John Sparkman. Nevertheless, the state's Democrats were denied the chance to vote for electors pledged to support their party's presidential nominee, ironically, the first from the South in more than a century. Instead the Democrat electors, though ostensibly unpledged, were in reality Wallacites. Durr was distressed, though hardly unsurprised. He was extremely angry, though, when someone tore an "LBJ for the USA" sticker from his car, replacing it with a "Goldwater—64" one. He did not want to be mistaken for a Goldwaterite for a minute, even through political skulduggery, he complained bitterly. He need not have worried. No one who knew him would ever have thought that.[25]

Durr did his bit for LBJ at the Forum Club as well, speaking for the president in a Goldwater-Johnson debate. "To me, an Arizona Carpetbagger dressed in grey, is not a very convincing image of a Southern leader" was his contemptuous dismissal of the Republican nominee. Earlier that year he had taken the affirmative in another Forum Club debate on the proposition "That the Civil Rights Bill Now Pending before the United States Senate Should Be Enacted into Law," comparing himself to an Aztec human sacrifice in arguing the case and admitting that his "enthusiasm for the Bill is less than wholehearted." It would not have been necessary to bring it in, however, if Southerners had obeyed existing laws, including those flowing from the Thirteenth, Fourteenth and Fifteenth amendments. They had not done so, and the 1964 legislation was the result. Durr kept on putting forward his views in the atmosphere of the Forum Club even after the move to the Pea Level. In 1972 he took the negative on the resolution "That President Nixon Should Be Re-elected," claiming that the President lacked "moral and intellectual integrity." His last appearance there was in 1974, after the president's disgrace and resignation. Then, he argued against the proposition "The United States Is in an Irrevocable Moral Decline," using the Nixon resignation as a hopeful sign. He did not believe that corruption in government was any greater in the present era than in past periods of American history, he said, though perhaps it was more concentrated. Nevertheless, the propensity for its discovery was also greater, as the Watergate affray had shown.[26]

Toward the end of his life, Durr also saw signs of regeneration for his beloved South. Even at the height of the crisis surrounding the Selma-Montgomery march in 1965, with its "Bloody Sunday" and the subsequent murder of Mrs. Viola Liuzzo, there were some signs of hope. In a long magazine article, he spoke of the actual march as "a remarkable combination of good humor, goodwill, and enthusiasm, an impressive demonstration of nationwide insistence that old and obvious injustices be corrected now," and even the most intransigent of white Southerners were at last beginning to realize this. Repeating his familiar theme that the problem of the South was basically one of civil liberties and that dissent in the white community had for far too long been silenced by "the pressure of conformity," he predicted that the recent federal legislation on civil rights and voting guarantees would eventually put an end to that. It was one of the reasons he maintained his friendship with and admiration for Lyndon Johnson, despite the trauma of the Vietnam War, namely, the conviction that Johnson, more than any other politician, "freed the South from its generations of bondage to racism"—indeed, made it, at last, a region where he and others like him could finally live in increasing serenity.[27]

Nevertheless, there were some things Durr could not be serene about. One was the war in Vietnam, which he thought a disastrous mistake, the very antithesis of what America's global role should be. As late as 1973, the suicide of a young relative, in part the result of his Vietnam experience, could bring out the passionate intensity with which he had always opposed American involvement there.

The blame for the young man's death, he wrote Ann, should be put "where it belonged, in Vietnam." The experiences he had had there, what he had done, what he had seen, had permanently destroyed him. "God Damn Kennedy and his 'Best and Brightest' as well as Nixon and his palace guard" was his angry conclusion.[28]

The very fact that Richard Nixon was in the White House was, of course, anathema to him, for he had bitterly opposed him since the days of the postwar HUAC investigations, when Nixon, like McCarthy, used the climate of fear to make his national reputation. A lawyer soliciting funds for Nixon's 1972 reelection campaign received the tart response from Durr that, "having followed the career and methods of Richard Nixon rather closely since his first campaign for Congress in 1946, I will take my chances with the Democratic nominee." He believed, he went on to say, that the country would survive some honesty in government and "some truth to the people about its operation." As the Watergate scandal unraveled, he felt at once vindicated and alarmed. He did not for one moment believe, he told his daughter Lucy, that Nixon was the "mere victim of overzealous underlings," for he knew from bitter experience what "a past master in the art of dirty tricks" the president was. Knowing this made him fearful, for he was convinced Nixon's disregard for the law was such that he would call out the military rather than release the damning Watergate tapes.[29]

In 1974, Durr, along with the rest of the country, sat glued to the television screen watching the death throes of the Nixon presidency. Cliff for a time savored the idea that Nixon could make "two historical firsts, the first President to be convicted and the first to serve time in the pen." He was, he wrote Virginia, who was away visiting the grandchildren, bothered that he might resign and that this might result in everything being called off in the desire to get back "to the everyday problems of business and life." Yet when that eventually happened, Cliff felt a twinge of compassion for one sunk so low—but only a twinge. Nevertheless, he was glad the whole thing was over. "Nixon is out, Ford is in and all's well with the world"—at least that seemed to be the mood of the moment, he told Virginia. To a degree, he shared it. The new president, he felt, was "not an evil man," unlike his predecessor. Perhaps, after decades of divisive turmoil, America had finally come home. He certainly hoped so.[30]

Retirement, therefore, was not unpleasant. Durr was more in tune with Alabama than he had ever been since he left it in 1933, he was finally receiving recognition for the public contributions he had made, he was blissfully happy about the Pea Level, there were no longer any money worries, and most important of all, he had lived for nearly fifty years, despite all the trepidations he and Virginia had shared, in a happy, sustaining marriage. Moreover, he was often surrounded by his family and his growing array of grandchildren, and as Virginia once said, "that delights his soul." Truly, as he looked back on his life, Cliff Durr saw so much to be thankful for.[31]

The one nagging problem, however, was Cliff's health. He had not been a really well man for a long time. In addition to his back problems, he had suffered often from colds and influenza, and there was also the slight heart condition which the tension of the New Orleans hearing had exacerbated. From 1966 on, he was plagued with a series of debilitating ailments, often requiring lengthy spells in the hospital. In that year he was hospitalized for a high white blood count and various complications resulting from that. There were respiratory problems as well, and he was advised to cut down drastically on his smoking. He really had been very sick, Virginia told Jim Dombrowski, and "gave us all a terrible fright." Cliff was on the mend, she said, but still "had to be babied and fed and looked after." The debilitating illness had left him low in spirit, and they were planning a trip to visit their children and grandchildren as soon as he was fit to travel, as this always cheered him up.[32]

In February 1968 he was back in the hospital, this time with a recurrence of his old back condition, and had to spend some time in traction. Again, he became terribly depressed, mainly because of the enforced inactivity it entailed; he could not garden, nor could he get on with the building of the new house. He had picked up by the middle of the year, however, and was out building concrete walls again. Virginia wished he would slow down, but she knew she could not make him do so. "You cannot MAKE him do anything," she told Clark Foreman ruefully.[33]

In 1969, after suffering chest pains, he was diagnosed as having severe angina and again solemnly warned that at least he must restrict his smoking. Apart from a series of colds and influenza, from which he always took a long time to recover, he maintained reasonably good health until 1972, when Cliff was again in the hospital from early October until the week before Christmas. During routine prostate surgery, cancer cells were detected, and this required another operation. While recovering from this, he developed a severe

"Relaxing at Pea Level," 1973 (Courtesy of Virginia Foster Durr)

infection of the urinary tract. He was left so weak that he was warned against traveling for three months, and not until the trip to Britain and the hearty Scottish breakfasts did he fully recover his strength. Even then Virginia wished he would try to slow down a little.[34]

The next year was reasonably illness-free. Cliff had a bad cough early in the year but recovered, and Virginia thought him stronger than he had been for some years. His back was fine, and he was able to do quite heavy work, including the building of a fence and a barn. In May 1975, he was again readmitted to the hospital, this time with a pulmonary embolism. While there was obviously cause for some concern, the family was not unduly alarmed, given his medical history of the past few years. Ann and Walter even sent him a facetious telegram chiding him for succumbing to a "Nixon illness" and confidently predicting a swift recovery. It never came. On May 12, 1975,

Cliff at Pea Level, 1973 (Courtesy of the Alabama State Department of Archives and History)

he seemed much better—in fact, he chuckled heartily at his favorite passages from *Catch 22,* which he was reading for the third time. Later in the day, however, he died, quickly and peacefully. He was buried in the Durr family plot in Greenwood Cemetery, Montgomery.[35]

CONCLUSION

When the news of Clifford Durr's death got around, letters and telegrams of condolence and tribute poured in. Their very extent and variety revealed much about his career and the extent of his influence. Old New Dealers remembered the dedicated public official with whom they had worked in the 1930s and 1940s; civil libertarians recalled the courageous stand he had taken against the assaults on the First Amendment in the post-1945 climate of fear and suspicion. Some of those whom he had defended before HUAC or loyalty review boards also wrote. There were tributes from blacks whom he had quietly helped during the days of the Montgomery bus boycott and the beginnings of the civil rights revolution; from many of the young English visitors who had made the Durr home a resting place during their Southern peregrinations in the early 1960s; from politicians, both friend and foe—even George Wallace sent his condolences—from lawyers, scholars, journalists, broadcasters, novelists, and folk singers, many much better known than he, yet all of whom had found something profoundly important in their association with this modest, principled, essentially decent Southern gentleman.[1]

The same point could be made about the memorial service held in Washington a month after Durr's death. There, more than three hundred people heard a succession of speakers discuss both the breadth and significance of his public career and the quality of his personal example. The Honorable Abe Fortas talked about his work with the RFC and the DPC, focusing in particular on his defense work and speaking of the struggle he waged "against private greed to protect the public interest." Without Cliff Durr, he claimed, "the purposes of the vast government financing which the Defense Plant program supplied might have been misdirected and diverted." Red James, his former FCC assistant, spoke of his contribution there, again of his fight for the public interest and against congressional investigatory committees. Thomas Emerson picked up the latter theme in his discussion of Durr's contribution to freedom of expression in the United States. "Cliff's position on political liberties was Jeffersonian in philosophy and pure in practice," he said. Embracing wholeheartedly the rights guaranteed by the First Amendment, Durr believed their legitimate exercise strengthened rather than weakened the body politic, and "he courageously acted out these beliefs, both in the conduct of his own affairs and in his defense of others." In the decade following World War II, Cliff Durr was one of the few who recognized early the danger to these liberties through fear's corrosive effect and fought against it.[2]

I. F. Stone, the newspaperman, also spoke about Durr's opposition to the climate of McCarthyism, emphasizing the twin sources of his beliefs, Jefferson and Jesus. "Without ever acquiescing in the shame and superstitions of institutionalized religion," he said, "he drew sustenance from the Gospel and for him Jefferson and the First Amendment were the secular equivalent of the American faith and the embodiment of universal values." Charles G. Gomillion, Negro educator, recalled how the commitment to civil liberties embraced the drive for civil rights. Judge Rives talked of his skills and dedication as a lawyer and also of his confidence "in the underlying sense of fairness of his fellow Southerners." It had, he said, not been misplaced. Many were now coming to think as he had thought. He had "fought the good fight," and he had won it. Jessica Mitford and Tilla both spoke movingly about Cliff's human qualities—of his gentleness, his utter integrity, and his love for his family.[3]

If those who spoke on this occasion attempted to survey the scope of Clifford Durr's life, those who listened provided a visual reinforcement of the point. Lady Bird Johnson was there; so were Frank Oppenheimer, Eric Sevareid, and Studs Terkel. Virginia made sure that Rosa Parks was introduced to the gathering; she was sitting not far from one of the others whom the bus boycott made famous, Fred Gray. Politicians were there—old New Dealers like Benjamin Cohen, civil libertarians such as Linus Pauling and Corliss Lamont, radical lawyers like Leonard Boudin, civil rights activists like Anne Braden, Charles Morgan, and John Doar. The young black Georgia state legislator Julian Bond was prevented at the last minute from participating. By their presence, they testified to the significance of Durr's life for them.[4]

Those who spoke on that occasion managed to get across very well both the flavor of Durr's life and the impulsions which lay behind it and which gave meaning to his actions and opinions. Certainly I. F. Stone was close to the mark when he talked about Jesus and Jefferson being the twin sources of his beliefs. Durr lived his life a convinced and committed Christian. Perhaps the consequence of the New Orleans hearing of 1954 which saddened him the most was losing his Sunday school class. His Christianity led him into more than just church attendance; it led him, too, into a close involvement with the church as an institution wherever he was living. When he returned to Montgomery, he quickly became a deacon at First Presbyterian and left it in 1965, only after the greatest of torment, because of its refusal to admit blacks as worshipers. It hurt Cliff intensely to do this, all the more so because his brother James was the church's most prominent layman, and he hated causing him distress. Though he never joined another church and rarely attended thereafter, this certainly did not mean that his Christian witness had been diminished. A belief in the social and egalitarian aspects of the Christian message remained part of his life until its ending.[5]

Stone talked also about Jefferson, saying that, like most Southerners, Durr had grown up with an almost instinctive reverence for Jeffersonian concepts of democracy and a corresponding distrust of bigness, whether in government or in business. Though his New Deal experiences moderated somewhat the second of these precepts, the first remained throughout his life. Jefferson's beliefs in basic civil liberties, as exemplified by the Bill of Rights, became even more important to Durr as he saw them challenged. "I was always emotionally for the Bill of Rights," he recalled toward the end of his life, "and all these traditions and could recite them as well as anybody." But, like Wilbur Cash, he believed that Southerners had great difficulty dealing with abstractions, and he was no different from anyone else. The Jeffersonian principles and precepts had to be "made solid" with the "flesh and blood" of personal experience before he could appreciate fully their enduring importance. This was what the Goodwin Watson incident did to him. He said it provided the first practical example in his experience of what could happen when Jeffersonian guarantees were abandoned. The rest of his life was spent trying to ensure that they would be sustained. For example, Durr always denied that he had ever been specifically concerned with "improving the lot of black people." Rather, as he often said, he wished only to ensure that they, like every other American, were able to live with the protection the Constitution afforded them.[6]

When he spoke about the law and his reverence for it, it was always with a tincture of Jeffersonianism. Lawyers as a group he had little regard for, but the law was something different—a body of enduring principle and precedent, derived from a host of sources, but in the end answerable to the Constitution. The law, however, "like the house built on the sand," would "not hold up too long without a basis of accepted morality," and at times this base seemed disturbingly absent. That was where the Jeffersonian principles underlying the Bill of Rights were so enduringly important. In the end they continued to provide that base when all else had failed.[7]

Clifford Durr remained all his life as he had been born—an Alabamian and a Southerner. Unlike many others who went to Washington, he retained his identification with things Southern, including his accent, all the time he was away. He continued to vote absentee in Alabama rather than switch allegiances, and though he enjoyed his government work to the full, he always "felt I belonged down here in Alabama." When he decided to close up the Washington law practice in 1950, it was only Virginia's obvious unhappiness at the prospect that prevented him returning home then and there, and when he eventually did come back, he determined never to move away again. "I have the need of roots," he explained, "and I've got my roots down here." Moreover, "as ornery" as they were, he always liked the Southern people he lived with, even though at times "they didn't seem to love me so much." But "this is home to me," he said, no matter what.[8]

Virginia came to understand this deep, spiritual attachment to his roots, even if she could not always share it. Even at the height of their troubles in Montgomery, she said, he would wake up and say, "Thank God I am back in Alabama." It may have been a brier patch, he would often assert, but it was his brier patch, and the "s.o.b.s" in it were people with whom he was familiar. No one described better this intense love for his place and its people, even when they did not love him, than his wife. "He felt that he owned Alabama," she wrote perceptively. "It was his. The South was his. He didn't regard the Southern people as his enemy or the South as his enemy. It was his, and if they did wrong, well, that was his fault, too." When he felt ashamed of the South, as he came to do during the civil rights struggle, he did not except himself from the shame. How could he, for he was so much a part of the South, its history and its agony. Nevertheless, he never lost his faith in the ultimate sense of justice of Southern people and lived just long enough to see this faith at least partially vindicated. Clifford Durr's Southernness, the depth of the traditions in his background and his continuing love for his region, explained much about the man personally and the way he lived his life.[9]

To place Durr within the context of Southern liberalism is difficult. By nature a moderate, it was his commitment to civil liberties, not any passionate adherence to the cause of civil rights, which in the end placed him in opposition to the white supremacists of his region. His frequent insistence that he had little particular concern with the aspirations of black people as such but simply wished to ensure that they, like any other American, received equal protection of the laws has to be accepted; it set him apart to a degree from other Southern liberals, including his close friends Aubrey Williams and James Dombrowski, and even from Virginia. For they, and those like them, believed that the key to political, economic, and social change in the South could be found in the legitimate aspirations of its black citizens for full equality, and they worked actively and specifically to further that end, particularly through the SCHW and SCEF, its successor. Cliff Durr never joined these organizations; it was not in his nature to do so. He did not share their single-minded commitment to the realization of black civil rights or their insistence that "civil rights" and "civil liberties" could be readily separated. Still, it would have to be said that the end result was the same. Clifford Durr, no less than his wife or his friends, ended up as one of those few lonely souls who stood bravely against the rampant white racism of the post-Brown South. It was just that he arrived at this position from his civil liberties perspective, they from another, less eclectic point of view.

There were other factors in the formation of Durr's attitudes which should be mentioned. He arrived in Washington in 1933 without any deep commitment to public service as a career, and certainly without any philosophy of serving the public interest. When he left it in 1948, it was with the conviction that public service was a trust and should be regarded as such with the utmost seriousness. Moreover, there was such a concept as "the public interest," and it was the duty of the public servant both to promote and to defend it. It was this developing perspective that motivated his opposition to

Jesse Jones when in the DPC. It was the guiding impulse of his years on the FCC, manifesting itself in his vigorous advocacy of policies aimed at breaking the power of the radio networks and their sponsors in determining what was broadcast, in his insistence that applicants for radio licenses and for their renewal should be able to convince the commission of their concern for quality and breadth in programming, and in his tireless advocacy of the causes of educational and public radio. By the time his term on the FCC had finished, he had become clearly identified as the leading spokesperson for the public interest in radio, and as such a figure of some concern to the broadcasting executives, to the commercial station owners, and to their sponsors. It was also the time of his greatest public visibility.

Working for the New Deal gave Clifford Durr this sense of the public interest, as it did so many others. William Leuchtenburg has discussed well the effect the concentration on public concerns had on those who saw themselves as working with FDR for a better America, and Durr was no exception. He talked often about the selflessness of the early New Deal years, with everyone "performing above our own rated capacity," with little concern for salary and status, and with a real sense of being part of a cooperative enterprise of almost transcendental importance. If later, once the emergency had passed, more mundane concerns of position and place began to surface, public service nevertheless remained an "exciting and satisfying" way to work, and Durr never lost the sense of having taken part in a great public concern. The New Deal had a profound and permanent influence on him.[10]

Clifford Durr came from a large and loving family, and he established one of his own. He and Virginia shared nearly fifty years of marriage; she was, as their daughter Tilla once said, "his best friend." To Jessica Mitford, the Durrs seemed when first she met them to be "an amazingly ill-assorted couple"—she the firebrand, "one of nature's rebels," he "the Southerner with a conscience . . . conservative by nature, yet flung by history into a radical role." But she soon found out they were made for each other. "Like two trees of totally disparate species," they "supported and fortified each other" throughout their eventful and wonderfully successful marriage. As to his daughters, they loved him and thought him a hero. He delighted in them as individuals and as part of an extended family unit which included his mother, his brothers, and his sisters, and was easily expandable to include his growing number of grandchildren.

If Clifford Durr was serene in adversity, one reason was the strength and support his personal and family life gave him.[11]

Durr's friend Ray Jenkins finished his obituary for Durr with the following paragraph: "Hemingway . . . once wrote that the world will not tolerate the very good, the very gentle or the very brave, that it will break them or kill them. Cliff Durr proved that Hemingway was wrong about that, because he was all three, and he never broke, but lived life with zest and good humor to the very end."[12] He could not have had a better epitaph.

Notes

Preface

1. Various versions of this tale are scattered throughout the Durr Papers. This one comes from the transcript of a memorial service for Cliff Durr held in Washington on June 12, 1975. I found it in papers held privately by his eldest daughter, Ann Durr Lyon, and I thank her for making these available to me.

1. A Southern Boy

1. Interview with Clifford J. Durr, Columbia Oral History Collection, Columbia University, New York (henceforth Durr Interview, COHC).

2. Most of the genealogical information comes from a long letter Clifford Durr wrote to his first granddaughter, Nancy Lyon, on the occasion of her birth, December 5, 1958; see Cliff Durr to Nancy Lyon, December 5, 1958, Judkins-Durr Family Papers, Alabama Department of Archives and History (old classification; henceforth Judkins-Durr Papers), Box 1.

3. Ibid.

4. Ibid. See also J. Wayne Flynt, *Montgomery: An Illustrated History* (Woodland Hills, Calif.: Windsor Publications, 1980), p. 169.

5. Durr to Nancy Lyon, December 5, 1958; J. H. Judkins to Thomas M. Owen, March 31, 1908, Judkins-Durr Papers, Box 1.

6. J. H. Judkins to Thomas M. Owen, March 31, 1908; Durr to Nancy Lyon, December 5, 1958, Judkins-Durr Papers, Box 1.

7. Lucy Judkins Durr to Cliff Durr, March 27, 1945, Clifford J. Durr Papers, Alabama Department of Archives and History (old classification; henceforth Clifford Durr Papers), Box 3; Cliff Durr to Nancy Lyon, December 5, 1958, Judkins-Durr Papers, Box 1.

8. Judkins to Cliff Durr, October 12, 1915, Judkins-Durr Papers, Box 2.

9. Drafts of an autobiography, Clifford Durr Papers (old classification), Box 12.

10. Ibid.

11. Hollinger F. Barnard, ed., *Outside the Magic Circle: The Autobiography of Virginia Foster Durr* (University: University of Alabama Press, 1985), p. 211; interview with Virginia Foster Durr (henceforth Virginia Durr Interview), May 13, 1987.

12. Lucy Durr to Virginia Durr, September 12, 1976, Virginia Durr Papers, Alabama Department of Archives and History (new classification; henceforth Virginia Durr Papers [Alabama]), Box 2, Folder 5 (henceforth 2/5).

13. Clifford Durr Papers (new classification), 15/20, speeches and writings, fragments; Barnard, *Outside the Magic Circle*, p. 210.

14. Drafts of an autobiography, Clifford Durr Papers (old classification), Box 12.

15. Flynt, *Montgomery*, pp. 54–56; *A Brief History of Montgomery, Alabama* (Montgomery: Montgomery Chamber of Commerce, 1953), pp. 11–13; *Official Guide to the City of Montgomery* (Montgomery: Tintagel Club, 1948), pp. 56–57, 105; J. Mills Thornton III, "Challenge and Response in the Montgomery Bus Boycott of 1955–56," *Alabama Review* 33, no. 3 (July 1980): 166.

16. Flynt, *Montgomery*, pp. 53, 76.

17. Ibid., p. 80; Barnard, *Outside the Magic Circle*, pp. 212–13; *Official Guide*, p. 80; *Brief History of Montgomery*, p. 12.

18. J. M. Starke to John Wesley Durr, January 24, 1913; report cards from Starke University School, May 10, June 12, November 8, 1912, Judkins-Durr Papers, Box 1.

19. Drafts of an autobiography, Clifford Durr Papers (old classification), Box 12.

20. Ibid. See also Judkins-Durr Papers, Box 1, clipping from *Montgomery Advertiser*, 1906.

21. Drafts of an autobiography, Clifford Durr Papers (old classification), Box 12.

22. Ibid. See also Cliff Durr to his mother, July 9, September 3, 1912, October 22, 1913, Judkins-Durr Papers, Box 1.

23. Barnard, *Outside the Magic Circle*, p. 210; Cliff Durr speech "The Relevance of Morality," Washington, University of St. Louis, November 3, 1965, Clifford Durr Papers (new classification), 14/6, speeches; Kate Durr to Lucy Durr, July 28, 1913; Cliff Durr to his mother, July 28, 1913, Judkins-Durr Papers, Box 1; drafts of an autobiography, Clifford Durr Papers (old classification), Box 12.

24. Drafts of an autobiography, Clifford Durr Papers (old classification), Box 12.

25. Barnard, *Outside the Magic Circle*, pp. 295–96.

26. Ibid., p. 210; drafts of an autobiography, Clifford Durr Papers (old classification), Box 12.

27. Drafts of an autobiography, Clifford Durr Papers (old classification), Box 12.

28. Ibid.

29. *Montgomery Advertiser,* May 29, 1915; Kent E. Scislaw, ed., *When Mother Calls* (University: University of Alabama Press, 1981), pp. 31–32.

30. Scislaw, *When Mother Calls,* pp. 98–99; Albert B. Moore, *History of Alabama* (University, Ala.: Supply Store, 1934), p. 752. See also James B. Sellers, *History of the University of Alabama,* vol. 1, *1818–1902* (University: University of Alabama Press, 1953), pp. 357–59, 399–400, 434, 507–12.

31. John Wesley Durr to Cliff Durr, September 18, 1915; Cliff Durr to his mother, September 10, October 11, 1915; to his sister Lucy, October 1, 10, 1915, all in Judkins-Durr Papers, Boxes 1 and 2.

32. John Wesley Durr to Cliff Durr, January 11, 1916; Cliff Durr to Lucy Durr, November 4, 1915, Judkins-Durr Papers, Box 2.

33. Cliff Durr to his mother, November 17, 1915; to his father, November 20, 1915; John Wesley Durr II to Cliff Durr, November 22, 1915, Judkins-Durr Papers, Box 2.

34. Cliff Durr to Lucy Durr, October 1, 1915; to James Durr, October 22, 1915; to his father May 1, 1916; to Henrietta Walker, May 2, 1916, all in Judkins-Durr Papers, Box 2.

35. Cliff Durr to his mother, September 19, 1916, February 27, 1917; to his father, September 27, 1916, February 19, 1917; John Wesley Durr II to Cliff Durr, January 16, 1917, all in Judkins-Durr Papers, Box 2.

36. Cliff Durr to his father, March 2, 1917; to his mother, March 24, April 1, 1917, Judkins-Durr Papers, Box 2.

37. Cliff Durr to his mother, April 24, 1917, Judkins-Durr Papers, Box 2.

38. Cliff Durr to his father, April 8, 1917, Judkins-Durr Papers, Box 2.

39. Cliff Durr to his father, May 9, 1918, Judkins-Durr Papers, Box 2.

40. Cliff Durr to his mother, June 3, 1918, Judkins-Durr Papers, Box 2.

41. Cliff Durr to Lucy Durr, November 10, 1918, Judkins-Durr Papers, Box 2.

42. Cliff Durr to his mother, November 16, 1918, Judkins-Durr Papers, Box 2.

43. Cliff Durr to Lucy Durr, January 10, 1919, Judkins-Durr Papers, Box 3.

44. Cliff Durr to Lucy Durr, February 2, 1919, Judkins-Durr Papers, Box 3.

45. Cliff Durr to his father, April 21, 1919; John Wesley Durr to Clifford Durr, May 13, 1919, Judkins-Durr Papers, Box 3.

46. James J. Doster to Cliff Durr, May 13, 1919; Durr to Rhodes Secretariat, August 9, 1919, Judkins-Durr Papers, Box 3.

47. C. H. Bonneau to Durr, September 1, 1919; to "To Whom It May Concern," October 14, 1919; Addison White to Durr, October 15, 1919, all in Judkins-Durr Papers, Box 3.

48. Prof. Frank Aydelotte to Rhodes Scholars Elect, December 9, 1919, Judkins-Durr Papers, Box 3; *Montgomery Advertiser,* November 3, 1919.

2. Johnny Reb at Oxford

1. Cliff Durr to his father, December 31, 1919; Clifford Durr passport, Judkins-Durr Papers, Box 3.

2. Cliff Durr to his mother, January 4, 1920; to Lucy Durr, January 8, 1920; to Aunt Florence, January 11, 1920; to James H. Judkins, January 10, 1920, all in Judkins-Durr Papers, Box 3.

3. Cliff Durr to his mother, February 15, 18, 1920, Judkins-Durr Papers, Box 3.

4. Cliff Durr to his father, January 27, 1920; to James H. Judkins, February 16, 1920; to Aunt Florence, March 11, 1920, all in Judkins-Durr Papers, Box 3.

5. Cliff Durr to his mother, March 10, 1920; to James Durr, April 15, 1920, both in Judkins-Durr Papers, Box 3.

6. Cliff Durr to his mother, March 21, 1920, Judkins-Durr Papers, Box 3.

7. Cliff Durr to Little Auntie, July 5, 1920; to his father, August 8, 1920, Judkins-Durr Papers, Box 3.

8. Cliff Durr to James Durr, September 21, 1920; to his mother, September 12, 1920, Judkins-Durr Papers, Box 3.

9. Cliff Durr to his mother, October 16, December 18, 1920; to Little Auntie, November 24, 1920; to John Durr, December 24, 1920, all in Judkins-Durr Papers, Box 3.

10. Cliff Durr to his mother, January 23, 1921, Judkins-Durr Papers, Box 3.

11. Cliff Durr to his father, January 30, 1921, Judkins-Durr Papers, Box 3.

12. Cliff Durr to his mother, February 27, October 4, 1921, Judkins-Durr Papers, Box 3.

13. Cliff Durr to his father, April 3, 1921; to Lucy Durr, April 10, 1921, Judkins-Durr Papers, Box 3.

14. Cliff Durr to his father, April 3, 1921, Judkins-Durr Papers, Box 3.

15. Cliff Durr to his mother, April 22, 1921; to Lucy Durr, June 16, 1921, Judkins-Durr Papers, Box 3.

16. Cliff Durr to Lucy Durr, June 16, 1921; to James H. Judkins, July 19, 1921, Judkins-Durr Papers, Box 3; Virginia Durr Interview, February 1985.

17. Cliff Durr to his mother, July 1, 1921, Judkins-Durr Papers, Box 3.

18. Cliff Durr to his father, July 26, 1921; to his mother, August 22, 1921, Judkins-Durr Papers, Box 3.

19. Cliff Durr to James H. Judkins, July 19, 1921, January 24, 1922; to his mother, August 22, 1921, Judkins-Durr Papers, Box 3.

20. Cliff Durr to James H. Judkins, July 19, 1921; to his father, July 26, 1921, Judkins-Durr Papers, Box 3.

21. Cliff Durr to his mother, August 6, 15, 1921, Judkins-Durr Papers, Box 3.

22. Cliff Durr to James Durr, August 24, 1921; to James H. Judkins, September 2, 1921, Judkins-Durr Papers, Box 3.

23. Cliff Durr to his mother, October 4, 1921, Judkins-Durr Papers, Box 3.

24. Ibid.

25. Cliff Durr to his mother, September 25, 1921, Judkins-Durr Papers, Box 3.

26. Cliff Durr to his mother, October 25, November 6, 13, 1921; to Lucy Durr, October 30, 1921, Judkins-Durr Papers, Box 3.

27. Cliff Durr to his mother, December 26, 1921, January 18, 1922, Judkins-Durr Papers, Box 3.

28. Cliff Durr to his mother, May 15, June 5, 16, 1922; to Lucy Durr, March 16, April 19, 1922; to his father, March 26, 1922, all in Judkins-Durr Papers, Box 3.

29. Cliff Durr to his mother, July 4, 1922, Judkins-Durr Papers, Box 3; Barnard, *Outside the Magic Circle,* p. 213.

30. Cliff Durr to his mother, April 19, 1922, Judkins-Durr Papers, Box 3.

3. Learning the Law—and Other Things

1. Barnard, *Outside the Magic Circle,* p. 213; Virginia Durr Interview, May 13, 1987.

2. Barnard, *Outside the Magic Circle,* p. 213; Virginia Durr Interview, May 13, 1987. For Sara Mayfield, see Flynt, *Montgomery,* p. 86.

3. Barnard, *Outside the Magic Circle,* p. 214; Virginia Durr Interview, May 13, 1987.

4. Cliff Durr to his mother, October 17, November 15, December 3, 1923; to his father, September 10, October 11, 1923; to Lucy Durr Dunn, October 4, 1923; to James Durr, November 20, 1923, Judkins-Durr Papers, Box 3.

5. Clifford Durr to his father, May 20, July 29, August 18, 23, 1924; to his mother, April 16, December 1, 1924, Judkins-Durr Papers, Box 3.

6. Cliff Durr to John W. Durr III, February 18, 1924, Judkins-Durr Papers, Box 3.

7. Cliff Durr to Lucy Durr Dunn, February 6, 1924, Judkins-Durr Papers, Box 3.

8. Cliff Durr to Lucy Durr Dunn, March 10, November 16, 1924; to his mother, October 19, 1924, Judkins-Durr Papers, Box 3.

9. Cliff Durr to his mother, November 15, 1923, June 9, 1924, Judkins-Durr Papers, Box 3; Virginia Durr to author, May 4, 1988, letter in author's possession.

10. Cliff Durr to his mother, March 19, 1924, Judkins-Durr Papers, Box 3.

11. Cliff Durr to his mother, July 1, November 9, 1924, Judkins-Durr Papers, Box 3.

12. Cliff Durr to his mother, December 1, 7, 1924, Judkins-Durr Papers, Box 3; Barnard, *Outside the Magic Circle,* p. 214.

13. Leah Rawls Atkins, *The Valley and the Hills: An Illustrated History of Birmingham and Jefferson County* (Woodland Hills, Calif.: Windsor Publications, 1981), pp. 129–38.

14. Ibid., pp. 178–79.

15. Barnard, *Outside the Magic Circle,* pp. 66–67, 214; Virginia Durr Interview, May 13, 1987.

16. Cliff Durr to his mother, November 19, 1925, Judkins-Durr Papers, Box 3; Lucy Durr Dunn to Virginia Foster Durr, November 26, 1925; Lucy Judkins Durr to Virginia Foster Durr, November 21, 1925, Virginia Durr Papers (Alabama), 1/2. *Birmingham Age-Herald,* April 6, 1926; Barnard, *Outside the Magic Circle,* p. 70.

17. Barnard, *Outside the Magic Circle,* pp. 3–14. The quotation is from page 5.

18. Ibid., pp. 21–22, 31.

19. Ibid., pp. 30–34, 41–42. See also Virginia Van der Veer Hamilton, *Hugo Black: The Alabama Years* (Baton Rouge: Louisiana State University Press, 1972), pp. 81–82.

20. Barnard, *Outside the Magic Circle,* pp. 50–63; Jessica Mitford to Virginia Durr, May 13, 1975, Virginia Durr Papers, Schlesinger Library, Radcliffe College (henceforth, Virginia Durr Papers [Radcliffe]), Box 1.

21. Barnard, *Outside the Magic Circle,* pp. 43, 46–47.

22. Ibid., pp. 72–74.

23. Ibid.; Cliff Durr to Virginia Durr, June 20, July 9, 1930, Virginia Durr Papers (Alabama), 1/2.

24. Barnard, *Outside the Magic Circle,* p. 74; Virginia Durr Interview, May 13, 1987; Cliff Durr to his mother, March 6, 1928, Durr Family Papers, Alabama Department of Archives and History (new classification), 4/3.

25. Hugo Black to Cliff Durr, July 18, October 3, 1932; Durr to Black, February 26, 1932, Hugo L. Black Papers, Library of Congress (henceforth Black Papers). I consulted copies of the Library of Congress collection held privately by Clifford Durr's eldest daughter, Ann Durr Lyon, and I thank her for permitting me to do so. See also Barnard, *Outside the Magic Circle,* pp. 78–81.

26. Barnard, *Outside the Magic Circle,* pp. 74–79; Virginia Durr Interview, May 13, 1987.

27. Barnard, *Outside the Magic Circle,* pp. 83–84; Cliff Durr to his mother, March 29, 1933, Clifford Durr Papers (old classification), Box 1.

28. Ibid.

29. Ibid.

30. Barnard, *Outside the Magic Circle,* p. 85.

31. Cliff Durr to Virginia Durr, April 29, 1933, Virginia Durr Papers (Alabama), 1/2.

32. Ibid.

33. Ibid., and Cliff Durr to Virginia Durr, undated 1933, Virginia Durr Papers (Alabama), 1/2.

4. New Dealer

1. James S. Olson, "Reconstruction Finance Corporation," in *Government Agencies*, ed. Donald R. Whitnah (Westport, Conn.: Greenwood Press, 1983), pp. 462–66; Susan Estabrook Kennedy, *The Banking Crisis of 1933* (Lexington: University Press of Kentucky, 1973), pp. 19, 36–40.

2. Olson, "Reconstruction Finance Corporation," pp. 463–64; Kennedy, *Banking Crisis*, p. 44; James S. Olson, *Herbert Hoover and the Reconstruction Finance Corporation, 1931–33* (Ames: Iowa State University Press, 1977), pp. 106–12.

3. Kennedy, *Banking Crisis*, pp. 189–90; William E. Leuchtenburg, *Franklin D. Roosevelt and the New Deal, 1932–1940* (New York: Harper and Row, 1963), p. 71.

4. Leuchtenburg, *Roosevelt and the New Deal*, pp. 71–72; Albert U. Romasco, *The Politics of Recovery: Roosevelt's New Deal* (New York: Oxford University Press, 1983), pp. 54–56.

5. Kennedy, *Banking Crisis*, p. 192; Romasco, *Politics of Recovery*, p. 57.

6. Kennedy, *Banking Crisis*, p. 194.

7. Cliff Durr to his mother, May 5, July 13, October 29, 1933, Clifford Durr Papers (old classification), Box 1.

8. Barnard, *Outside the Magic Circle*, pp. 89–90, 116–20.

9. Leuchtenburg, *Roosevelt and the New Deal*, p. 76; Barnard, *Outside the Magic Circle*, pp. 109, 152, 188; Virginia Durr Interview, February 1985.

10. Jerold S. Auerbach, *Unequal Justice: Lawyers and Social Change in Modern America* (New York: Oxford University Press, 1976), pp. 168, 173.

11. Cliff Durr to William H. Trueman, Birmingham, Alabama, February 1, 1935; to Brobeck, Phleger, and Harrison, San Francisco, January 18, 1934, April 11, 1935; to Ralph B. Jones, Boston, April 7, 1934; Fleming, Hamilton, Diver, and Lichliter, Miami, to Cliff Durr, July 23, 1934, all in Records of the Reconstruction Finance Corporation, National Archives, Washington D.C. (henceforth RFC Records), Group 46, Legal Files, Box 1 (henceforth 46/1).

12. Memo for Cliff Durr, Carter Council Commercial Bank, Olive Hill, Kentucky, November 12, 1935; A. J. Hobson, assistant secretary, RFC, to the treasurer, June 11, 1935, both in RFC Records, 46/13.

13. Cliff Durr to his mother, October 29, 1933, July 7, December 9, 1934, Clifford Durr Papers (old classification), Box 1.

14. Cliff Durr to his mother, February 12, 1935, Clifford Durr Papers (old classification), Box 1.

15. Cliff Durr to his mother, July 7, 1934, March 17, 1936, Clifford Durr Papers (old classification), Box 1.

16. Cliff Durr to his mother, July 7, 1934, February 12, 1935, February 17, 1936, Clifford Durr Papers (old classification), Box 1.

17. Durr Interview, COHC; Cliff Durr to Harry E. Meek, Loan Agency, RFC, Little Rock, Arkansas, December 3, 1936; to J. W. Jones, Federal Reserve Branch Bank, Denver, Colorado, December 23, 1936, RFC Records, 46/1.

18. Cliff Durr to Thomas Schneider, Loan Agency, RFC, New York, June 17, 1938, RFC Records, 46/4; to George R. Wilbur, agency counsel, Loan Agency, RFC, Portland, Oregon, January 19, 1938, RFC Records, 46/9.

19. Cliff Durr to Walter R. Wolf, City Bank Farmers Trust Co., New York, May 27, 1937, RFC Records, 46/9; to Larry L. Gelbach, acting manager, Loan Agency, RFC, Cleveland, June 1, 1936, RFC Records, 46/13.

20. Cliff Durr to his mother, January 16, March 10, 1937; to his father, February 9, 1937, in Clifford Durr Papers (old classification), Box 1.

21. Cliff Durr to his mother, May 29, 1939, Clifford Durr Papers (old classification), Box 1; Auerbach, *Unequal Justice*, p. 225.

22. Cliff Durr to his mother, May 29, 1939; Advisory Committee on Lawyers—Drafts and Suggestions, both in Clifford Durr Papers (old classification), Box 1; Presidential Advisory Committee on Lawyers, Durr memo, May 13, 1939, and final report, both in Clifford Durr Papers (new classification), 27/4.

23. Barnard, *Outside the Magic Circle*, pp. 89, 116–20; file "Economic Needs of the South," in Clifford Durr Papers (new classification), 27/5.

24. Barnard, *Outside the Màgic Circle*, pp. 90–94.

25. Ibid., p. 90; Cliff Durr to his mother, September 18, October 26, 1935, May 31, 1936, January 13, 1937; to his father, February 9, 1937, all in Clifford Durr Papers (old classification), Box 1.

26. Barnard, *Outside the Magic Circle*, p. 108; Clifford Durr to his mother, April 18, 1938, Clifford Durr Papers (old classification) Box 1; Virginia Durr to Jessica Mitford, June 3, 1959, Jessica Mitford Papers, Ohio State University Library, Columbus (henceforth Mitford Papers), Virginia Durr Correspondence, Folder 3.

27. Leuchtenburg, *Roosevelt and the New Deal*, p. 149; Barnard, *Outside the Magic Circle*, pp. 97–99, 103–6.

28. Barnard, *Outside the Magic Circle*, pp. 94–95; Cliff Durr to his mother, December 9, 1934, November 13, 1937, Clifford Durr Papers (old classification), Box 1; *New York Times*, September 30, October 1, 1937; Clifford J. Durr, "Hugo L. Black: A Personal Appraisal," *Georgia Law Review* 6, no. 1 (1971): 13–14.

29. Leuchtenburg, *Roosevelt and the New Deal*, p. 242; Barnard, *Outside the Magic Circle*, pp. 99–102, 106.

30. Virginia Durr to Andrew Roberts, December 10, 1973, Virginia Durr Papers (Radcliffe), Carton 2; Jessica Mitford to Virginia Durr, July 5, 1977, Virginia Durr Papers (Radcliffe), Box 1.

31. Cliff Durr to his mother, September 9, 1939, April 19, 1940, Clifford Durr Papers (old classification), Box 1.

32. For DPC, see Gerald T. White, "The Defense Plant Corporation," in *Government Agencies,* ed. Donald R. Whitnah (Westport, Conn.: Greenwood Press, 1983), pp. 81–86. See also White's monograph, *Billions for Defense: Government Financing by the Defense Plant Corporation during World War II* (University: University of Alabama Press, 1980).

33. White, *Billions for Defense,* p. 1.

34. Ibid., pp. 1–2.

35. *New York Times,* May 27, 1940.

36. White, *Billions for Defense,* pp. 3–5.

37. Leuchtenburg, *Roosevelt and the New Deal,* p. 318; White, *Billions for Defense,* pp. 4–7.

38. White, *Billions for Defense,* p. 16; Virginia Durr Interview, February 1985. See also Gerald T. White, "Financing Industrial Expansion for War: The Origin of the Defense Plant Corporation Leases," *Journal of Economic History* 9, no. 2 (November 1949): 156–83.

39. Clifford J. Durr, "A History of the Defense Plant Corporation," unpublished manuscript, first draft, p. 2, Clifford Durr Papers (old classification), Box 20. There are several drafts of this paper in the Durr collection. I shall identify them by successive drafts, when I am able.

40. White, *Billions for Defense,* p. 16; Durr, "History of the DPC," first draft, p. 3.

41. Durr, "History of the DPC," first draft, pp. 4–5.

42. White, *Billions for Defense,* p. 19; Durr, "History of the DPC," second draft, pp. 11–12.

43. Durr, "History of the DPC," first draft, pp. 5–8; Durr to Jesse Jones, June 29, 1940, Clifford Durr Papers (new classification), 27/6.

44. Durr, "History of the DPC," second draft, p. 16.

45. Ibid.

46. Ibid., first draft, p. 18; White, *Billions for Defense,* p. 24; Records of the Defense Plant Corporation, National Archives, Washington, D.C. (henceforth DPC Records), Group 145, Minutes, vol. 6, Meeting of Board of Directors, May 9, 1941; Durr Interview, COHC.

47. Cliff Durr to his mother, August 27, 1940, Clifford Durr Papers (old classification), Box 1.

48. White, *Billions for Defense,* pp. 26–29; White, "Defense Plant Corporation," p. 82.

49. White, *Billions for Defense,* pp. 28, 34; Virginia Durr Interview, May 13, 1987; *Washington Post,* January 13, 1941.

50. White, "Defense Plant Corporation," p. 83. See Cliff Durr to R. J. Grigsby, August 15, 1941; to W. Drager, July 26, 1941, Clifford Durr Papers (new classification), 28/1; Cliff Durr to Edward T. Dixon, January 24, 1941, Clifford Durr Papers (new classification) 27/8; DPC Records, Group 145, Minutes.

51. Cliff Durr to his mother, February 9, May 30, 1941, Clifford Durr Papers (old classification), Box 1.

52. White, *Billions for Defense,* p. 39; Jones to Schram, February 7, 1941, Clifford Durr Papers (new classification), 27/8.

53. White, *Billions for Defense,* pp. 42–49; Cliff Durr to Jones, July 26, August 2, 1941; to Husbands, September 26, 1941, Clifford Durr Papers (new classification), 28/5.

54. White, *Billions for Defense,* p. 47; Knudsen to Jones, October 16, 1941; Minutes of Special Meeting of Board of Directors, October 16, 1941, in DPC Records, Group 145, Minutes, vol. 11, pt. 1.

55. Cliff Durr to Sheldon Hackney, January 16, 1971, Clifford Durr Papers (old classification), Box 9; Jesse H. Jones, with Edward Angby, *Fifty Billion Dollars: My Thirteen Years with the RFC* (New York: Macmillan, 1951), pp. 340–41.

56. Cliff Durr to David Lilienthal, November 27, 1941, Clifford Durr Papers (new classification), 28/5.

57. Cliff Durr to his mother, February 7, September 12, 1939, July 12, 1940; W. O. Aydelotte to Cliff Durr, July 9, 1940, all in Clifford Durr Papers (old classification), Box 1; Barnard, *Outside the Magic Circle,* p. 140.

58. Jessica Mitford, *Daughters and Rebels* (Boston: Houghton Mifflin, 1960), p. 283; Barnard, *Outside the Magic Circle,* pp. 137–41.

59. Mitford, *Daughters and Rebels,* pp. 255, 283; Barnard, *Outside the Magic Circle,* pp. 145–46; Jessica Mitford, *A Fine Old Conflict* (London: Michael Joseph, 1977), pp. 30–31; Cliff Durr to his mother, December 20, 1941, Clifford Durr Papers (old classification), Box 1.

5. Wave-Length Warrior

1. Kent Anderson, "Federal Communications Commission," in *Government Agencies,* ed. Donald R. Whitnah (Westport, Conn.: Greenwood Press, 1983), pp. 219–23.

2. James L. Baughman, *Television's Guardians: The FCC and the Politics of Programming, 1958–1967* (Knoxville: University of Tennessee Press, 1985), pp. 6–9; Charles A. Siepmann, *Radio's Second Chance* (Boston: Little Brown, 1946), pp. 8–10.

3. Anderson, "Federal Communications Commission," pp. 221–22; Erik Barnouw, *The Golden Web: A History of Broadcasting in the United States,* vol. 2, *1933–1953* (New York: Oxford University Press, 1968), pp. 169–73.

4. Barnouw, *Golden Web,* pp. 169–70.

5. Baughman, *Television's Guardians,* p. 9; Barnouw, *Golden Web,* p. 180; Charles A. Siepmann, *Radio, Television, and Society* (New York: Oxford University Press, 1950), pp. 27–33.

6. James H. Rowe to Franklin D. Roosevelt, June 10, 1941; Roosevelt to

Rowe, June 16, 1941; Lister Hill to General Watson, September 26, 1941, all in Franklin D. Roosevelt Papers, Franklin D. Roosevelt Library, Hyde Park, New York (henceforth FDR Papers), Personal Subject File 1059-A Durr. For Durr's remarks on the fortieth anniversary of the FCC, see *Federal Communications Commission Bar Journal* 27, no. 2 (1974): 117–23, copy in Clifford Durr Papers (new classification), Box 25.

7. FCC press release, February 1, 1942; Rep. Lyndon B. Johnson to Roosevelt, October 14, 1941, both in Clifford Durr Papers (old classification), Box 1.

8. "Dissent by Durr," *Tide,* November 1, 1945, clipping in Clifford Durr Papers (new classification), 11/6.

9. Merger of Western Union Telegraph Company and Postal Telegraph Company, FCC decision, September 27, 1943, in Clifford Durr Papers (old classification), Box 4; Records of the Federal Communications Commission, National Archives, Washington D.C. (henceforth FCC Records), Record Group 173 Minutes, Minutes of Special Meeting, September 27, 1943; *Washington News,* September 28, 1943; *Birmingham News,* October 4, 1943, clippings in Clifford Durr Papers (new classification), 11/5.

10. Barnouw, *Golden Web,* pp. 224–27.

11. Powel Crosley for transferer to the Aviation Corporation, transferee—Record of FCC decision, August 2, 1945, Clifford Durr Papers (old classification), Box 4.

12. Ibid. See also Barnouw, *Golden Web,* pp. 225–26.

13. Powel Crosley for transferer to the Aviation Corporation, transferee—Record of FCC decision, August 2, 1945, Clifford Durr Papers (old classification), Box 4. See also Barnouw, *Golden Web,* pp. 225–26.

14. Powel Crosley for transferer to the Aviation Corporation, transferee—Dissent of Clifford J. Durr, Clifford Durr Papers (old classification), Box 4.

15. Ibid.

16. Barnouw, *Golden Web,* p. 227; *Broadcasting Magazine,* June 4, September 12, 1945; *Washington Evening Star,* September 22, 1945; *Montgomery Advertiser,* October 4, 1945; *Birmingham News,* January 2, 1945, all clippings in Clifford Durr Papers (new classification), 11/6.

17. Stephen Rich Rintoul, transferer, Western Connecticut Broadcasting, transferee, FCC decision, December 19, 1945, in Clifford Durr Papers (old classification), Box 4.

18. Stephen Rich Rintoul, transferer, Western Connecticut Broadcasting, transferee, Durr dissent, December 1945, in Clifford Durr Papers (old classification), Box 4; *Broadcasting Magazine,* January 28, 1946, clipping in Clifford Durr Papers (new classification), Box 21.

19. Interview with Clifford J. Durr, December 29, 1974, Southern Oral History Collection, University of North Carolina at Chapel Hill (henceforth Durr Interview, SOHC).

20. Ibid.

21. Luther Bentley III, "A Critical Study of the Federal Communications Commission Career of Clifford Judkins Durr, Emphasizing His Support for the Public Interest As It Applies to Broadcasting" (Master's thesis, Auburn University, 1972), p. 60, copy in Clifford Durr Papers (old classification), Box 13; Petition of Robert J. Harold Scott, FCC Decision, July 19, 1946, Clifford Durr Papers (old classification), Box 4.

22. Durr Interview, SOHC; John and Lorraine Frank, "Cliff Durr: Wave-Length Warrior," *The Progressive* (Madison, Wis.), September 18, 1944, clipping in Clifford Durr Papers (old classification), Box 3.

23. Durr Interview, SOHC; Cliff Durr to his mother, June 16, 1944, Clifford Durr Papers (old classification), Box 3; Candace Ward and Allan Tullos, "Clifford Durr, the FCC Years," *Southern Exposure* 2, no. 4 (Winter 1975): 14–22.

24. Siepmann, *Radio's Second Chance,* pp. 246–49.

25. FCC press release, August 24, 1945, in Clifford Durr Papers (old classification), Box 1.

26. Ibid.

27. Ibid.

28. Cliff Durr to Charles Siepmann, September 6, 1945; *Time,* June 24, 1946, clipping, both in Clifford Durr Papers (old classification), Box 3.

29. Cliff Durr to his mother, November 16, 1944; to Cecil Sarver, January 4, 1945, Clifford Durr Papers (old classification), Box 3.

30. Speech to the Independent Citizens Committee of the Arts, Sciences, and Professions, June 23, 1945, Clifford Durr Papers (new classification), 13/5.

31. *Broadcasting Magazine,* May 15, 1944, clipping in Clifford Durr Papers (new classification), 11/5; Cliff Durr to his mother, November 16, 1944, Clifford Durr Papers (old classification), Box 3.

32. *New Republic,* December 25, 1944, clipping in Clifford Durr Papers (old classification), Box 3; Cliff Durr to Lucien Hilmer, April 28, 1943; Sen. Homer T. Bone to Durr, September 25, 1944, both in Clifford Durr Papers (new classification), 29/9, 30/2.

33. "Public Service Responsibility of Broadcast Licensees," FCC Report, March 7, 1946, copy in Clifford Durr Papers (old classification), Box 3; Clifford Durr Interview, SOHC.

34. Clifford Durr Interview, SOHC; Barnouw, *Golden Web,* pp. 227–31.

35. Clifford Durr Interview, SOHC; Barnouw, *Golden Web,* pp. 227–31.

36. Clifford Durr Interview, SOHC; Barnouw, *Golden Web,* pp. 229–32; Blue Book drafts and final copy, Leah E. McClelland to Charles R. Denny, March 8, 1946, all in Clifford Durr Papers (old classification), Box 3; Bentley, "FCC Career of Durr," p. 45.

37. See the file of letters in Clifford Durr Papers (old classification), Box 3; *Time,* June 24, 1946, clipping in Clifford Durr Papers (old classification), Box 13; *Montgomery Advertiser,* June 24, 1946.

38. Clifford Durr Interview, SOHC; Barnouw, *Golden Web,* pp. 233–36.

39. Cliff Durr to his mother, May 14, 1946, Clifford Durr Papers (old classification), Box 3; Virginia Durr to Ann Durr, April 30, 1947, Ann Durr Lyon Papers.

40. "The Post War Relationship between Government and Business," speech to American Economic Association, January 5, 1943, Clifford Durr Papers (new classification), 13/3.

41. "Some Economic Problems of Radio Broadcasting," speech to Nieman Fellows, March 10, 1944; "Radio and Women's Responsibility," speech to the New York Federation of Women's Clubs, October 29, 1944, both in Clifford Durr Papers (new classification), 13/4; "Responsibility of Radio to Education," speech to the Conference on FM Education, Austin, Texas, September 27, 1945, Clifford Durr Papers (new classification), 13/5; "The Social Significance of Radio," speech to the Joint Radio Committee of the Congregational Christian, Methodist, and Presbyterian U.S.A. Churches, January 27, 1946, Clifford Durr Papers (new classification), 13/6.

42. Press release, Heinl Radio News Service, March 20, 1947; *Radio Daily,* October 29, 1947; *Billboard,* May 15, 1948, all clippings from Clifford Durr Papers (new classification), 11/8, 12/1.

43. Cliff Durr to Virginia Durr, October 9, 14, 1946, Virginia Durr Papers (Alabama), 1/4; to his mother, October 2, 1946; to Charles Siepmann, November 12, 1946, both in Clifford Durr Papers (old classification), Box 3.

44. Cliff Durr, notes on Moscow trip, Clifford Durr Papers (old classification), Box 3; Virginia Durr Interview, May 13, 1987; Barnard, *Outside the Magic Circle,* p. 192.

45. Cliff Durr to Virginia Durr, October 22, 30, 1946, Virginia Durr Papers (Alabama), 1/4; to his mother, October 25, November 9, 1946; notes on Moscow trip, all in Clifford Durr Papers (old classification), Box 3.

46. Cliff Durr to his mother, June 1, 17, 18, August 3, 1943; to his sister Lucy, July 28, 1943, Clifford Durr Papers (old classification), Box 2.

47. Barnard, *Outside the Magic Circle,* pp. 152–70.

48. Ibid., pp. 153–54.

49. Lucy Judkins Durr to Clifford Durr, March 27, 1945, Clifford Durr Papers (old classification), Box 3.

50. Cliff Durr to his mother, March 31, 1945, Clifford Durr Papers (old classification), Box 3.

51. Ibid.

52. Cliff Durr to his mother, November 16, 1944, Clifford Durr Papers (old classification), Box 3; James M. Barnes to William P. Hassett, April 6, 1945; Franklin D. Roosevelt to James M. Barnes, April 9, 1945, FDR Papers, PSF, Wallace Folder 2–45.

53. Sen. John Bankhead to Durr, April 12, September 5, 1945; Durr to Bankhead, April 17, 1945, Clifford Durr Papers (old classification), Box 3; Virginia Durr Interview, February 1985.

54. Cliff Durr to Thurman Arnold, April 17, 1945, Clifford Durr Papers (old classification), Box 3; James M. Barnes to Roosevelt, April 11, 1945, FDR Papers, PSF, Wallace Folder 2–45.

55. Address by Wayne F. Coy, Washington Hotel, June 19, 1948, copy in Clifford Durr Papers (old classification), Box 5.

56. *Washington Post*, April 28, 1948; *New York Times*, May 2, 1948; *Newsweek*, July 19, 1948, clipping in Clifford Durr Papers (new classification), 12/1; fragment of letter, Clifford Durr Papers (new classification), 15/20.

57. Address by Wayne F. Coy, June 19, 1948, Clifford Durr Papers (old classification), Box 5.

6. The Loyalty Issue

1. Cliff Durr to his mother, January 29, 1942, Clifford Durr Papers (old classification), Box 1; Leuchtenburg, *Roosevelt and the New Deal*, pp. 280–81; Athan Theoharis, *Seeds of Repression: Harry S. Truman and the Origins of McCarthyism* (Chicago: Quadrangle Books, 1971), p. 7.

2. James L. Fly to Martin Dies, November 19, 1941, Clifford Durr Papers (new classification), 35/7; drafts of an autobiography, Clifford Durr Papers (old classification), Box 12; Durr Interviews, COHC, SOHC.

3. Dies to Fly, November 18, 1941; Fly to Dies, November 19, 1941, Clifford Durr Papers (new classification), 35/7; Virginia Durr Interview, February 1985.

4. Drafts of an autobiography, Clifford Durr Papers (old classification), Box 12; *Broadcasting Magazine*, December 8, 1941, clipping in Clifford Durr Papers (new classification), 35/7.

5. Barnouw, *Golden Web*, p. 178; drafts of an autobiography, Clifford Durr Papers (old classification), Box 12; Clifford Durr, Memoranda for Commissioners on Dr. Goodwin Watson, December 17, 30, 1941, Clifford Durr Papers (new classification), 35/7.

6. Clifford Durr, Memorandum for Commissioners on Dr. Goodwin Watson, December 30, 1941, Clifford Durr Papers (new classification), 35/7.

7. Drafts of an autobiography, Clifford Durr Papers (old classification), Box 12.

8. Ibid.; Barnouw, *Golden Web*, p. 176; Durr Interview, SOHC.

9. FCC press conference, January 26, 1942, Clifford Durr Papers (new classification), 35/7; Cliff Durr to his mother, January 29, 1942, Clifford Durr Papers (old classification), Box 1.

10. Cliff Durr to Sen. James Mead, February 2, 20, 1942; to Sen. Lister Hill, February 18, 1942; to Sen. Harry S. Truman, February 9, 14, 1942; to William

F. Russell, February 5, 1942; Truman to Durr, February 21, 1942, all in Clifford Durr Papers (new classification), 35/7; drafts of an autobiography, Clifford Durr Papers (old classification), Box 12.

11. Clifford Durr, memo for files, May 1, 1942, Clifford Durr Papers (new classification), 35/7; drafts of an autobiography, Clifford Durr Papers (old classification), Box 12.

12. Cliff Durr to Rep. Joe Hendricks, June 15, 1942, Clifford Durr Papers (new classification), 35/7.

13. Watson to Cliff Durr, May 14, 1942, Clifford Durr Papers (old classification), Box 1; drafts of an autobiography, Clifford Durr Papers (old classification), Box 12; Durr Interview, SOHC.

14. Drafts of an autobiography, Clifford Durr Papers (old classification), Box 12; Durr Interview, SOHC; Barnouw, *Golden Web*, p. 180.

15. Durr Interview, COHC; Cliff Durr to Francis Biddle, March 18, 1942, Clifford Durr Papers (old classification), Box 1.

16. Hoover to Fly, March 28, 1942; Cliff Durr to Rep. Joe Starnes, April 2, 1942, both in Clifford Durr Papers (old classification), Box 1.

17. Cliff Durr to Edwin D. Dickinson, July 28, 1942; to his mother, July 10, 1942, both in Clifford Durr Papers (old classification), Box 1.

18. "FBI File," Virginia Durr Papers (Radcliffe), 2/93; Barnard, *Outside the Magic Circle*, pp. 146–48.

19. Raoul Berger to Neil Anderson, acting chief, trial section, Department of Justice, April 29, 1942; Wendell Berge, Jr., assistant attorney general to attorney general, April 29, 1942, both in Eugene Meyer Papers, Manuscript Division, Library of Congress (henceforth Meyer Papers), Box 105, FCC Matters.

20. Cliff Durr to his mother, January 23, 29, 1943; to Samuel T. Rayburn, September 24, 1943, Clifford Durr Papers (old classification), Box 2.

21. Eugene Meyer, "A Public Letter to Speaker Rayburn," *Washington Post*, September 27, 1943; *Washington Post*, October 15, 1943.

22. *New York Times*, April 11, 18, 1943.

23. Cliff Durr to John W. Durr, May 27, 1943; to James Durr, June 21, 1943; to Rayburn, May 13, 1943; Durr press release, May 13, 1943, all in Clifford Durr Papers (old classification), Box 2.

24. *Washington Post*, September 27, 1943; Durr to Rayburn, September 24, 1943; Durr press release, September 24, 1943, both in Clifford Durr Papers (old classification), Box 2.

25. *Washington Post*, September 27, 1943; Durr Interview, COHC; Barnouw, *Golden Web*, p. 179; Nathan Green to Eugene Meyer, September 17, 1943, Meyer Papers, Box 105.

26. *Washington Post*, September 27, 1943; copies of letters, telegrams, and press clippings, including clipping from *Louisville Courier Journal*, October 2, 1943, all in Meyer Papers, Box 105.

27. *Washington Evening Star*, September 30, 1943; *Washington Post*, Oc-

tober 1, 1943; *Louisville Courier Journal*, October 2, 1943, clippings in Meyer Papers, Box 105.

28. *Christian Science Monitor*, September 29, 1943; *P.M.*, October 1, 1943; "The Case against Cox," *Nation*, October 9, 1943, p. 397, all clippings in Meyer Papers, Box 105; Cliff Durr to his sister Lucy, October 1, 1943; "The Dogged Durr," clipping from *Birmingham Age-Herald*, October 2, 1943, in Clifford Durr Papers (old classification), Box 2.

29. *Washington Post*, October 19, 20, 1943; Robert D. Leigh, "Politicians vs Bureaucrats: The Case of FCC Chairman Fly and Congressman Cox," *Harpers Magazine* 190, no. 1136 (January 1945): 97–105.

30. Cliff Durr to Eugene Meyer, September 30, 1943; Meyer to Durr, October 1, 1943, Meyer Papers, Box 105.

31. Barnouw, *Golden Web*, pp. 246–48; drafts of an autobiography, Clifford Durr Papers (old classification), Box 12; Hollywood Community Radio Group Inc., interoffice memorandum, January 14, 1948, Clifford Durr Papers (old classification), Box 4.

32. Hoover to Paul A. Porter, October 1, 1946, Clifford Durr Papers (old classification), Box 4.

33. Charles R. Denny to Hoover, November 26, 1946; Hoover to Denny, December 18, 1946, Clifford Durr Papers (old classification), Box 4.

34. FBI Report on Hollywood Community Radio Group, Clifford Durr Papers (old classification), Box 4.

35. Drafts of an autobiography, Clifford Durr Papers (old classification), Box 12.

36. Raymond Lewis to Harry Plotkin, FCC interoffice memorandum, February 12, 1947, Clifford Durr Papers (old classification), Box 4.

37. Bernard Koteen to FCC general counsel, April 15, 1947, Clifford Durr Papers (old classification), Box 4; drafts of an autobiography, Clifford Durr Papers (old classification), Box 12.

38. Speech to Annual Dinner of the National Association of Educational Broadcasters, October 26, 1947, Clifford Durr Papers (old classification), Box 4.

39. *Washington Post*, November 19, 1947.

40. J. Edgar Hoover press statement, November 21, 1947, Clifford Durr Papers (old classification), Box 4; *New York Times*, November 22, 1947.

41. Paul A. Walker to Hoover, December 1, 1947, Clifford Durr Papers (old classification), Box 4.

42. Position of Clifford J. Durr on letter to Mr. J. Edgar Hoover, December 1, 1947, Clifford Durr Papers (old classification), Box 4.

43. Ibid.

44. Statement of Sen. Homer Capehart, December 5, 1947, Clifford Durr Papers (old classification), Box 4; *New York Times*, December 6, 1947.

45. Jennings Perry, "Durr's Derring," and I. F. Stone, "Another Victory for the Thought Police," both in *P.M.*, December 3, 1947, clippings; Cliff Durr to his mother, December 19, 1947; to Felix Frankfurter, November 28,

1947; M. S. Novik to Durr, December 3, 1947; Robert W. Hudson to Durr, December 6, 1947; Thomas Emerson to Durr, December 12, 1947, all in Clifford Durr Papers (old classification), Box 4.

46. Marquis Childs, "Freedom of Conscience," *Washington Post*, November 19, 1947.

47. David Caute, *The Great Fear: The Anti-Communist Purge under Truman and Eisenhower* (New York: Simon and Schuster, 1978); Theoharis, *Seeds of Repression*, pp. 98–99.

48. Theoharis, *Seeds of Repression*, pp. 99–100.

49. Ibid., pp. 101–3, 106–7.

50. Earl Latham, *The Communist Controversy in Washington: From the New Deal to McCarthy* (Cambridge: Harvard University Press, 1966), esp. pp. 365–68; Alan D. Harper, *The Politics of Loyalty: The White House and the Communist Issue, 1946–1952* (Westport, Conn.: Greenwood Press, 1969), pp. 47–51.

51. Dissenting Views of Commissioner Clifford J. Durr Re Proposed Rules Governing FCC Loyalty Procedures, Clifford Durr Papers (old classification), Box 4.

52. Ibid.

53. Ibid.

54. Ibid.

55. Ibid.

56. "Freedom and Fear," speech by Clifford J. Durr at the annual luncheon of the Associated Church Press and the National Religious Publicity Council, Hotel Commodore, New York, April 17, 1947, Clifford Durr Papers (old classification), Box 4.

57. See "Freedom and Fear," *Birmingham Age Herald*, September 13, 1947, clipping in Clifford Durr Papers (new classification), 11/8; "Where We Stand Today," speech to the National Citizens Conference on Civil Liberties, April 14, 1948; "Science and the Bill of Rights," speech to the Acoustical Society of America, April 23, 1948, both in Clifford Durr Papers (new classification), 13/7; *Washington Post*, September 3, 1947.

58. Cliff Durr to William Rice, June 24, 1947; to Harold McCarty, August 29, 1947, Clifford Durr Papers (old classification), Box 4.

59. Richard B. Hull, president, National Association of Educational Broadcasters, to Truman, March 30, 1948; John Haynes Holmes to Truman, March 24, 1948; Mrs. Marion L. Stern to Truman, January 25, 1947, all in Harry S. Truman Papers, Harry S. Truman Library, Independence, Missouri (henceforth Truman Papers), Official File—FCC; *Variety*, March 31, 1948; *Billboard*, April 3, 17, 1948, Clifford Durr Papers (new classification), 11/9; Sen. Joseph McCarthy to Cliff Durr, May 27, 1947; Durr to McCarthy, June 3, 1947, both in Clifford Durr Papers (old classification), Box 4.

60. Cliff Durr to his brother James, April 15, 1948; to his mother, April 23, 1948, Clifford Durr Papers (old classification), Box 5; *New York Times*, April 23, 1948; Durr Interview, SOHC.

7. Civil Liberties Lawyer

1. William Rice, University of Wisconsin Law School, to Cliff Durr, June 14, 1947, Clifford Durr Papers (old classification), Box 4; Wilbur G. Katz, University of Chicago Law School, to Cliff Durr, March 10, 1948; Durr to his brother James, April 15, 1948; George A. Graham, Department of Politics, Princeton University, to Cliff Durr, May 4, 1948; Durr to Graham, May 14, 1948, all in Clifford Durr Papers (old classification), Box 5; Barnard, *Outside the Magic Circle,* p. 219.

2. Graham to Cliff Durr, June 18, 1948; Cliff Durr to his mother, July 12, 1948, Clifford Durr Papers (old classification), Box 5.

3. Barnard, *Outside the Magic Circle,* p. 196; Cliff Durr to his mother, July 12, 1948; Jacques F. Ferand to Cliff Durr, July 17, 1948, both in Clifford Durr Papers (old classification), Box 5.

4. Cliff Durr to his mother, July 27, August 22, 1948, Clifford Durr Papers (old classification), Box 5.

5. Cliff Durr to his mother, August 31, 1948; notes on his trip, August 23, September 4, 1948, both in Clifford Durr Papers (old classification), Box 5.

6. Cliff Durr, notes on his trip, Clifford Durr Papers (old classification), Box 5.

7. Cliff Durr to his mother, August 31, 1948, Clifford Durr Papers (old classification), Box 5; Barnard, *Outside the Magic Circle,* p. 197.

8. Barnard, *Outside the Magic Circle,* p. 8; Cliff Durr, notes on his trip, Clifford Durr Papers (old classification), Box 5.

9. Cliff Durr to Mrs. Rainey, October 8, 1948; to Milo Perkins, October 26, 1948; to Wayne Coy, November 4, 1948, all in Clifford Durr Papers (old classification), Box 5; drafts of an autobiography, Clifford Durr Papers (old classification), Box 12.

10. Drafts of an autobiography, Clifford Durr Papers (old classification), Box 12.

11. Ibid.; Barnard, *Outside the Magic Circle,* p. 221.

12. Drafts of an autobiography, Clifford Durr Papers (old classification), Box 12; Durr Interview, COHC.

13. Drafts of an autobiography, Clifford Durr Papers (old classification), Box 12; Durr Interview, COHC.

14. Drafts of an autobiography, Clifford Durr Papers (old classification), Box 12; Durr Interview, COHC.

15. Barnard, *Outside the Magic Circle,* pp. 221–22; Durr Interview, COHC.

16. Drafts of an autobiography, Clifford Durr Papers (old classification), Box 12.

17. Ibid.

18. Ibid.; Durr Interview, COHC.

19. Drafts of an autobiography, Clifford Durr Papers (old classification), Box 12; Durr Interview, COHC.

20. Ibid. See also Cliff Durr to John F. Lukens, assistant executive secretary, Central Loyalty Security Board, Department of the Air Force, October 28, 1948, Clifford Durr Papers (old classification), Box 6.

21. Drafts of an autobiography, Clifford Durr Papers (old classification), Box 12; Durr Interview, COHC.

22. Drafts of an autobiography, Clifford Durr Papers (old classification), Box 12; Durr Interview, COHC.

23. Drafts of an autobiography; clipping from *Washington Times Herald*, June 14, 1947, in Clifford Durr Papers (old classification), Box 12.

24. Drafts of an autobiography, Clifford Durr Papers (old classification), Box 12.

25. Ibid.

26. Oppenheimer, press release, Clifford Durr Papers (old classification), Box 12.

27. *Hearings Regarding Communist Infiltration of Radiation Laboratory and Atomic Bomb Project at the University of California, Berkeley, California*, vols. 1, 2, and 3, *Hearings before the Committee on Un-American Activities, House of Representatives*, 81st Cong., 1st sess., April 22, 26, May 25, June 10, 14, 1949 (Washington, D.C.: Government Printing Office, 1949), 1:355–77 (henceforth *Radiation Laboratory Hearings*); drafts of an autobiography; clipping file; Oppenheimer to Dean Acheson, February 20, 1950; to Cliff Durr, June 20, 1949, undated February 1950, all in Clifford Durr Papers (old classification), Box 12.

28. Ellen W. Schrecker, *No Ivory Tower: McCarthyism and the Universities* (New York: Oxford University Press, 1986), p. 143.

29. *Radiation Laboratory Hearings* 1:321–26, 347–51.

30. Bohm to Cliff Durr, December 12, 1950, Clifford Durr Papers (old classification), Box 12; Barnard, *Outside the Magic Circle*, p. 223.

31. Malcolm Hobbs, "The Subversive Drugstore," *Nation*, November 26, 1949, clipping in Clifford Durr Papers (old classification), Box 6; Virginia Durr Interview, May 13, 1987.

32. Hobbs, "Subversive Drugstore"; file on sale of Investment Pharmacy Inc., both in Clifford Durr Papers (old classification), Box 6; *Hearings Regarding Communism in the District of Columbia*, pt. 1; *Hearings before the Committee on Un-American Activities, House of Representatives*, 81st Cong., 1st sess., June 28, 29, July 6, 12, 28, 1949 (Washington, D.C.: Government Printing Office, 1949), pp. 695–98.

33. Durr Interview, SOHC; "FBI File," Virginia Durr Papers (Radcliffe), 2/93.

34. Auerbach, *Unequal Justice*, pp. 158, 198–200. See also Percival R. Bailey, "The Case of the National Lawyers Guild, 1939–1958," in *Beyond the Hiss Case: The FBI, Congress, and the Cold War*, ed. Athan Theoharis (Philadelphia: Temple University Press, 1982), pp. 129–75.

35. Bailey, "National Lawyers Guild," p. 132; Auerbach, *Unequal Justice*, pp. 203–4.

36. Virginia Durr Interview, May 13, 1987; *New York Times*, February 23, 1949; "The Voice in Democracy," address to National Lawyers Guild, February 21, 1948, Clifford Durr Papers (new classification), 13/7.

37. Kenneth O'Reilly, *Hoover and the Un-Americans: The FBI, HUAC, and the Red Menace* (Philadelphia: Temple University Press, 1983), pp. 133–35; Athan Theoharis, *Spying on Americans: Political Surveillance from Hoover to the Huston Plan* (Philadelphia: Temple University Press, 1978), pp. 100–103.

38. Cliff Durr to Truman, June 20, 1949, Truman Papers, CF 10-B.

39. Bailey, "National Lawyers Guild," p. 137; O'Reilly, *Hoover and the Un-Americans*, pp. 135–39; Truman to Cliff Durr, June 23, 1949, Truman Papers, OF-10B; *New York Times*, June 29, 1949.

40. Report of the Special Committee of the National Lawyers Guild Appointed to Study Certain Alleged Practices of the FBI, Truman Papers, OF—Legal Cases.

41. Bailey, "National Lawyers Guild," pp. 162–63; O'Reilly, *Hoover and the Un-Americans*, pp. 135–39.

42. "FBI File," Virginia Durr Papers (Radcliffe), 2/93; John Rosenberg, "The FBI Shreds Its Files," *Nation* 226, no. 4 (February 4, 1978): 108–11.

43. Statement of Clifford J. Durr, president of the National Lawyers Guild, on the North Atlantic Pact, for the Senate Committee on Foreign Relations; The Bill of Rights and the Mundt-Ferguson Bills (S.1194 and S.1196): An Analysis of the Provisions and Opinion on Their Constitutionality, prepared by the National Lawyers Guild; Clifford J. Durr, "Keynote Address," *Lawyers Guild Review* 10, no. 2 (Spring 1950): 2–6, all in National Lawyers Guild Papers, Alexander Meiklejohn Civil Liberties Institute, Berkeley, California; *Control of Subversive Activities: Hearings before a Subcommittee of the Senate Committee on the Judiciary, United States Senate*, 81st Cong., 1st sess., on S.1194 and S.1196, *Bills to Protect the United States against Certain Un-American and Subversive Activities*, April 29, May 4, 6, 18, 19, 20, June 10, 1949 (Washington, D.C.: Government Printing Office, 1949), pp. 126–50; Virginia Durr Interview, May 13, 1987.

44. Freda Kirchwey to Cliff Durr, February 21, 1949; Durr to Kirchwey, February 28, 1949, Clifford Durr Papers (old classification), Box 6; Clifford J. Durr, "How to Measure Loyalty," *Nation* 209, no. 17 (April 23, 1949): 470–73, copy in Clifford Durr Papers (new classification), 16/5.

45. Clifford J. Durr, "The Loyalty Order's Challenge to the Constitution," *University of Chicago Law Review* 16, no. 2 (Winter 1949): 298–306.

46. "Trial by Terror," a Palm Sunday sermon delivered at the First Unitarian Church of Denver, Colorado, March 18, 1951, published in 1960 by Southern Farm and Home, Inc. (Montgomery, Alabama), copy in Clifford Durr Papers (old classification), Box 12.

47. Ibid. See also Nona S. Brown to Cliff Durr, April 15, 1949; Bruce Bli-

ven to Durr, April 22, 1949; Jerry Tallmer to Durr, May 4, 1949; Guy Shipler to Durr, November 16, 1949, all in Clifford Durr Papers (old classification), Box 6; Durr, "Jesus a Free Speech Victim: Trial by Terror Two Thousand Years Ago," *The Churchman*, July 1960, pp. 7–8, August 1960, pp. 7–9; pamphlets from National Emergency Civil Liberties Committee (1960, 1982), all in Clifford Durr Papers (new classification), 16/7.

48. Clifford J. Durr, *Three Biblical Lessons in Civil Liberties* (Yellow Springs, Ohio: American Humanist Association, n.d.).

49. "The Loyalty Order and Due Process," "The Declaration of Independence," "Should the FBI Methods of Investigation Be Made Public?" Clifford Durr Papers (new classification), 13/8, 13/9; CBS People's Platform, March 26, 1950; American Town Meeting, April 25, 1950, transcripts in Clifford Durr Papers (new classification), 14/1.

50. Cliff Durr to his mother, November 10, December 4, 1948, Clifford Durr Papers (old classification), Box 5; Barnard, *Outside the Magic Circle*, pp. 224–25.

51. Cliff Durr to his mother, March 15, 1949; to George Graham, April 13, 1949, Clifford Durr Papers (old classification), Box 6.

52. Cliff Durr to his mother, June 20, December 30, 1949; to George Graham, May 2, 1950, Clifford Durr Papers (old classification), Box 6; Virginia Durr to Ann Durr, October 10, 1948, undated 1949, Ann Durr Lyon Papers; Barnard, *Outside the Magic Circle*, p. 233.

8. Colorado Interlude

1. Barnard, *Outside the Magic Circle*, p. 244; James Durr to Cliff Durr, June 9, 1949; Cliff Durr to James Durr, June 15, 1949, Clifford Durr Papers (old classification), Box 6; Virginia Durr to Ann Durr, January 21, 1950, Ann Durr Lyon Papers.

2. Virginia Durr to Ann Durr, March 24, 1950, Ann Durr Lyon Papers.

3. Virginia Durr to Ann Durr, April 24, 1950, Ann Durr Lyon Papers; to Clark Foreman, undated 1950, Virginia Durr Papers (Radcliffe), 1/24; Barnard, *Outside the Magic Circle*, p. 224; Virginia Durr Interview, February 1985.

4. John A. Salmond, *A Southern Rebel: The Life and Times of Aubrey Willis Williams, 1890–1965* (Chapel Hill: University of North Carolina Press, 1983), pp. 179–81; drafts of an autobiography, Clifford Durr Papers (old classification), Box 12; Barnard, *Outside the Magic Circle*, p. 233.

5. James Patton to Cliff Durr, April 25, 1950; C. E. Huff to Durr, May 8, 1950; Cliff Durr to Huff, May 2, 1950; to his mother, May 22, 1950; to John Durr, May 24, 1950; to Leonard Boudin, May 24, 1950, all in Clifford Durr Papers (old classification), Box 6; Virginia Durr to Ann Durr, April 24, 1950, Ann Durr Lyon Papers.

6. Cliff Durr to his mother, July 16, 23, August 30, 1950; to Tex Gold-

schmidt, October 19, 1950; Ann Durr to Mrs. John Durr, October 10, 1950, all in Clifford Durr Papers (old classification), Box 6.

7. Sen. Styles Bridges, "The Communist Invasion of Agriculture," speech to United States Senate, September 7, 1950, clipping from *Congressional Record,* in Clifford Durr Papers (old classification), Box 6.

8. Cliff Durr to Bridges, September 27, 1950, Clifford Durr Papers (old classification), Box 6; to Edward Harris, September 28, 1950, Clifford Durr Papers (old classification), Box 7; drafts of an autobiography, Clifford Durr Papers (old classification), Box 12.

9. Cliff Durr to his mother, November 13, 1937, March 18, 1940, Clifford Durr Papers (old classification), Box 1; to his mother, July 23, 1950, Clifford Durr Papers (old classification), Box 6.

10. Ann Durr to Mrs. John Durr, January 3, 1951, Clifford Durr Papers (old classification), Box 6; Cliff Durr to Frank Oppenheimer, October 30, 1950; Russell L. Shepherd to Durr, November 14, 20, 1950, all in Clifford Durr Papers (old classification), Box 7; drafts of an autobiography, Clifford Durr Papers (old classification), Box 12; Barnard, *Outside the Magic Circle,* pp. 233–34.

11. Barnard, *Outside the Magic Circle,* p. 234.

12. Initiators, American Peace Crusade to Sponsors, February 7, 1951; pamphlet, "Let the People Speak for Peace," both in Clifford Durr Papers (old classification), Box 7.

13. Cliff Durr to Edwin Hoyt, May 5, 1951, Clifford Durr Papers (old classification), Box 12; Barnard, *Outside the Magic Circle,* p. 234.

14. Barnard, *Outside the Magic Circle,* pp. 234–35; Virginia Durr to Ann Durr, undated 1951, Ann Durr Lyon Papers.

15. Virginia Durr to Ann Durr, undated 1951, Ann Durr Lyon Papers.

16. Minutes of meeting of Alabama Farmers Union, April 12, 1951, Clifford Durr Papers (old classification), Box 12; Williams to Patton, May 14, 1951, Aubrey W. Williams Papers, Franklin D. Roosevelt Library, Hyde Park, New York (henceforth Williams Papers), Box 33.

17. Dallas Smythe to Cliff Durr, March 7, 1951; Eugene Cotton to Durr, March 13, 1951; Karl Heiser to Durr, March 16, 1951; Don Riddle to Durr, March 17, 1951, all in Clifford Durr Papers (old classification), Box 7.

18. Cliff Durr to Hugh Wilson, March 4, 1951, Clifford Durr Papers (old classification), Box 7.

19. Ibid.

20. Edwin Hoyt to Cliff Durr, April 12, 1951; Durr to Hoyt, May 5, 1951, Clifford Durr Papers (old classification), Box 12.

21. Cliff Durr to Edwin Hoyt, May 5, 1951, Clifford Durr Papers (old classification), Box 12.

22. Drafts of an autobiography, Clifford Durr Papers (old classification), Box 12; Virginia Durr to Ann Durr, undated 1951, Ann Durr Lyon Papers.

23. Virginia Durr to Mrs. Durr and Little Auntie, March 29, 1951, Clifford

Durr Papers (old classification), Box 7; Virginia Durr to Clark Foreman, undated 1951, Virginia Durr Papers (Radcliffe), 1/24.

24. Cliff Durr to his mother, April 7, 20, 1951; Virginia Durr to Mrs. Durr, April 19, 1951; Virginia Durr to Lucy Durr, April 27, 1951, all in Clifford Durr Papers (old classification), Box 7.

25. Cliff Durr to his mother, May 12, 1951; Virginia Durr to Mrs. Durr, April 19, 1951, Clifford Durr Papers (old classification), Box 7; Barnard, *Outside the Magic Circle,* p. 238.

9. Montgomery and New Orleans

1. Henry F. Bedford, *Trouble Downtown: The Local Context of Twentieth Century America* (New York: Harcourt Brace, 1978), pp. 134–35; Thornton, "Challenge and Response," pp. 166–68, 185.

2. Bedford, *Trouble Downtown,* pp. 134–35.

3. Drafts of an autobiography, Clifford Durr Papers (old classification), Box 12; Barnard, *Outside the Magic Circle,* pp. 241–42.

4. Cliff Durr to Ann and Walter Lyon, December 1, 1951, Ann Durr Lyon Papers.

5. Cliff Durr to Rudy Gilbert, January 25, 1952; to Houston Waring, January 31, 1952, Clifford Durr Papers (old classification), Box 7.

6. Cliff Durr to James L. Jones, March 21, 1952; to Hugh Wilson, May 1952; to Beanie Baldwin, June 4, 1952; to J. K. Galbraith, July 2, 1952, all in Clifford Durr Papers (old classification), Box 7; Barnard, *Outside the Magic Circle,* p. 243.

7. Virginia Durr to Clark Foreman, March 6, 1952, Virginia Durr Papers (Radcliffe), 1/25; to Otto Nathan, August 29, November 5, 1951, January 25, April 30, 1952, Virginia Durr Papers (Radcliffe), 1/63.

8. Cliff Durr to Claims Department, George Rogers Clark Mutual Casualty Company, August 6, 1952; to Rosell Hyde, August 30, 1952; to the First National Bank of Wetumpka, October 27, 1952; to Max Goldman, September 11, 1953; to George Graham, September 17, 1953; Walter M. Beale to Durr, August 27, 1952, all in Clifford Durr Papers (old classification), Box 7.

9. Cliff Durr to Rudy Gilbert, April 21, 1953; to Judge Wolfe, April 24, 1953, Clifford Durr Papers (old classification), Box 7.

10. Virginia Durr to Clark Foreman, April 14, September 16, November 23, 1953, Virginia Durr Papers (Radcliffe), 1/26.

11. Virginia Durr to Ann Durr Lyon, December 4, 1953, March 7, April 14, 1954, Ann Durr Lyon Papers.

12. Barnard, *Outside the Magic Circle,* pp. 254–55. A full account of this hearing and the events leading up to it can also be found in Salmond, *Southern Rebel,* pp. 229–46.

13. Barnard, *Outside the Magic Circle,* p. 255; Virginia Durr to Ann Durr Lyon, March 7, 1954, Ann Durr Lyon Papers.

14. Salmond, *Southern Rebel,* p. 219; Barnard, *Outside the Magic Circle,* pp. 152–70.

15. Salmond, *Southern Rebel,* pp. 220–25. See also Morton Sosna, *In Search of the Silent South: Southern Liberals and the Race Issue* (New York: Columbia University Press, 1977), pp. 88–104, 140–49; Thomas A. Kreuger, *And Promises to Keep: The Southern Conference for Human Welfare, 1938–1948* (Nashville: Vanderbilt University Press, 1967).

16. Salmond, *Southern Rebel,* pp. 227–29.

17. Barnard, *Outside the Magic Circle,* pp. 254–55; Robert E. Griffith, *The Politics of Fear: Joseph R. McCarthy and the Senate* (Lexington: University Press of Kentucky, 1970), pp. 118–20, 208–10; Theoharis, *Seeds of Repression,* p. 15.

18. Salmond, *Southern Rebel,* pp. 231–33; Barnard, *Outside the Magic Circle,* pp. 256–57; *New Orleans Times Picayune,* March 10, 1954. Professor Taylor was later excused from attendance on medical grounds.

19. Salmond, *Southern Rebel,* p. 233; *New Orleans Times Picayune,* March 10, 18, 1954; Joseph and Stewart Alsop, "Information on the Informer," *Washington Post,* April 16, 1954.

20. *Southern Conference Educational Fund Inc. Hearings before the Subcommittee to Investigate the Administration of the Internal Security Act and Other Internal Security Laws of the Committee of the Judiciary, United States Senate,* 83d Cong., 2d sess., *On Subversive Influence in the Southern Conference Educational Fund Inc.,* March 18, 19, 20, 1954 (Washington, D.C.: Government Printing Office, 1955), pp. 6–80 (henceforth *SCEF Hearing*); *New Orleans Times Picayune,* March 10, 1954.

21. *SCEF Hearing,* pp. 84–90.

22. Ibid., pp. 90–95.

23. Salmond, *Southern Rebel,* p. 236; Durr Interview, COHC.

24. *SCEF Hearing,* pp. 100–20.

25. Ibid., pp. 122–33.

26. Ibid., pp. 133.

27. Ibid., pp. 139–44.

28. Ibid., pp. 144–45.

29. Ibid., pp. 145–48; *St. Louis Post Dispatch,* March 19, 1954; *Atlanta Constitution, Washington Post, New York Times,* and *New York Herald Tribune,* all March 20, 1954.

30. *SCEF Hearing,* pp. 150–51, 162; *Washington Post,* March 21, 1954.

31. Barnard, *Outside the Magic Circle,* pp. 263–64; *Washington Post* and *New York Times,* March 21, 1954; Durr Interview, COHC.

32. *Montgomery Advertiser,* March 21, 25, 1954; *New Orleans Times Picayune,* March 21, 24, 1954.

33. Hubert Wilson to Cliff Durr, March 21, 1954; Allan Barth to Durr, March 20, 1954; Decca to Virginia, undated; Tilla and Lulah to the Durrs,

undated; Clark Foreman to Durr, March 21, 1954; Ruth E. Moore to Durr, April 11, 1954, all in Clifford Durr Papers (old classification), Box 7.

34. Barnard, *Outside the Magic Circle,* p. 267; Virginia Durr to Ann Durr Lyon, April 14, 1954, Ann Durr Lyon Papers.

35. Barnard, *Outside the Magic Circle,* pp. 267–69; Virginia Durr to Jessica Mitford, May 1, 1954, Mitford Papers, Durr Correspondence, Folder 2; Virginia Durr Interview, May 13, 1987.

36. Durr to Hubert Wilson, May 18, 1954, Clifford Durr Papers (old classification), Box 7; Barnard, *Outside the Magic Circle,* p. 269.

37. Virginia Durr to Ann Durr Lyon, April 14, 1954, Ann Durr Lyon Papers; to Jessica Mitford, May 1, 1954, Mitford Papers, Durr Correspondence, Folder 2.

38. Cliff Durr to Lister Hill, July 3, 1954, Clifford Durr Papers (old classification), Box 7.

39. Clifford Durr, "FBI File," Virginia Durr Papers (Radcliffe), 2/93.

40. Salmond, *Southern Rebel,* pp. 242–43; *I. F. Stones Weekly,* December 12, 1955.

10. The Civil Rights Revolution

1. Cliff Durr to Frank and Tilla Parker, November 30, 1965, Clifford Durr Papers (old classification), Box 9. See also Durr to Charles Siepmann, December 30, 1958, Clifford Durr Papers (old classification), Box 7.

2. Barnard, *Outside the Magic Circle,* p. 251; Jessica Mitford to Ring Lardner, Jr., April 7, 1977, Mitford Papers, Virginia Durr Correspondence, Folder 9.

3. Cliff Durr to Foreman, May 18, 1955, Clifford Durr Papers (old classification), Box 7.

4. Virginia Durr to Foreman, undated 1955, Virginia Durr Papers (Radcliffe), 1/27.

5. David J. Garrow, *Bearing the Cross: Martin Luther King Jr. and the Southern Christian Leadership Conference* (New York: Morrow, 1986), pp. 13–15; David J. Garrow, ed., *The Montgomery Bus Boycott and the Women Who Started It: The Memoirs of Jo Ann Gibson Robinson* (Knoxville: University of Tennessee Press, 1987), pp. 22–30; Thornton, "Challenge and Response," pp. 173–85, 230–34.

6. Garrow, *Bearing the Cross,* pp. 14–15.

7. Ibid., p. 15; Garrow, *Montgomery Bus Boycott,* pp. 37–39.

8. Virginia Durr to Jessica Mitford, undated and May 5, 1955, Mitford Papers, Virginia Durr Correspondence, Folder 2; Garrow, *Bearing the Cross,* p. 15.

9. Garrow, *Bearing the Cross,* pp. 15–16; Garrow, *Montgomery Bus Boycott,* p. 40; Virginia Durr to Jessica Mitford, undated 1955, Mitford Papers, Virginia Durr Correspondence, Folder 2.

10. Garrow, *Bearing the Cross*, p. 16; Garrow, *Montgomery Bus Boycott*, p. 42; Virginia Durr to Jessica Mitford, May 6, 1955, Mitford Papers, Virginia Durr Correspondence, Folder 2.

11. Garrow, *Bearing the Cross*, pp. 11–12.

12. Drafts of an autobiography, Clifford Durr Papers (old classification), Box 12; Durr Interview, COHC; Barnard, *Outside the Magic Circle*, pp. 278–79; Garrow, *Bearing the Cross*, pp. 11–13.

13. Drafts of an autobiography, Clifford Durr Papers (old classification), Box 12; Garrow, *Bearing the Cross*, pp. 13–14.

14. Garrow, *Montgomery Bus Boycott*, pp. 44–47.

15. Drafts of an autobiography, Clifford Durr Papers (old classification), Box 12; Virginia Durr to Clark Foreman, February 9, April 12, May 1, 29, 1956, Virginia Durr Papers (Radcliffe), 1/27.

16. Gray to Bryce Rucker, January 30, 1973, Clifford Durr Papers (old classification), Box 9.

17. Cliff Durr to Leonard Boudin, April 12, 1956, Virginia Durr Papers (Radcliffe), 1/27; Garrow, *Montgomery Bus Boycott*, p. 104.

18. Virginia Durr to Clark Foreman, September 20, 1954, June 9, 1955, Virginia Durr Papers (Radcliffe), 1/26, 1/27; Barnard, *Outside the Magic Circle*, pp. 269–70.

19. Virginia Durr to Clark Foreman, June 9, 1955, February 9, March 15, May 7, 1956, Virginia Durr Papers (Radcliffe), 1/27; to Otto Nathan, March 7, July 18, 1956, Virginia Durr Papers (Radcliffe), 1/63; to Jessica Mitford, April 16, 1956, Mitford Papers, Virginia Durr Correspondence, Folder 2.

20. Virginia Durr to Clark Foreman, January 7, July 1, 1957, Virginia Durr Papers (Radcliffe), 1/27.

21. Virginia Durr to Jessica Mitford, August 6, 1957, Mitford Papers, Virginia Durr Correspondence, Folder 2; to Clark Foreman, March 11, 1957, Virginia Durr Papers (Radcliffe), 1/28; Jessica Mitford to Ring Lardner, Jr., April 7, 1977, Mitford Papers, Virginia Durr Correspondence, Folder 9.

22. Virginia Durr to Clark Foreman, July 8, 1957; Cliff Durr to Robert Foreman, January 10, 1958, Virginia Durr Papers (Radcliffe), 1/28.

23. Virginia Durr Interview, May 13, 1987; Virginia Durr to Clark Foreman, January 1958 and undated 1958, Virginia Durr Papers (Radcliffe), 1/28, 1/29.

24. "In Defense of the Fifth," Unity Club, April 26, 1955; "Eisenhower v. Stevenson," Forum Club, 1956; "That the Fourteenth Amendment Is Invalid," Forum Club, September 25, 1958, all in Clifford Durr Papers (new classification), 14/3.

25. Virginia Durr Interview, February 1985; Barnard, *Outside the Magic Circle*, pp. 246–50, 304–5.

26. Barnard, *Outside the Magic Circle*, pp. 312–14.

27. Nat Hentoff, "A Conversation in Alabama," *New Yorker*, July 16, 1960; clipping in Clifford Durr Papers (new classification), 16/7.

28. Barnard, *Outside the Magic Circle*, pp. 312–14; *Montgomery Adver-*

tiser, August 7, 1960; Cliff Durr to Grover Hall, August 8, 1960, Clifford Durr Papers (old classification), Box 8.

29. Virginia Durr to Nat Hentoff, July 20, 1960; to Clark Foreman, August 29, 1960, both in Virginia Durr Papers (Radcliffe), 1/32.

30. Durr Interview, COHC.

31. Rufus Horne File, Clifford Durr Papers (old classification), Box 8.

32. Ibid.

33. Ibid.

34. Ibid.; Cliff Durr to Robert Foreman, January 10, 1958, Virginia Durr Papers (Radcliffe), 1/28.

35. Willie Howard File, Clifford Durr Papers (old classification), Box 8.

36. *Caesar Davis* v. *City of Montgomery* File, Clifford Durr Papers (old classification), Box 8; Jessica Mitford to Ring Lardner, Jr., April 7, 1977, Mitford Papers, Virginia Durr Correspondence, Folder 9.

37. *Caesar Davis* v. *City of Montgomery* File, Clifford Durr Papers (old classification), Box 8; *Montgomery Advertiser,* June 20, 1961.

38. *Bessie May Prince* v. *B. G. Bryant,* Clifford Durr Papers (old classification), Box 8.

39. Ibid.

40. Ibid.; Cliff Durr to Ira De Ment, July 26, 1963; Walter Knable to Durr, August 28, 1963, both in Clifford Durr Papers (old classification), Box 8.

41. Virginia Durr to Clark Foreman, May 22, 1959, February 8, July 26, December 8, 1961, Virginia Durr Papers (Radcliffe), 1/31, 1/33.

42. Garrow, *Bearing the Cross,* pp. 155–56.

43. Ibid.

44. *City of Montgomery* v. *Anna Gach*; *City of Montgomery* v. *Frederick Gach,* Clifford Durr Papers (old classification), Box 8.

45. *City of Montgomery* v. *Anna Gach,* Clifford Durr Papers (old classification), Box 8. See also James Dombrowski to Cliff Durr, May 25, June 16, 1961; Cliff Durr to Robert Truehaft, September 16, 1961, in Clifford Durr Papers (old classification), Box 8.

46. *City of Montgomery* v. *Anna Gach*; *City of Montgomery* v. *Frederick Gach*; Cliff Durr to Robert Truehaft, September 16, 1961, all in Clifford Durr Papers (old classification), Box 8.

47. Virginia Durr to Jessica Mitford, undated, Mitford Papers, Virginia Durr Correspondence, Folder 3; "Nesmith v. Alford: A Constructive Legal Encounter," in drafts of an autobiography, Clifford Durr Papers (old classification), Box 12.

48. "Nesmith v. Alford."

49. Ibid.

50. Ibid.; Barnard, *Outside the Magic Circle,* pp. 290–91; Durr Interview, COHC; Virginia Durr to Jessica Mitford, undated 1960, Mitford Papers, Virginia Durr Correspondence, Folder 3.

51. "Nesmith v. Alford."

52. Ibid.

53. Ibid.; Virginia Durr to Clark Foreman, November 15, 1961, July 3, 1963, Virginia Durr Papers (Radcliffe), 1/33.

54. "Nesmith v. Alford"; "Negroes and the Police"; drafts of an autobiography, all in Clifford Durr Papers (old classification), Box 12.

55. Virginia Durr to Clark Foreman, April 7, 20, 1960, June 12, September 27, 1962, Virginia Durr Papers (Radcliffe), 1/32, 1/33.

56. Virginia Durr to Clark Foreman, March 23, 1962, Virginia Durr Papers (Radcliffe), 1/33; to Jessica Mitford, December 18, 1961, Mitford Papers, Virginia Durr Correspondence, Folder 4; Garrow, *Bearing the Cross*, p. 158; Cliff Durr to Sheldon and Lucy, June 29, 1966, Clifford Durr Papers (old classification), Box 9; Barnard, *Outside the Magic Circle*, p. 323.

57. Christopher Bacon File, Clifford Durr Papers (old classification), Box 8.

58. Virginia Durr to Jessica Mitford, August 11, 1961, Mitford Papers, Virginia Durr Correspondence, Folder 4; Cliff Durr to Anthony Lester, June 3, October 24, 1963; Louis Schweitzer to Durr, November 14, 1963, Clifford Durr Papers (old classification), Box 8.

59. Lester to Cliff Durr, October 10, 19, November 19, 20, December 10, 1963, all in Clifford Durr Papers (old classification), Box 8.

60. Cliff Durr to Lucy Hackney, March 2, 1964; to Louis Schweitzer, April 24, 1964, Clifford Durr Papers (old classification), Box 8.

61. Cliff Durr to his sister Lucy, February 5, 17, March 9, 1964; to his brother James, February 22, 1964; to Louis Schweitzer, April 24, 1964; to the clerk of accounts, Queens College, Oxford, April 16, 1964, all in Clifford Durr Papers (old classification), Box 8.

62. Virginia Durr to Clark Foreman, May 7, October 8, 1964, Virginia Durr Papers (Radcliffe), 1/33.

11. Retirement and Reflection

1. Virginia Durr to Clark Foreman, October 8, 1964, Virginia Durr Papers (Radcliffe), 1/33; G. C. Harcourt to Cliff Durr, January 30, March 5, April 28, May 6, 1964, all in Clifford Durr Papers (old classification), Box 8.

2. Durr Interview, COHC; Clifford Durr "FBI File," Virginia Durr Papers (Radcliffe), 2/9; Anthony Thorley to Cliff Durr, October 16, 1964; Ruth Glass to Virginia Durr, October 7, 1964; Cliff Durr to Mrs. Michael Roberts, October 12, 1964; to Lucy Dunn, November 17, 1964, all in Clifford Durr Papers (old classification), Box 8.

3. "A Southerner Looks at the South," speech at University of Sussex, November 12, 1964, Clifford Durr Papers (new classification), 15/9.

4. Dallas Smythe to Cliff Durr, May 21, August 27, October 14, 1964; Maynard Gestler to Durr, September 8, November 20, 1964; Carol Peterson to Durr, February 26, 1965; John Rosenberg to Durr, January 15, 1965; Allan

Hart to Durr, February 19, 1965; Durr to Dallas Smythe, February 10, 1965, all in Clifford Durr Papers (old classification), Boxes 8 and 9.

5. Cliff Durr to Robert Conzoneri, February 15, 1965; copy of "The Relevance of Morality"; clipping from *St. Louis Post Dispatch,* November 4, 1965, all in Clifford Durr Papers (old classification), Box 9.

6. Doris W. Havice to Cliff Durr, February 17, 1967; Bob Bailey to Durr, March 10, 1967; Durr to Doris Havice, March 1, 1967, Clifford Durr Papers (old classification), Box 9; Barnard, *Outside the Magic Circle,* pp. 328–30; Virginia Durr to Clark Foreman, undated 1971, Virginia Durr Papers (Radcliffe), 1/3.

7. Jonathan Steele to Virginia Durr, March 27, July 26, 1967; Robert L. Johnston to Cliff Durr, September 13, 1967, Clifford Durr Papers (old classification), Box 9.

8. Jessica Mitford to Virginia Durr, November 12, 1967; Virginia Durr to Jessica Mitford, November 13, 1967, Mitford Papers, Virginia Durr Correspondence, Folder 6.

9. Virginia Durr to Clark Foreman, August 19, 1973, Virginia Durr Papers (Radcliffe), 1/38; to Jessica Mitford, July 24, 1973, Mitford Papers, Virginia Durr Correspondence, Folder 9.

10. Aubrey Williams to Lyndon Johnson, April 15, 1964, Clifford Durr Papers (old classification), Box 8. See Mrs. Elmer T. Wilmer to Lyndon Johnson, May 25, 1964, Lyndon Baines Johnson Papers, Lyndon Baines Johnson Library, Austin, Texas (henceforth Lyndon B. Johnson Papers), White House Central File, Name File, Clifford and Virginia Durr, Container 333; Virginia Durr to Clark Foreman, March 25, 1964, Virginia Durr Papers (Radcliffe), 1/33.

11. Cliff Durr to Lyndon Johnson, May 12, 25, 1964; to Aubrey Williams, May 26, 1964; Lyndon Johnson to Aubrey Williams, May 19, 1964; to Cliff Durr, May 20, 1964, all in Clifford Durr Papers (old classification), Box 8.

12. Memo in files, February 11, 1975, Lady Bird Johnson Papers, Lyndon Baines Johnson Library, Austin, Texas (henceforth Lady Bird Johnson Papers), Mrs. Johnson's Files, Durr, Virginia; oral histories of Clifford and Virginia Durr, Lyndon B. Johnson Papers.

13. *Alabama Journal,* January 31, 1966.

14. *New York Times,* February 23, 1966; Saul Carson to Cliff Durr, January 21, 1966; "The Conscience of a Lawyer," clipping from the *Nation,* February 21, 1966, both in Clifford Durr Papers (old classification), Box 9.

15. Cliff Durr to Charles Siepmann, December 9, 1965; Hugo Black, letter to *Nation,* April 18, 1966; extract from *Congressional Record,* April 26, 1966, all in Clifford Durr Papers (old classification), Box 9.

16. Virginia Durr to James Dombrowski, November 5, 1973, James A. Dombrowski Papers, State Historical Society of Wisconsin (henceforth Dombrowski Papers), 4/2.

17. Studs Terkel to Cliff Durr, February 6, 1967; Miss Gail Brown to Durr, December 3, 1968; David A. Bagwell to Durr, January 18, 1972; Gene L. Gres-

sley to Durr, April 19, 1973; Durr to Sheldon Hackney, January 17, July 8, 1971; to Charles Siepmann, January 24, 1966, all in Clifford Durr Papers (old classification), Box 9; Virginia Durr Interview, May 13, 1987.

18. Cliff Durr to Dombrowski, December 7, 1964, Dombrowski Papers, 1/4; Virginia Durr to Dombrowski, April 28, 1965, Virginia Durr Papers (Radcliffe), 1/20; Virginia Durr to Clark Foreman, February 12, 1965, Virginia Durr Papers (Radcliffe), 1/35.

19. Anne Barrett to Cliff Durr, March 8, April 7, 1965, March 22, April 5, 1968; to Ed Brecher, October 23, 1967, March 19, 1968; Cliff Durr to Anne Barrett, April 1, 1965, March 29, April 15, 1968; Ed Brecher to Durr, January 22, 1967, all in Clifford Durr Papers (old classification), Box 12.

20. Anne Barrett to Cliff Durr, April 24, November 20, 1969; Bryce Rucker to Durr, February 14, December 29, 1972, June 17, 1974; Durr to Anne Barrett, May 6, 1969; to Charles Siepmann, December 9, 1965, all in Clifford Durr Papers (old classification), Box 9; Virginia Durr to Clark Foreman, January 23, 1967, Virginia Durr Papers (Radcliffe), 1/35.

21. Barnard, *Outside the Magic Circle,* pp. 286, 324. Virginia Durr to Hugo Black, February 20, 1968, Virginia Durr Papers (Alabama), 1/8; Clifford Durr to Walter Lyon, June 4, 1966; to Ann Durr Lyon, October 10, 1966, Ann Durr Lyon Papers; Virginia Durr to Clark Foreman, June 16, 1967, Virginia Durr Papers (Radcliffe), 1/35.

22. Virginia Durr to Clark Foreman, June 17, 1971, March 1, June 21, 1972, March 6, 1974, all in Virginia Durr Papers (Radcliffe), 1/36, 1/37, 1/38; Virginia Durr to James Dombrowski, January 24, 1975, Dombrowski Papers, 5/1.

23. Virginia Durr to Clark Foreman, June 17, 1971, Virginia Durr Papers (Radcliffe), 1/37; Virginia Durr to James Dombrowski, January 24, 1975, Dombrowski Papers, 5/1.

24. Cliff Durr to Sheldon and Lucy, June 29, 1966; to Ann Durr Lyon, February 15, March 7, 1971; to Lulah, May 9, 1971; to Tilla, September 9, 1971, Clifford Durr Papers (old classification), Box 9.

25. Sen. John Sparkman to Cliff Durr, July 21, 1964; Cliff Durr to Sparkman, July 23, 1964; to Rep. George Huddlestone, June 11, 1964; to the Editor, *Alabama Journal,* October 6, 1964, all in Clifford Durr Papers (old classification), Box 8.

26. "That the Civil Rights Bill Now Pending before the United States Senate Should Be Enacted into Law," April 23, 1964; "Goldwater vs. Johnson," October 22, 1964; "That President Nixon Should Be Re-elected," October 19, 1972; "That the United States Is in an Irrevocable Moral Decline," November 11, 1974, all Forum Club speeches in Clifford Durr Papers (new classification), 14/6, 14/8.

27. Cliff Durr to Lyndon Johnson, January 6, 1973; Virginia Durr to Lady Bird Johnson, February 5, May 13, 1974, both in Lady Bird Johnson Papers, Mrs. Johnson's Files, Durr, Virginia; Clifford and Virginia Durr Interview, Lyndon B. Johnson Papers; Clifford J. Durr, "Report from Alabama: The Af-

fair on Highway 80," *Rights* 12, no. 4 (June 1965): 7–10; Garrow, *Bearing the Cross,* 406–14.

28. Cliff Durr to Ann Durr Lyon, August 26, 1973, Ann Durr Lyon Papers.

29. J. Foy Guin to Cliff Durr, August 4, 1972; Durr to Guin, August 16, 1972; to Lucy Hackney, August 24, 1973, all in Clifford Durr Papers (old classification), Box 9; Virginia Durr to Clark Foreman, September 6, 1973, Virginia Durr Papers (Radcliffe), 1/38.

30. Cliff Durr to Virginia Durr, August 7, 12, 1974, Virginia Durr Papers (Alabama), 2/2.

31. Virginia Durr to Clark Foreman, December 20, 1972, Virginia Durr Papers (Radcliffe), 1/37.

32. Virginia Durr to James Dombrowski, October 24, November 2, 18, 1966, Virginia Durr Papers (Radcliffe), 1/20.

33. Virginia Durr to Clark Foreman, March 7, May 28, June 23, 1968, Virginia Durr Papers (Radcliffe), 1/37.

34. Virginia Durr to John and Jessica Abt, January 26, 1973; to Clark Foreman, November 3, 1969, December 20, 1972, January 11, August 19, 1973, Virginia Durr Papers (Radcliffe), 1/6, 1/37, 1/38.

35. Virginia Durr to Clark Foreman, March 6, 1974; Clark Foreman to Virginia Durr, May 12, 1975, Virginia Durr Papers (Radcliffe), 1/38, 1/39; Ann and Walter Lyon to Clifford Durr, May 6, 1975, Clifford Durr Papers (old classification), Box 9; Virginia Durr to author, May 4, 1988.

Conclusion

1. Condolence File, Clifford Durr Papers (new classification), Box 9.

2. Memorial Service for Clifford J. Durr, June 12, 1975, record of proceedings, in Dombrowski Papers, 8/28; *New York Times,* June 13, 1975.

3. Memorial Service for Clifford J. Durr, June 12, 1975, record of proceedings, in Dombrowski Papers, 8/28.

4. Ibid.

5. Barnard, *Outside the Magic Circle,* p. 295; Virginia Durr to Dombrowski, Virginia Durr Papers (Radcliffe), 1/20.

6. Durr Interview, COHC.

7. Ibid.; Cliff Durr to Ann and Walter Lyon, April 1, 1965, Ann Durr Lyon Papers.

8. Durr Interview, COHC.

9. Barnard, *Outside the Magic Circle,* p. 335; Virginia Durr Interview, May 13, 1987.

10. Leuchtenburg, *Roosevelt and the New Deal,* pp. 342–43; Durr Interview, COHC.

11. Memorial Service for Clifford J. Durr, June 12, 1975, record of proceedings, in Dombrowski Papers, 8/28.

12. *Alabama Journal,* May 13, 1975.

BIBLIOGRAPHY

ESSAY ON SOURCES

Manuscripts

This book is based mainly on manuscript sources. By far the most important of these was the Clifford J. Durr Papers, held at the Alabama Department of Archives and History in Montgomery. This large collection contains material on all aspects of Durr's life and career but is particularly strong on his period with the DPC, his years with the FCC, and his legal practices in both Washington, D.C., and Montgomery. All his case files are held there, as is his personal correspondence from the early 1930s till the time of his death. Of particular value were the successive drafts of his unpublished autobiography, of which I have made extensive use. The way I have cited this collection in the notes needs some explanation. I have visited the archives to use the collection on three occasions—in 1976, 1985, and 1987—and on my second visit arranged to have a substantial part of it microfilmed. Between 1985 and 1987, the whole collection was completely rearranged, to the extent that notes I had taken on my earlier visits could not be adapted to the new system without working through the whole collection again. Consequently, any reference to material I had gathered prior to 1987 is referred to in accordance with the way it had been previously filed (old classification), while material collected in 1987 is referred to under the rubric new classification.

Also held at the Alabama Department of Archives and History are the Judkins-Durr Papers (old classification), now called the Durr Family Papers (new classification), and a small collection deposited there by Durr's widow, Virginia Foster Durr. Both collections were of great value to me. The Judkins-Durr Papers contain a wealth of material about Cliff's early life. Of particular importance were his letters home from the University of Alabama, during his army training, and while he was working in Milwaukee. Perhaps the most fascinating aspect of the collection, however, are the scores of letters written from Oxford during his time as a Rhodes Scholar. Durr wrote home often and at length, describing Oxford life, the English, and, when on his travels, the sights and sounds of a Europe recovering from the devastation of the First World War. These letters are a delight to read, as well as being a prime source for the biographer. The Virginia Durr collection has some items of interest to do with Durr's appointment to the RFC and his trip to the Soviet Union in 1946.

The much larger Virginia Durr collection at the Schlesinger Library, Radcliffe College, was invaluable, especially for the post-Washington period of the Durrs' lives. Virginia commented in voluminous detail to a wide variety of correspondents on most aspects of their lives in Montgomery, both public and private. Her letters are a rich source of Southern history and are particularly valuable on the events surrounding the Montgomery bus boycott and the civil rights movement of the 1960s. Cliff Durr's FBI file can also be found there. Virginia's correspondence with Jessica Mitford, contained in the Jessica Mitford Papers at Ohio State University, was likewise of importance for helping me understand Durr's role in those crucial years. Ann Durr Lyon graciously allowed me to see family papers which she holds privately. Again, they were particularly valuable for the post-Washington period of their lives.

The records of the Legal Division of the Reconstruction Finance Corporation, at the National Archives, contained sufficient items to enable me to gain a flavor of Durr's work for the RFC, but those of the DPC proved somewhat disappointing. I found little of interest in the records of the Federal Communications Commission. The Durr file in the Hugo Black Papers, Manuscripts Division, Library of Congress, was of interest for the light it threw on certain family matters, as well as what it revealed of the political climate of the times. The Eugene Meyer Papers were invaluable in helping me understand Durr's crucial role in removing Rep. Eugene Cox from the chairmanship of the congressional committee set up in 1943 to investigate the FCC.

The Franklin D. Roosevelt Papers contained a few items of interest, principally to do with Durr's appointment to the FCC and his prospects of becoming federal loans administrator in 1945. There were also some useful items in the Harry S. Truman Library to do with loyalty review matters, with Durr's decision to leave the FCC, and with the National Lawyers Guilds' criticism of the FBI during Durr's term as president of that body. The Lyndon Baines Johnson and Lady Bird Johnson Papers both contain material to do with the friendship between the Johnsons and the Durrs.

The James A. Dombrowski Papers were of some value in rounding out the details of Durr's later life, mainly because Virginia wrote to him frequently about their lives generally. There was little of importance in the records of the National Lawyers Guild.

Interviews

I made considerable use of the interviews Durr recorded for the Columbia Oral History Collection and for the Southern Oral History Collection at the University of North Carolina at Chapel Hill. The COHC interview contains important material on just about every aspect of Durr's life, while the SOHC interview is particularly useful for his years with the FCC. I should also acknowledge at this time how important a source Virginia Durr's own autobiography, *Outside the Magic Circle,* proved to be. Superbly edited by Hollinger Barnard from a series of interviews Mrs. Durr had given over the years, it constantly enriched and informed my own work. Almost every chapter draws on it to some degree. Furthermore, Virginia Durr and I have often spoken about Cliff, his life, his work, his character, and I have drawn on these discussions, too, in my book.

Other Sources

Though this book has been written primarily from manuscripts, it is obvious from the bibliography that I have also used other sources. I used the *New York Times* and *Washington Post* throughout and made use of other newspapers for particular purposes. I used the *Montgomery Advertiser* for the period of the bus boycott and civil rights activities and read the *New Orleans Times Picayune,* the *Atlanta Constitution,* and the *St. Louis Post Dispatch* for their coverage of the SCEF hearings. I read *Broadcasting Magazine* for the years Durr was with the FCC and used the *Nation* and the *New Republic* selectively, usually when referred to them by a reference in another source.

After nearly thirty years of teaching and writing about the New Deal and the twentieth-century South, to list the books that have influenced one's general thinking about the period would be time consuming for me and probably tedious for the reader. Nevertheless, there were some books and articles which I found particularly useful for this study, which I discuss briefly. J. Wayne Flynt's excellent *Montgomery: An Illustrated History* helped me understand the city in which Durr grew up and to which he returned in 1951. The illustrations were particularly effective in giving one a "feel" for the city. James B. Sellers's detailed *History of the University of Alabama* helped me understand the milieu in which he was educated.

There is no complete history of the Reconstruction Finance Corporation, but James S. Olson's *Herbert Hoover and the Reconstruction Finance Corporation* is good on its origins, while Susan Estabrook Kennedy, in *The Banking Crisis of 1933,* discusses its increased role under Jesse Jones. Albert Romasco provides the best overview of its general importance in *The Politics of Recovery: Roosevelt's New Deal.* Gerald T. White's *Billions For Defense:*

Government Financing by the Defense Plant Corporation during World War II is the standard treatment of the subsidiary and deals fully with Durr's crucial role in its creation. I found it particularly helpful. There is no standard history of the Federal Communications Commission, but Erik Barnouw, in *The Golden Web,* vol. 2, provides a useful and entertaining overview of Durr's years as a commissioner. In *Unequal Justice: Lawyers and Social Change in Modern America,* Jerold S. Auerbach discusses superbly the effect of the New Deal on the legal profession and describes the troubled creation and growth of the National Lawyers Guild. There are useful articles on each of the three federal agencies with which Durr was associated in *Government Agencies,* edited by Donald R. Whitnah.

David E. Caute's sprawling *The Great Fear* is still the best introduction to understanding the climate of opinion in America after World War II which made loyalty hearings and Senators McCarthy and Eastland possible. Athan Theoharis, in *Seeds of Repression,* writes about the origins of Truman's loyalty program. I find his argument generally persuasive, though, for balance, I also used Earl Latham, *The Communist Conspiracy in Washington,* and Allan Harper, *The Politics of Loyalty.* In *Spying on Americans,* Theoharis discusses the harassment of the National Lawyers Guild by the FBI during Durr's tenure of office as president of that organization, as does Percival Bailey in a fine essay in *Beyond the Hiss Case,* edited by Theoharis. Kenneth O'Reilly covers the same ground in considerable detail, and perhaps a little less passion, in *Hoover and the Un-Americans: The FBI, HUAC, and the Red Menace.* Ellen Schrecker's excellent recent study *No Ivory Tower: McCarthyism and the Universities* uncompromisingly chronicles the failure of the nation's greatest institutions of higher learning to take a stand against the erosion of basic civil liberties during the "climate of fear."

For background to the Montgomery bus boycott and the civil rights years I drew on David Garrow's magisterial biography of Martin Luther King, Jr., as well as *The Montgomery Bus Boycott and the Women Who Started It: The Memoirs of Jo Ann Robinson,* which Garrow edited. The memoir brings out the importance of the Women's Political Council in initiating the boycott. Also of value was J. Mills Thornton III's lengthy article "Challenge and Response in the Montgomery Bus Boycott of 1955–56," a superb discussion of Montgomery's changing political demography, which deserves to be much more widely read than it has been.

The comparatively few works discussed above are but the most important of those that helped me understand the context of Clifford Durr's life. Others have been cited in the text and are also listed in the bibliography. Still others have been neither cited nor placed in the bibliography because, as earlier mentioned, to do so would be to list the literally thousands of books and articles read over a long period and often only half-remembered, yet which together form the topography, the set of ideas, the context, within which scholarly work occurs.

SOURCES CITED IN TEXT

Manuscripts

Black, Hugo L. Papers. Library of Congress. Washington, D.C.
Defense Plant Corporation. Records. National Archives. Washington, D.C.
Dombrowski, James A. Papers. State Historical Society of Wisconsin. Madison.
Durr, Clifford J. Papers. Alabama Department of Archives and History. Montgomery.
Durr, Virginia Foster. Papers. Alabama Department of Archives and History. Montgomery.
———. Papers. Schlesinger Library. Radcliffe College. Cambridge, Massachusetts.
Federal Communications Commission. Records. National Archives. Washington, D.C.
Johnson, Lady Bird. Papers. Lyndon Baines Johnson Library. Austin, Texas.
Johnson, Lyndon Baines. Papers. Lyndon Baines Johnson Library. Austin, Texas.
Judkins-Durr Family Papers (now called Durr Family Papers). Alabama Department of Archives and History. Montgomery.
Lyon, Ann Durr. Papers. Privately held.
Meyer, Eugene. Papers. Library of Congress. Washington, D.C.
Mitford, Jessica. Papers. Ohio State University Library. Columbus.
National Lawyers Guild. Papers. Alexander Meiklejohn Civil Liberties Institute. Berkeley, California.
Reconstruction Finance Corporation. Records. National Archives. Washington, D.C.
Roosevelt, Franklin Delano. Papers. Franklin Delano Roosevelt Library. Hyde Park, New York.
Truman, Harry S. Papers. Harry S. Truman Library. Independence, Missouri.
Williams, Aubrey W. Papers. Franklin Delano Roosevelt Library. Hyde Park, New York.

Government Documents

Control of Subversive Activities: Hearings before a Subcommittee of the Senate Committee on the Judiciary, United States Senate. 81st Cong., 1st sess., on S.1194 and S.1196. *Bills to Protect the United States against Certain Un-American and Subversive Activities,* April 29, May 4, 6, 18, 19, 20, June 10, 1949. Washington, D.C.: Government Printing Office, 1949.

Hearings Regarding Communism in the District of Columbia, pt. 1. *Hearings before the Committee on Un-American Activities, House of Representatives.* 81st Cong., 1st sess., June 28, 29, July 6, 12, 28, 1949. Washington, D.C.: Government Printing Office, 1949.

Hearings Regarding Communist Infiltration of Radiation Laboratory and Atomic Bomb Project at the University of California, Berkeley, California, vols. 1, 2, and 3. *Hearings before the Committee on Un-American Activities, House of Representatives.* 81st Cong., 1st sess., April 22, 26, May 25, June 10, 14, 1949. Washington, D.C.: Government Printing Office, 1949.

Southern Conference Educational Fund Inc. Hearings before the Subcommittee to Investigate the Administration of the Internal Security Act and Other Internal Security Laws of the Committee of the Judiciary, United States Senate. 83d Cong. 2d sess., *On Subversive Influence in the Southern Conference Educational Fund Inc.,* March 18, 19, 20, 1954. Washington, D.C.: Government Printing Office, 1955.

Newspapers and Periodicals

Alabama Journal
Atlanta Constitution
Billboard
Birmingham Age-Herald
Birmingham News
Broadcasting Magazine
Christian Science Monitor
I. F. Stones Weekly
Louisville Courier Journal
Montgomery Advertiser
Nation
New Orleans Times Picayune
New Republic
Newsweek
New York Herald Tribune
New York Times
P.M.
St. Louis Post Dispatch
Time
Variety
Washington Evening Star
Washington News
Washington Post
Washington Times-Herald

Interviews

Durr, Clifford J. Columbia Oral History Collection. Columbia University, New York.
———. Southern Oral History Collection. University of North Carolina at Chapel Hill.
Durr, Clifford and Virginia. Oral Histories. Lyndon Baines Johnson Library. Austin, Texas.
Durr, Virginia Foster. Interview by author, May 29, 31, 1976; December 9, 1981; February 1–12, 1985; May 13, 1987.

Thesis

Bentley, Luther III. "A Critical Study of the Federal Communications Commission Career of Clifford Judkins Durr, Emphasizing His Support for the Public Interest As It Applies to Broadcasting." Master's thesis, Auburn University, 1972.

Articles

Durr, Clifford J. "How to Measure Loyalty." *Nation* 209, no. 17 (April 23, 1949): 470–73.
———. "Hugo L. Black: A Personal Appraisal." *Georgia Law Review* 16, no. 1 (1971): 1–16.
———. "Jesus a Free Speech Victim: Trial by Terror Two Thousand Years Ago." *The Churchman*, July 1960, pp. 7–8; August 1960, pp. 7–9.
———. "The Loyalty Order's Challenge to the Constitution." *University of Chicago Law Review* 16, no. 2 (Winter 1949): 298–306.
———. "Report from Alabama: The Affair on Highway 80." *Rights* 12, no. 4 (June 1965): 7–10.
Hentoff, Nat. "A Conversation in Alabama." *New Yorker*, July 16, 1960.
Leigh, Robert D. "Politicians vs Bureaucrats: The Case of FCC Chairman Fly and Congressman Cox." *Harpers Magazine* 190, no. 1136 (January 1945): 95–105.
Rosenberg, John. "The FBI Shreds Its Files." *Nation* 226, no. 4 (February 4, 1976): 108–11.
Thornton, J. Mills III. "Challenge and Response in the Montgomery Bus Boycott of 1955–56." *Alabama Review* 33, no. 3 (July 1980): 163–235.
Ward, Candace, and Allan Tullos. "Clifford Durr, the FCC Years." *Southern Exposure* 2, no. 4 (Winter 1975): 14–22.

White, Gerald T. "Financing Industrial Expansion for War: The Origin of the Defense Plant Corporation Leases." *Journal of Economic History* 9, no. 2 (November 1949): 156–83.

Books

Atkins, Leah Rawls. *The Valley and the Hills: An Illustrated History of Birmingham and Jefferson County.* Woodland Hills, Calif.: Windsor Publications, 1981.

Auerbach, Jerold S. *Unequal Justice: Lawyers and Social Change in Modern America.* New York: Oxford University Press, 1976.

Barnard, Hollinger F., ed. *Outside the Magic Circle: The Autobiography of Virginia Foster Durr.* University: University of Alabama Press, 1985.

Barnouw, Erik. *The Golden Web: A History of Broadcasting in the United States.* Vol. 2, *1933–1953.* New York: Oxford University Press, 1968.

Baughman, James L. *Television's Guardians: The FCC and the Politics of Programming, 1958–1967.* Knoxville: University of Tennessee Press, 1985.

Bedford, Henry F. *Trouble Downtown: The Local Context of Twentieth Century America.* New York: Harcourt Brace, 1978.

A Brief History of Montgomery, Alabama. Montgomery: Montgomery Chamber of Commerce, 1953.

Caute, David. *The Great Fear: The Anti-Communist Purge under Truman and Eisenhower.* New York: Simon and Schuster, 1978.

Durr, Clifford J. *Three Biblical Lessons in Civil Liberties.* Yellow Springs, Ohio: American Humanist Association, n.d.

Flynt, J. Wayne. *Montgomery: An Illustrated History.* Woodland Hills, Calif.: Windsor Publications, 1980.

Garrow, David J. *Bearing the Cross: Martin Luther King Jr. and the Southern Christian Leadership Conference.* New York: Morrow, 1986.

———, ed. *The Montgomery Bus Boycott and the Women Who Started It: The Memoirs of Jo Ann Gibson Robinson.* Knoxville: University of Tennessee Press, 1987.

Griffith, Robert E. *The Politics of Fear: Joseph R. McCarthy and the Senate.* Lexington: University Press of Kentucky, 1970.

Hamilton, Virginia Van der Veer. *Hugo Black: The Alabama Years.* Baton Rouge: Louisiana State University Press, 1972.

Harper, Allan D. *The Politics of Loyalty: The White House and the Communist Issue, 1946–1952.* Westport, Conn.: Greenwood Press, 1969.

Jones, Jesse H., with Edward Angby. *Fifty Billion Dollars: My Thirteen Years with the RFC.* New York: Macmillan, 1951.

Kennedy, Susan Estabrook. *The Banking Crisis of 1933.* Lexington: University Press of Kentucky, 1973.

Krueger, Thomas A. *And Promises to Keep: The Southern Conference for*

Human Welfare, 1938–1948. Nashville: Vanderbilt University Press, 1967.

Latham, Earl. *The Communist Controversy in Washington: From the New Deal to McCarthy.* Cambridge: Harvard University Press, 1966.

Leuchtenburg, William E. *Franklin D. Roosevelt and the New Deal, 1932–1940.* New York: Harper and Row, 1963.

Mitford, Jessica. *Daughters and Rebels.* Boston: Houghton Mifflin, 1960.

———. *A Fine Old Conflict.* London: Michael Joseph, 1977.

Moore, Albert B. *History of Alabama.* University, Ala.: Supply Store, 1934.

Official Guide to the City of Montgomery. Montgomery: Tintagel Club, 1948.

Olson, James S. *Herbert Hoover and the Reconstruction Finance Corporation, 1931–33.* Ames: Iowa State University Press, 1977.

O'Reilly, Kenneth. *Hoover and the Un-Americans: The FBI, HUAC, and the Red Menace.* Philadelphia: Temple University Press, 1983.

Romasco, Albert U. *The Politics of Recovery: Roosevelt's New Deal.* New York: Oxford University Press, 1983.

Salmond, John A. *A Southern Rebel: The Life and Times of Aubrey Willis Williams, 1890–1965.* Chapel Hill: University of North Carolina Press, 1983.

Schrecker, Ellen W. *No Ivory Tower: McCarthyism and the Universities.* New York: Oxford University Press, 1986.

Scislaw, Kent E., ed. *When Mother Calls.* University: University of Alabama, 1981.

Sellers, James B. *History of the University of Alabama.* Vol. 1, *1818–1902.* University: University of Alabama Press, 1953.

Siepmann, Charles A. *Radio's Second Chance.* Boston: Little Brown, 1946.

———. *Radio, Television, and Society.* New York: Oxford University Press, 1950.

Sosna, Morton. *In Search of the Silent South: Southern Liberals and the Race Issue.* New York: Columbia University Press, 1977.

Theoharis, Athan. *Seeds of Repression: Harry S. Truman and the Origins of McCarthyism.* Chicago: Quadrangle Books, 1971.

———. *Spying on Americans: Political Surveillance from Hoover to the Huston Plan.* Philadelphia: Temple University Press, 1978.

———, ed. *Beyond the Hiss Case: The FBI, Congress, and the Cold War.* Philadelphia: Temple University Press, 1982.

White, Gerald T. *Billions for Defense: Government Financing by the Defense Plant Corporation during World War II.* University: University of Alabama Press, 1980.

Whitnah, Donald R., ed. *Government Agencies.* Westport, Conn.: Greenwood Press, 1983.

INDEX